The Psalms
New American Bible 1991

Annotated Edition

Authorized by the Board of Trustees
of the Confraternity of Christian Doctrine

and

Approved by the Administrative Committee/Board
of the National Conference of Catholic Bishops
and the United States Catholic Conference

A Liturgical Press Book

 THE LITURGICAL PRESS
Collegeville, Minnesota

IMPRIMATUR:
Most Reverend Daniel E. Pilarczyk
President, National Conference of Catholic Bishops
September 10, 1991

Published by The Liturgical Press, Collegeville, Minnesota.

Cover design by Ann Blattner
Cover photograph by Sr. Annette Brophy

ISBN 0-8146-2156-2

1   2   3   4   5   6   7   8   9

CONTENTS

COLLABORATORS
ON THE REVISED PSALMS
of the NEW AMERICAN BIBLE

BISHOPS' AD HOC COMMITTEE

Most Rev. Enrique San Pedro, S.J.
Most Rev. Richard Sklba, D.D.
Most Rev. Donald W. Troutman, S.T.D., S.S.L.
Most Rev. Emil A. Wcela
Most Rev. John F. Whealon, S.S.L., Chairman

BOARD OF EDITORS

Rev. Richard Clifford, S.J.
Br. Aloysius Fitzgerald, F.S.C.
Rev. Joseph Jensen, O.S.B.
Rev. Roland Murphy, O. Carm.
Sr. Irene Nowell, O.S.B.
Dr. Judith Sanderson

REVISERS

Prof. Gary Anderson
Rev. Michael L. Barré
Rev. Christopher T. Begg
Dr. Joseph Blenkinsopp
Rev. Anthony R. Ceresko, O.S.F.S.
Rev. Richard J. Clifford, S.J.
Rev. Aelred Cody, O.S.B.
Prof. Michael D. Coogan
Rev. Alexander A. Di Lella, O.F.M.
Dr. Robert A. Di Vito
Br. Aloysius Fitzgerald, F.S.C.
Rev. Michael D. Guinan, O.F.M.
Rev. William L. Holladay
Rev. William Irwin, C.S.B.
Rev. Joseph Jensen, O.S.B.

Rev. John S. Kselman
Dr. Conrad E. L'Heureux
Rev. Leo Laberge, O.M.I.
Dr. Paul G. Mosca
Rev. Dr. Roland E. Murphy, O. Carm.
Dr. Michael Patrick O'Connor
Rev. Brian J. Peckham, S.J.
Prof. Jimmy J. Roberts
Sr. Eileen M. Schuller, O.S.U.
Dr. Byron E. Shafer
Prof. Mark S. Smith
Prof. Matitiahu Tsevat
Dr. Eugene C. Ulrich
Prof. James C. VanderKam
Rev. Jerome T. Walsh

ENGLISH CONSULTANTS

Dr. Catherine Dunn
Br. Daniel Burke, F.S.C.

BUSINESS MANAGER

Charles A. Buggé

5

Introduction

The Hebrew Psalter numbers 150 songs. The corresponding number in the LXX differs because of a different division of certain psalms. Hence the numbering in the Greek Psalter (which was followed by the Latin Vulgate) is usually one digit behind the Hebrew. In the New American Bible the numbering of the verses follows the Hebrew numbering; many of the traditional English translations are often a verse number behind the Hebrew because they do not count the superscriptions as a verse.

The superscriptions derive from pre-Christian Jewish tradition, and they contain technical terms, many of them apparently liturgical, which are no longer known to us. Seventy-three psalms are attributed to David, but there is no sure way of dating any psalm. Some are pre-exilic (before 587 B.C.), and others are post-exilic (after 539 B.C.), but not as late as the Maccabean period (ca. 165 B.C.). The psalms are the product of many individual collections (e.g., Songs of Ascents, Pss 120–134), which were eventually combined into the present work in which one can detect five "books," because of the doxologies which occur at 41:14; 72:18-19; 89:53; 106:48.

Two important features of the psalms deserve special notice. First, the majority were composed originally precisely for liturgical worship. This is shown by the frequent indication of liturgical leaders interacting with the community (e.g., 118:1-4). Secondly, they follow certain distinct patterns or literary forms. Thus, the hymn is a song of praise, in which a community is urged joyfully to sing out the praise of God. Various reasons are given for this praise (often introduced by "for" or "because"): the divine work of creation and sustenance (Pss 8, 104), or the divine acts in Israel's favor (Pss 135:1-12; 136). Some of the hymns have received a more specific classification, based on content. The "Songs of Zion" are so called because they exalt Zion, the city in which God dwells among the people (Pss 46, 48). Others are termed "enthronement" psalms because they re-enact or re-present in the liturgy the kingship of the Lord (Pss 47; 96-99). Characteristic of the songs of praise is the joyful summons to get involved in the activity; Ps 104 is an exception to this, although it remains universal in its thrust.

Another type of psalm is similar to the hymn: the thanksgiving psalm. This too is a song of praise acknowledging the Lord as the rescuer of the psalmist from a desperate situation. Very often the psalmist will give a flash-back, recounting the past distress, and the plea that was uttered (Pss 30; 116). The setting for such prayers seems to have been the offering of a *todah* (a "praise" sacrifice) with friends in the Temple.

There are more psalms of lament than of any other type. They may be individual (e.g., Pss 3-7; 22) or communal (e.g., Ps 44). Although they usually begin with a cry for help, they develop in various ways. The description of the distress is couched in the broad imagery typical of the Bible (one is in Sheol, the Pit, or is afflicted by enemies or wild beasts, etc.)—in such a way that one cannot pinpoint the exact nature of the psalmist's plight. However, Ps 51 (cf. also Ps 130) seems to refer clearly to deliverance from sin. Several laments end on a note of certainty that the Lord has heard the prayer (cf. Ps 7, but contrast Ps 88), and the Psalter has been characterized as a movement from lament to praise. If this is somewhat of an exaggeration, it serves at least to emphasize the frequent expressions of trust which characterize the lament. In some cases it would seem as if the theme of trust has been lifted out to form a literary type all its own; cf. Pss 23, 62, 91. Among the communal laments can be counted Pss 74 and 79. They complain to the Lord about some national disaster, and try to motivate God to intervene in favor of the suffering people.

Other psalms are clearly classified on account of content, and they may be in themselves laments or psalms of thanksgiving. Among the "royal" psalms, that deal directly with the currently reigning king, are Pss 20, 21, and 72. Many of the royal psalms were given a messianic interpretation by Christians. In Jewish tradition they were preserved, even after kingship had disappeared, because they were read in the light of the Davidic covenant reported in 2 Samuel 7. Certain psalms are called wisdom psalms because they seem to betray the influence of the concerns of the sages (cf. Pss 37, 49), but there is no general agreement as to the number of these prayers. Somewhat related to the wisdom psalms are the "torah" psalms, in which the *torah* (instruction or law) of the Lord is glorified (Pss 1, 19:8-14; 119). Pss 78, 105 and 106 can be considered as "historical" psalms. Although the majority of the psalms have a liturgical setting, there are certain prayers that may be termed "liturgies," so clearly does their structure reflect a liturgical incident (e.g., Pss 15, 24).

It is obvious that not all of the psalms can be pigeon-holed into neat classifications, but even a brief sketch of these types help us to catch the structure and spirit of the psalms we read. It has been rightly said that the psalms are "a school of prayer." They not only provide us with models to follow, but inspire us to voice our own deepest feelings and aspirations.

FIRST BOOK—PSALMS 1-41

Psalm 1
True Happiness in God's Law

I

1 Happy those who do not follow
   the counsel of the wicked,
   Nor go the way of sinners,
   nor sit in company with scoffers.[a]
2 Rather, the law of the LORD is their joy;
   God's law they study day and night.[b]
3 They are like a tree[c]
   planted near streams of water,
   that yields its fruit in season;
   Its leaves never wither;
   whatever they do prospers.

II

4 But not the wicked!
   They are like chaff driven by the wind.[d]
5 Therefore the wicked will not survive judgment,
   nor will sinners in the assembly of the just.
6 The LORD watches over the way of the just,[e]
   but the way of the wicked leads to ruin.

---

[a] Pss 26, 4-5; 40, 5.
[b] Jos 1, 8; Ps 119; Sir 39, 1.
[c] Pss 52, 10; 92, 13-15; Jer 17, 8.

[d] Pss 35, 5; 83, 14-16; Jb 21, 18.
[e] Ps 37, 18.

Ps 1: A preface to the whole Book of Psalms, contrasting with striking similes the destiny of the good and the wicked. The psalm views life as activity, as choosing either the good or the bad. Each "way" brings its inevitable consequences. The wise through their good actions will experience rootedness and life, and the wicked, rootlessness and death.
   1, 1: *Those:* literally, "the man." That word is used here and in many of the Psalms as typical, and therefore is translated "they." *The way:* a common biblical term for manner of living or moral conduct (Pss 32, 8; 101, 2. 6; Prv 2, 20; 1 Kgs 8, 36).
   1, 2: *The law of the LORD:* either the Torah, the first five books of the Bible, or, more probably, divine teaching or instruction. 1, 4: *The wicked:* those who by their actions distance themselves from God's life-giving presence.

11

Psalm 2
A Psalm for a Royal Coronation

1 Why do the nations protest
     and the peoples grumble in vain?[f]
2 Kings on earth rise up
     and princes plot together
     against the LORD and his anointed:[g]
3 "Let us break their shackles
     and cast off their chains!"[h]
4 The one enthroned in heaven laughs;
     the LORD derides them,[i]
5 Then speaks to them in anger,
     terrifies them in wrath:
6 "I myself have installed my king
     on Zion, my holy mountain."
7 I will proclaim the decree of the LORD,
     who said to me, "You are my son;
     today I am your father.[j]
8 Only ask it of me,
     and I will make your inheritance the nations,
     your possession the ends of the earth.
9 With an iron rod you shall shepherd them,
     like a clay pot you will shatter them."[k]
10 And now, kings, give heed;
     take warning, rulers on earth.

---

[f] Rv 11, 18.
[g] Ps 83, 6.
[h] Ps 149, 8.

[i] Pss 37, 13; 59, 9; Wis 4, 18.
[j] Pss 89, 27; 110, 2-3; Is 49, 1.
[k] Rv 2, 27; 12, 5; 19, 15.

Ps 2: A royal psalm. To rebellious kings (1-3) God responds vigorously (4-6). A speaker proclaims the divine decree (in the legal adoption language of the day), making the Israelite king the earthly representative of God (7-9) and warning kings to obey (10-11). The psalm has a messianic meaning for the Church; the New Testament understands it of Christ (Acts 4, 25-27; 13, 33; Heb 1, 5).

2, 2: *Anointed:* in Hebrew *mashiah,* "anointed"; in Greek *christos,* whence English Messiah and Christ. In Israel kings (Jgs 9, 8; 1 Sm 9, 16; 16, 12-13) and high priests (Lv 8, 12; Nm 3, 3) received the power of their office through anointing.

11 Serve the LORD with fear;
    with trembling bow down in homage,
    Lest God be angry and you perish from the way
    in a sudden blaze of anger.
    Happy are all who take refuge in God![1]

Psalm 3
Threatened but Trusting

1 *A psalm of David, when he fled from his son Absalom.*[m]

I
2 How many are my foes, LORD!
   How many rise against me!
3 How many say of me,
   "God will not save that one."[n]   *Selah*
4 But you, LORD, are a shield around me;
   my glory, you keep my head high.[o]

II
5 Whenever I cried out to the LORD,
   I was answered from the holy mountain.   *Selah*
6 Whenever I lay down and slept,
   the LORD preserved me to rise again.[p]
7 I do not fear, then, thousands of people
   arrayed against me on every side.

---

[1] Pss 34, 9; 146, 5; Prv 16, 20.
[m] 2 Sm 15, 13ff.
[n] Ps 71, 11.

[o] Pss 7, 11; 18, 3; 62, 7-8; Dt 33, 29;
Is 60, 19.
[p] Ps 4, 9; Prv 3, 24.

Ps 3: An individual lament complaining of enemies who deny that God will come to the rescue (2-3). Despite such taunts the psalmist hopes for God's protection even in sleep (4-7). The psalm prays for an end to the enemies' power to speak maliciously (8) and closes peacefully with an expression of trust (9).

3, 1: The superscription, added later, relates the psalm to an incident in the life of David.

3, 3. 5. 9: *Selah:* the term is generally considered a direction to the cantor or musicians but its exact meaning is not known. It occurs 71 times in 39 psalms.

13

III
8 Arise, Lord! Save me, my God!
   You will shatter the jaws of all my foes;
   you will break the teeth of the wicked.[q]
9 Safety comes from the Lord!
   Your blessing for your people![r]   *Selah*

Psalm 4
Trust in God

1 *For the leader; with stringed instruments. A psalm of David.*

I
2 Answer when I call, my saving God.
   In my troubles, you cleared a way;
   show me favor; hear my prayer.[s]

II
3 How long will you people mock my honor,
   love what is worthless, chase after lies?[t]   *Selah*
4 Know that the Lord works wonders for the faithful;
   the Lord hears when I call out.
5 Tremble and do not sin;
   upon your beds ponder in silence.[u]
6 Offer fitting sacrifice
   and trust in the Lord.[v]

---

q Ps 58, 7.   t Ps 62, 4.
r Ps 28, 9; Jon 2, 10.   u Eph 4, 26.
s Ps 118, 5.   v Ps 51, 19.

Ps 4: An individual lament emphasizing trust in God. The petition is based upon the psalmist's vivid experience of God as savior (2). That experience of God is the basis for the warning to the wicked: revere God who intervenes on the side of the faithful (3-6). The faithful psalmist exemplifies the blessings given to the just (7-9).

4, 1: *For the leader:* many psalm headings contain this rubric. Its exact meaning is unknown but may signify that such psalms once stood together in a collection of "the choirmaster." Cf 1 Chr 15, 21.

4, 5: *Tremble:* be moved deeply with religious awe. The Greek translation understood the emotion to be anger, and it is so cited in Eph 4, 26.

III

7 Many say, "May we see better times!
        LORD, show us the light of your face!"[w]   *Selah*
8 But you have given my heart more joy
        than they have when grain and wine abound.
9 In peace I shall both lie down and sleep,[x]
        for you alone, LORD, make me secure.

Psalm 5
Prayer for Divine Help

1 *For the leader; with wind instruments. A psalm of David.*

I

2 Hear my words, O LORD;
        listen to my sighing.[y]
3 Hear my cry for help,
        my king, my God!
   To you I pray, O LORD;
4   at dawn you will hear my cry;
         at dawn I will plead before you and wait.[z]

II

5 You are not a god who delights in evil;
        no wicked person finds refuge with you;
6   the arrogant cannot stand before you.
   You hate all who do evil;
7   you destroy all who speak falsely.[a]
   Murderers and deceivers
        the LORD abhors.

III

8 But I can enter your house
        because of your great love.

---

[w] Pss 31, 17; 44, 4; 67, 1; 80, 4; Jb 13, 24; Nm 6, 25; Dn 9, 17.
[x] Ps 3, 6.
[y] Pss 86, 6; 130, 1-2.
[z] Wis 16, 28.
[a] Ps 101, 7; Wis 14, 9; Hb 1, 13.

Ps 5: A lament contrasting the security of the house of God (8-9. 12-13) with the danger of the company of evildoers (5-7. 10-11). The psalmist therefore prays that God will hear (2-4) and grant the protection and joy of the temple.

I can worship in your holy temple
  because of my reverence for you, LORD.[b]
9 Guide me in your justice because of my foes;
  make straight your way before me.[c]

IV
10 For there is no sincerity in their mouths;
  their hearts are corrupt.
Their throats are open graves;[d]
  on their tongues are subtle lies.
11 Declare them guilty, God;
  make them fall by their own devices.[e]
Drive them out for their many sins;
  they have rebelled against you.

V
12 Then all who take refuge in you will be glad
  and forever shout for joy.[f]
Protect them that you may be the joy
  of those who love your name.
13 For you, LORD, bless the just;
  you surround them with favor like a shield.

Psalm 6
Prayer in Distress

1 *For the leader; with stringed instruments, "upon the eighth." A psalm*
of David.

I
2 Do not reprove me in your anger, LORD,
  nor punish me in your wrath.[g]

---

b Ps 138, 2; Jon 2, 5.
c Ps 23, 3; Prv 4, 11; Is 26, 7.
d Rom 3, 13.
e Ps 141, 10.
f Ps 64, 11.
g Ps 38, 2.

5, 10: *Their throats:* their speech brings harm to their hearers (cf Jer 5, 16). The verse mentions four parts of the body, each a source of evil to the innocent.

Ps 6: The first of the seven Penitential Psalms (Pss 6, 32, 38, 51, 102, 130, 143), a designation dating from the seventh century A.D. for psalms suitable to express repentance. The psalmist does not, as in many la-

3 Have pity on me, LORD, for I am weak;
     heal me, LORD, for my bones are trembling.[h]
4 In utter terror is my soul—
     and you, LORD, how long . . . ?[i]
5 Turn, LORD, save my life;
     in your mercy rescue me.
6 For who among the dead remembers you?
     Who praises you in Sheol?[j]

II

7 I am wearied with sighing;
     all night long tears drench my bed;
     my couch is soaked with weeping.
8 My eyes are dimmed with sorrow,
     worn out because of all my foes.[k]

III

9 Away from me, all who do evil![l]
     The LORD has heard my weeping.
10 The LORD has heard my prayer;
     the LORD takes up my plea.
11 My foes will be terrified and disgraced;
     all will fall back in sudden shame.[m]

---

[h] Jer 17, 14-15.
[i] Pss 13, 2-3; 74, 10; 89, 47.
[j] Pss 30, 10; 88, 11; 115, 17; Is 38, 18.
[k] Pss 31, 10; 38, 11; 40, 13.
[l] Ps 119, 115; Mt 7, 23; Lk 13, 27.
[m] Pss 35, 4. 26; 40, 15; 71, 13.

---

ments, claim to be innocent but appeals to God's mercy (5). Sin here, as often in the Bible, is both the sinful act and its injurious consequences; here it is physical sickness (3-4. 7-8) and the attacks of enemies (8. 9. 11). The psalmist prays that the effects of personal and social sin be taken away.

6, 1: *Upon the eighth:* apparently a musical notation, now lost.

6, 4: *How long?:* elliptical for "How long will it be before you answer my prayer?" Cf Ps 13, 2-3.

6, 5: *mercy:* Hebrew *hesed,* translated as "mercy" or "love," describes God's affectionate fidelity to human beings, which is rooted in divine and not human integrity.

6, 6: A motive for God to preserve the psalmist from death: in the shadowy world of the dead no one offers you praise. Sheol is the biblical term for the underworld where the insubstantial souls of dead human beings dwelt. It was similar to the Hades of Greek and Latin literature. In the second century B.C., biblical books begin to speak positively of life with God after death (Dn 12, 1-3; Wis 3).

Psalm 7
God the Vindicator

1 *A plaintive song of David, which he sang to the LORD concerning Cush, the Benjaminite.*

I

2 LORD my God, in you I take refuge;
rescue me; save me from all who pursue me,[n]

3 Lest they maul me like lions,
tear me to pieces with none to save.

II

4 LORD my God, if I am at fault in this,
if there is guilt on my hands,

5 If I have repaid my friend with evil—
I spared even those who hated me without cause—

6 Then let my enemy pursue and overtake me,
trample my life to the ground,
and leave me dishonored in the dust.[o]   *Selah*

III

7 Rise up, LORD, in your anger;
rise against the fury of my foes.[p]
Wake to judge as you have decreed.

8 Have the assembly of the peoples gather about you;
sit on your throne high above them,

9 O LORD, judge of the nations.
Grant me justice, LORD, for I am blameless,
free of any guilt.

10 Bring the malice of the wicked to an end;
uphold the innocent,

---

[n] Pss 6, 5; 22, 21.   [p] Pss 9, 4; 19, 20.
[o] Ps 143, 3.

Ps 7: An individual lament. The psalmist flees to God's presence in the sanctuary for justice and protection (2-3) and takes an oath that only the innocent can swear (4-6). The innocent psalmist can thus hope for the just God's protection (7-14) and be confident that the actions of the wicked will come back upon their own heads (15-17). The justice of God leads the psalmist to praise (18).

7, 4: *At fault in this:* in the accusation the enemies have made against the psalmist.

O God of justice,
>who tries hearts and minds.ᑫ

IV

11 A shield before me is God
>who saves the honest heart.ʳ
12 God is a just judge,
>who rebukes in anger every day.
13 If sinners do not repent,
>God sharpens his sword,
>strings and readies the bow,ˢ
14 Prepares his deadly shafts,
>makes arrows blazing thunderbolts.ᵗ

V

15 Sinners conceive iniquity;
>pregnant with mischief,
>they give birth to failure.ᵘ
16 They open a hole and dig it deep,
>but fall into the pit they have dug.ᵛ
17 Their mischief comes back upon themselves;
>their violence falls on their own heads.

VI

18 I praise the justice of the LORD;
>I celebrate the name of the LORD Most High.ʷ

Psalm 8
Divine Majesty and Human Dignity

1 *For the leader; "upon the* gittith.*" A psalm of David.*

ᑫ Pss 17, 3; 26, 2; 35, 24; 43, 1; 139,
  23; Jer 17, 10; 20, 12.
ʳ Ps 3, 4.
ˢ Ps 11, 2.
ᵗ Is 50, 11.

ᵘ Jb 15, 35; Is 59, 4.
ᵛ Pss 9, 16; 35, 8; 57, 7; Prv 26, 27; Eccl
  10, 8; Sir 27, 26.
ʷ Pss 18, 50; 30, 5; 135, 3; 146, 2.

Ps 8: While marvelling at the limitless grandeur of God (2-3), the psalmist is struck first by the smallness of human beings in creation (4-5), and then by the royal dignity and power that God has graciously bestowed upon them (6-10).

8, 1: *Upon the gittith:* probably the title of the melody to which the psalm was to be sung or a musical instrument.

2 O Lᴏʀᴅ, our Lord,
> how awesome is your name through all the earth!
> You have set your majesty above the heavens!

3 Out of the mouths of babes[x] and infants
> you have drawn a defense against your foes,
> to silence enemy and avenger.

4 When I see your heavens, the work of your fingers,
> the moon and stars that you set in place—

5 What are humans that you are mindful of them,[y]
> mere mortals that you care for them?[z]

6 Yet you have made them little less than a god,
> crowned them with glory and honor.

7 You have given them rule over the works of your hands,[a]
> put all things at their feet:

8 All sheep and oxen,
> even the beasts of the field,

9 The birds of the air, the fish of the sea,
> and whatever swims the paths of the seas.

10 O Lᴏʀᴅ, our Lord,
>   how awesome is your name through all the earth!

---

[x] Mt 21, 16; Wis 10, 21.
[y] Ps 144, 3; Jb 7, 17.
[z] Heb 2, 6ff.

[a] 7ff: Gn 1, 26. 28; Wis 9, 2; 1 Cor 15, 27.

8, 3: *Babes and infants:* the text is obscure. Some join this line to the last line of 2 (itself obscure) to read: "(you) whose majesty is exalted above the heavens / by the mouths of babes and infants." *Drawn a defense:* some prefer the Septuagint's "fashioned praise," which is quoted in Mt 21, 16. *Enemy and avenger:* probably cosmic enemies. The primeval powers of watery chaos are often personified in poetic texts (Pss 74, 13-14; 89, 11; Jb 9, 13; 26, 12-13; Is 51, 9).

8, 5: *Humans . . . mere mortals:* literally, "(mortal) person" . . . "son of man (in sense of a human being, Hebrew *'adam*)." The emphasis is on the fragility and mortality of human beings to whom God has given great dignity.

8, 6: *Little less than a god:* Hebrew *'elohim,* the ordinary word for "God" or "the gods" or members of the heavenly court. The Greek version translated *'elohim* by "angel, messenger"; several ancient and modern versions so translate. The meaning seems to be that God created human beings almost at the level of the beings in the heavenly world. Heb 2, 9 finds the eminent fulfillment of this verse in Jesus Christ, who was humbled before being glorified. Cf also 1 Cor 15, 27, where St. Paul applies to Christ the closing words of v 7.

Psalms 9-10
Thanksgiving for Victory and Prayer for Justice

1 *For the leader; according to* Muth Labben. *A psalm of David.*

A

I

2 I will praise you, LORD, with all my heart;
  I will declare all your wondrous deeds.
3 I will delight and rejoice in you;
  I will sing hymns to your name, Most High.
4 For my enemies turn back;
  they stumble and perish before you.

II

5 You upheld my right and my cause,
  seated on your throne, judging justly.
6 You rebuked the nations, you destroyed the wicked;
  their name you blotted out for all time.[b]
7 The enemies have been ruined forever;
  you destroyed their cities;
  their memory has perished.

III

8 The LORD rules forever,
  has set up a throne for judgment.
9 It is God who governs the world with justice,[c]
  who judges the peoples with fairness.
10 The LORD is a stronghold for the oppressed,
  a stronghold in times of trouble.[d]

---

[b] Jb 18, 17.
[c] Pss 96, 10; 98, 9.

[d] Ps 37, 39; Is 25, 4.

Pss 9-10: Pss 9 and 10 in the Hebrew text have been transmitted as separate poems but they actually form a single acrostic poem and are so transmitted in the Greek and Latin tradition. Each verse of the two psalms begins with a successive letter of the Hebrew alphabet (though several letters have no corresponding stanza). The psalm states loosely connected themes: the rescue of the helpless poor from their enemies, God's worldwide judgment and rule over the nations, the psalmist's own concern for rescue (14-15).
9, 1: *Muth Labben:* probably the melodic accompaniment of the psalm, now lost.

11 Those who honor your name trust in you;
        you never forsake those who seek you, LORD.

IV
12 Sing hymns to the LORD enthroned on Zion;
        proclaim God's deeds among the nations!
13 For the avenger of bloodshed remembers,
        does not forget the cry of the afflicted.ᵉ

V
14 Have mercy on me, LORD;
        see how my foes afflict me!
        You alone can raise me from the gates of death.ᶠ
15 Then I will declare all your praises,
        sing joyously of your salvation
        in the gates of daughter Zion.

VI
16 The nations fall into the pit they dig;
        in the snare they hide, their own foot is caught.
17 The LORD is revealed in this divine rule:
        by the deeds they do the wicked are trapped.ᵍ   *Higgaion.*
        Selah

VII
18 To Sheol the wicked will depart,
        all the nations that forget God.
19 The needy will never be forgotten,
        nor will the hope of the afflicted ever fade.ʰ
20 Arise, LORD, let no mortal prevail;
        let the nations be judged in your presence.
21 Strike them with terror, LORD;
        show the nations they are mere mortals.   *Selah*

ᵉ Jb 16, 18.   ᵍ Sir 27, 26.
ᶠ Wis 16, 13.   ʰ Prv 23, 18.

9, 15: *Daughter Zion:* an ancient Near Eastern city could sometimes be personified as a woman or a queen, the spouse of the god of the city.
9, 17: *The Lord is revealed in this divine rule:* God has so made the universe that the wicked are punished by the very actions they perform.

B

I

1 Why, LORD, do you stand at a distance
    and pay no heed to these troubled times?
2 Arrogant scoundrels pursue the poor;
    they trap them by their cunning schemes.[i]

II

3 The wicked even boast of their greed;
    these robbers curse and scorn the LORD.[j]
4 In their insolence the wicked boast:
    "God doesn't care, doesn't even exist."[k]
5 Yet their affairs always succeed;
    they ignore your judgment on high;
    they sneer at all who oppose them.
6 They say in their hearts, "We will never fall;
    never will we see misfortune."
7 Their mouths are full of oaths, violence, and lies;
    discord and evil are under their tongues.[l]
8 They wait in ambush near towns;
    their eyes watch for the helpless.
    to murder the innocent in secret.[m]
9 They lurk in ambush like lions in a thicket,
    hide there to trap the poor,
    snare them and close the net.[n]
10 The helpless are crushed, laid low;
    they fall into the power of the wicked,
11 Who say in their hearts, "God pays no attention,
    shows no concern, never bothers to look."[o]

III

12 Rise up, LORD God! Raise your arm!
    Do not forget the poor!
13 Why should the wicked scorn God,
    say in their hearts, "God doesn't care"?

---

[i] Is 32, 7.
[j] Ps 36, 2.
[k] Ps 14, 1; Jb 22, 13; Is 29, 15; Jer 5, 12; Zep 1, 12.
[l] Is 32, 7; Rom 3, 14.
[m] Ps 11, 2; Jb 24, 14.
[n] Ps 17, 12; Prv 1, 11; Jer 5, 26.
[o] Pss 44, 25; 64, 6; 73, 11; 94, 7; Ez 9, 9.

14 But you do see;
>   you do observe this misery and sorrow;[p]
>   you take the matter in hand.
> To you the helpless can entrust their cause;
>   you are the defender of orphans.[q]

15 Break the arms of the wicked and depraved;
>   make them account for their crimes;
>   let none of them survive.

   IV

16 The LORD is king forever;[r]
>   the nations have vanished from God's land.

17 You listen, LORD, to the needs of the poor;
>   you encourage them and hear their prayers.

18 You win justice for the orphaned and oppressed;[s]
>   no one on earth will cause terror again.

Psalm 11
Confidence in the Presence of God

1 *For the leader. Of David.*

   I

In the LORD I take refuge;
>   how can you say to me,
>   "Flee like a bird to the mountains![t]

2 See how the wicked string their bows,
>   fit their arrows to the string
>   to shoot from the shadows at the upright.[u]

3 When foundations are being destroyed,
>   what can the upright do?"

---

p Pss 31, 8; 56, 9; 2 Kgs 20, 5; Is 25, 8; Rv 7, 17.
q Ex 22, 21-22.
r Ps 145, 13; Jer 10, 10.
s Dt 10, 18.
t Pss 55, 7; 91, 4.
u Pss 7, 13; 37, 14; 57, 5; 64, 4.

Ps 11: A song of trust. Though friends counsel flight to the mountain country (a traditional hideout) to escape trouble (1-3), the innocent psalmist reaffirms confidence in God, who protects those who seek asylum in the temple (4-7).

11, 3: *Foundations:* usually understood of public order. Cf Ps 82, 5.

II

4 The Lord is in his holy temple;
   the Lord's throne is in heaven.[v]
   God's eyes keep careful watch;
   they test all peoples.
5 The Lord tests the good and the bad,
   hates those who love violence,
6 And rains upon the wicked
   fiery coals and brimstone,
   a scorching wind their allotted cup.[w]
7 The Lord is just and loves just deeds;
   the upright shall see his face.

Psalm 12
Prayer against Evil Tongues

1 *For the leader; "upon the eighth." A psalm of David.*

I

2 Help, Lord, for no one loyal remains;
   the faithful have vanished from the human race.[x]
3 Those who tell lies to one another
   speak with deceiving lips and a double heart.[y]

II

4 May the Lord cut off all deceiving lips,
   and every boastful tongue,

---

[v] Pss 14, 2; 102, 20; Hb 2, 20; Dt 26, 15; Is 66, 1; Mt 5, 34.
[w] Pss 120, 4; 140, 11; Prv 16, 27; Ez 38, 22; Rv 8, 5; 20, 10.
[x] Pss 14, 3; 116, 11; Is 59, 15; Mi 7, 2.
[y] Pss 28, 3; 55, 22; Is 59, 3-4; Jer 9, 7.

11, 6: *Their allotted cup:* the cup that God gives people to drink is a common figure for their destiny. Cf Pss 16, 5; 75, 9; Mt 20, 22; 26, 39; Rv 14, 10.

Ps 12: A lament. The psalmist, thrown into a world where lying and violent people persecute the just (2-3), prays that the wicked be punished (4-5). The prayer is not simply for vengeance but arises from a desire to see God's justice appear on earth. V 6 preserves the word of assurance spoken by the priest to the lamenter; it is not usually transmitted in such psalms. In vv 7-9 the psalmist affirms the intention to live by the word of assurance.

5   Those who say, "By our tongues we prevail;
        when our lips speak, who can lord it over us?"[z]

    III

6   "Because they rob the weak, and the needy groan,
        I will now arise," says the LORD;
        "I will grant safety to whoever longs for it."[a]

    IV

7   The promises of the LORD are sure,
        silver refined in a crucible,
        silver purified seven times.[b]

8   LORD, protect us always;
        preserve us from this generation.

9   On every side the wicked strut;
        the shameless are extolled by all.

Psalm 13
Prayer in Time of Illness

1   *For the leader. A psalm of David.*

    I

2   How long, LORD? Will you utterly forget me?
        How long will you hide your face from me?[c]

3   How long must I carry sorrow in my soul,
        grief in my heart day after day?
        How long will my enemy triumph over me?

    II

4   Look upon me, answer me, LORD, my God!
        Give light to my eyes lest I sleep in death,

---

[z] Sir 5, 3.
[a] Is 33, 10.
[b] Pss 18, 31; 19, 8; Prv 30, 5.

[c] Pss 6, 4; 44, 25; 77, 8; 79, 5; 89, 47;
    94, 3; Lam 5, 20.

12, 7: *A crucible:* literally, "in a crucible in the ground." The crucible was placed in the ground for support.

Ps 13: A lament in which the psalmist, seriously ill (4), expresses fear that enemies will interpret his or her death as a divine judgment. Hence the heartfelt prayer (2-3) is for healing that will signal to those enemies that the psalmist enjoys God's favor (4-5). The poem ends with a confession of trust in God and a statement of praise (6).

5 Lest my enemy say, "I have prevailed,"
>   lest my foes rejoice at my downfall.[d]

III

6 I trust in your faithfulness.
>   Grant my heart joy in your help,
> That I may sing of the LORD,
>   "How good our God has been to me!"[e]

Psalm 14
A Lament over Widespread Corruption

1 *For the leader. Of David.*

I

Fools say in their hearts,
>   "There is no God."[f]
Their deeds are loathsome and corrupt;
>   not one does what is right.
2 The LORD looks down from heaven
>   upon the human race,[g]
To see if even one is wise,[h]
>   if even one seeks God.
3 All have gone astray;
>   all alike are perverse.
Not one does what is right,
>   not even one.[i]

II

4 Will these evildoers never learn?
>   They devour my people as they devour bread;[j]

---

[d] Ps 38, 17.
[e] Ps 116, 7.
[f] Pss 10, 4; 36, 2; Is 32, 6; Jer 5, 12.
[g] Pss 11, 4; 102, 20.

[h] 2b-3: Rom 3, 11-12.
[i] Ps 12, 1.
[j] Ps 27, 2; Is 9, 11.

Ps 14: The lament (duplicated in Ps 53) depicts the world as consisting of two types of people: "the fools" (= the wicked, 1-3) and "the company of the just" (4-6; also called "my people," and "the poor"). The wicked persecute the just, but the psalm expresses the hope that God will punish the wicked and reward the good.

14, 1: *Fools:* literally, "the fool." The singular is used typically, hence the plural translation.

they do not call upon the LORD.[k]
5 They have good reason, then, to fear;
   God is with the company of the just.
6 They would crush the hopes of the poor,
   but the poor have the LORD as their refuge.

III
7 Oh, that from Zion might come
   the deliverance of Israel,
   That Jacob may rejoice, and Israel be glad
   when the LORD restores his people![l]

Psalm 15
The Righteous Israelite

1 *A psalm of David.*

I
LORD, who may abide in your tent?
   Who may dwell on your holy mountain?[m]

II
2 Whoever walks without blame,[n]
   doing what is right,
   speaking truth from the heart;
3 Who does not slander a neighbor,
   does no harm to another,
   never defames a friend;

---

[k] Ps 79, 6.   [m] Ps 56, 7.
[l] Ps 85, 2.   [n] Ps 119, 1.

14, 7: *Israel. . . Jacob. . . his people:* the righteous poor are identified with God's people.
Ps 15: The psalm records a liturgical scrutiny at the entrance to the temple court (cf Ps 24, 3-6; Is 33, 14b-16). The Israelite wishing to be admitted had to ask the temple official what conduct was appropriate to God's precincts. Note the emphasis on virtues relating to one's neighbor.
15, 1: *Your tent. . . your holy mountain:* the temple could be referred to as "tent" (Ps 61, 5; Is 33, 20), a reference to the tent of the wilderness period and the tent of David (2 Sm 6, 17; 7, 2), predecessors of the temple. *Holy mountain:* a venerable designation of the divine abode (Pss 2, 6; 3, 5; 43, 3; 48, 2; etc.).

4   Who disdains the wicked,
>   but honors those who fear the LORD;
>   Who keeps an oath despite the cost,
5   lends no money at interest,
>   accepts no bribe against the innocent.°

III
Whoever acts like this
>   shall never be shaken.

Psalm 16
God the Supreme Good

1   *A* miktam *of David.*

I
Keep me safe, O God;
>   in you I take refuge.ᵖ
2   I say to the LORD,
>   you are my Lord,
>   you are my only good.
3   Worthless are all the false gods of the land.
>   Accursed are all who delight in them.
4   They multiply their sorrows
>   who court other gods.
>   Blood libations to them I will not pour out,
>   nor will I take their names upon my lips.

° Ex 22, 24; 23, 8.   ᵖ Ps 25, 20.

15, 5: *Lends no money at interest:* lending money in the Old Testament was often seen as assistance to the poor in their distress, not as an investment; making money off the poor by charging interest was thus forbidden (Ex 22, 24; Lv 25, 36-37; Dt 23, 20).

Ps 16: In the first section, the psalmist rejects the futile worship of false gods (2-5), preferring Israel's God (1), the giver of the land (6). The second section reflects on the wise and life-giving presence of God (7-11).

16,1: *Miktam:* a term occurring six times in psalm superscriptions, always with "David." Its meaning is unknown.

16, 4: *Take their names:* to use the gods' names in oaths and hence to affirm them as one's own gods.

5 LORD, my allotted portion and my cup,
   you have made my destiny secure.^q

6 Pleasant places were measured out for me;
   fair to me indeed is my inheritance.

   II

7 I bless the LORD who counsels me;
   even at night my heart exhorts me.

8 I keep the LORD always before me;
   with the Lord at my right, I shall never be shaken.^r

9 Therefore my heart is glad, my soul rejoices;
   my body also dwells secure,

10 For you will not abandon me to Sheol,
   nor let your faithful servant see the pit.^s

11 You will show me the path to life,
   abounding joy in your presence,
   the delights at your right hand forever.

Psalm 17
Prayer for Rescue from Persecutors

1 *A prayer of David.*

   I

Hear, LORD, my plea for justice;
   pay heed to my cry;

---

q Pss 23, 5; 73, 26; Nm 18, 20; Lam 3, 24.

r Pss 73, 23; 121, 5. 8-12; Acts 2, 25-28.

s Pss 28, 1; 30, 4; 49, 16; 86, 13; Jon 2, 7; Acts 13, 35.

16, 6: *Pleasant places were measured out for me:* the psalmist is pleased with the plot of land measured out to the family, which was to be passed on to succeeding generations ("my inheritance").

16, 10: *Nor let your faithful servant see the pit:* Hebrew *shahath* means here the pit, a synonym for Sheol, the underworld. The Greek translation derives the word here and elsewhere from the verb *shahath,* "to be corrupt." On the basis of the Greek, Acts 2, 25-32 and 13, 35-37 apply the verse to Christ's resurrection, "Nor will you suffer your holy one to see corruption."

Ps 17: A lament of an individual unjustly attacked who has taken refuge in the temple. Confident of being found innocent, the psalmist cries out for God's just judgment (1-5) and requests divine help against ene-

Listen to my prayer
　　spoken without guile.
2 From you let my vindication come;
　　your eyes see what is right.
3 You have tested my heart,
　　searched it in the night.[t]
You have tried me by fire,
　　but find no malice in me.
My mouth has not transgressed
4　　as humans often do.
As your lips have instructed me,
　　I have kept the way of the law.
5 My steps have kept to your paths;
　　my feet have not faltered.[u]

II
6 I call upon you; answer me, O God.
　　Turn your ear to me; hear my prayer.
7 Show your wonderful love,
　　you who deliver with your right arm
　　those who seek refuge from their foes.
8 Keep me as the apple of your eye;
　　hide me in the shadow of your wings
9　　from the violence of the wicked.[v]

III
My ravenous enemies press upon me;[w]
10　　they close their hearts,
　　they fill their mouths with proud roaring.

---

[t] Pss 26, 2; 139, 23.
[u] Ps 18, 36; Jb 23, 11-12.
[v] Pss 36, 8; 57, 2; 61, 5; 63, 8; 91, 4;
　Dt 32, 10; Ru 2, 12; Zec 2, 12; Mt 23,
37.
[w] 9b-12: Pss 10, 9; 22, 14. 22; 35, 17;
　58, 7; Jb 4, 10-11.

---

mies (6-9a). Those ravenous lions (9b-12) should be punished (13-14).
The psalm ends with a serene statement of praise (15). The Hebrew text
of vv 3-4 and 14 is uncertain.
　17, 8: *Apple of your eye . . . shadow of your wings:* images of God's
special care. Cf Dt 32, 10; Prv 7, 2; Is 49, 2.
　17, 10-12. 14: An extended metaphor: the enemies are lions.

11 Their steps even now encircle me;
>   they watch closely, keeping low to the ground,
12 Like lions eager for prey,
>   like young lions lurking in ambush.
13 Rise, O LORD, confront and cast them down;
>   rescue me so from the wicked.
14 Slay them with your sword;
>   with your hand, LORD, slay them;
>   snatch them from the world in their prime.
>   Their bellies are being filled with your friends;
>   their children are satisfied too,
>   for they share what is left with their young.
15 I am just—let me see your face;
>   when I awake, let me be filled with your presence.ˣ

Psalm 18
A King's Thanksgiving for Victory

1 *For the leader. Of David, the servant of the* LORD, *who sang to the* LORD
the words of this song after the LORD *had rescued him from the clutches
of all his enemies and from the hand of Saul.* (2) *He said:*

I

I love you, LORD, my strength,
3   LORD, my rock, my fortress, my deliverer,ʸ

ˣ Pss 4, 7; 31, 17; 67, 2; 80, 4; Nm 6,   ʸ 2-51: 2 Sm 22, 2-51.
  25; Dn 9, 17.

17, 15: *When I awake:* probably the psalmist has spent the night in
the sanctuary (cf 3) and hopes to wake to an oracle assuring God's pro-
tective presence.

Ps 18: A royal thanksgiving for a military victory, duplicated in 2 Sm
22. Thanksgiving psalms are in essence reports of divine rescue. The
psalm has two parallel reports of rescue, the first told from a heavenly
perspective (5-20), and the second from an earthly perspective (36-46).
The first report adapts old mythic language of a cosmic battle between
sea and rainstorm in order to depict God's rescue of the Israelite king
from his enemies. Each report has a short hymnic introduction (2-4. 32-35)
and conclusion (21-31. 47-51).

18, 3: *My saving horn:* my strong savior. The horn referred to is the
weapon of a bull and the symbol of fertility. Cf 1 Sm 2, 10; Ps 132, 17;
Lk 1, 69.

My God, my rock of refuge,
my shield, my saving horn, my stronghold!^z

4 Praised be the LORD, I exclaim!
I have been delivered from my enemies.

II

5 The breakers of death surged round about me;
the menacing floods terrified me.

6 The cords of Sheol tightened;
the snares of death lay in wait for me.^a

7 In my distress I called out: LORD!
I cried out to my God.^b
From his temple he heard my voice;
my cry to him reached his ears.

8 The earth rocked and shook;
the foundations of the mountains trembled;
they shook as his wrath flared up.^c

9 Smoke rose in his nostrils,
a devouring fire poured from his mouth;
it kindled coals into flame.

10 He parted the heavens and came down,
a dark cloud under his feet.^d

11 Mounted on a cherub he flew,
borne along on the wings of the wind.

12 He made darkness the cover about him;
his canopy, heavy thunderheads.

---

^z Pss 3, 4; 31, 3-4; 42, 10; Gn 49, 24;
Dt 32, 4.
^a Pss 88, 8; 93, 3-4; 116, 3-4.
^b Jon 2, 3.

^c Pss 97, 3-4; 99, 1; Jgs 5, 4-5; Is 64,
1; Hab 3, 9-11.
^d Pss 104, 3; 144, 5; Is 63, 19.

18, 6: *Cords:* hunting imagery, the cords of a snare.
18, 7: *His temple:* his heavenly abode.
18, 8-16: God appears in the storm, which in Palestine comes from the west. The introduction to the theophany (vv 8-9) is probably a description of a violent, hot, and dry east-wind storm. In the fall transition period from the rainless summer to the rainy winter such storms regularly precede the rains. Cf Ex 14, 21-22.
18, 11: *Cherub:* a winged creature, derived from myth, in the service of the deity (Gn 3, 24; Ex 25, 18-20; 37, 6-9). Cherubim were the throne bearers of the deity (Pss 80, 2; 99, 1; 1 Kgs 6, 23-28; 8, 6-8).

13 Before him scudded his clouds,
    hail and lightning too.[e]
14 The LORD thundered from heaven;
    the Most High made his voice resound.[f]
15 He let fly his arrows and scattered them;
    shot his lightning bolts and dispersed them.[g]
16 Then the bed of the sea appeared;
    the world's foundations lay bare,[h]
  At the roar of the LORD,
    at the storming breath of his nostrils.
17 He reached down from on high and seized me;
    drew me out of the deep waters.[i]
18 He rescued me from my mighty enemy,
    from foes too powerful for me.
19 They attacked me on a day of distress,
    but the LORD came to my support.
20 He set me free in the open;
    he rescued me because he loves me.

    III
21 The LORD acknowledged my righteousness,
    rewarded my clean hands.[j]
22 For I kept the ways of the LORD;
    I was not disloyal to my God.
23 His laws were all before me,
    his decrees I did not cast aside.
24 I was honest toward him;
    I was on guard against sin.
25 So the LORD rewarded my righteousness,
    the cleanness of my hands in his sight.
26 Toward the faithful you are faithful;
    to the honest you are honest;[k]
27 Toward the sincere, sincere;
    but to the perverse you are devious.

---

[e] Ex 13, 21; 19, 16.
[f] Pss 29; 77, 19; Ex 19, 19; Jb 37, 3-4.
[g] Ps 144, 6; Wis 5, 21.
[h] Ps 77, 17; Zec 9, 14.
[i] Ps 144, 7.
[j] Ps 26; 1 Sm 26, 23.
[k] Ps 125, 4.

18, 15: *Arrows:* lightning.

28 Humble people you save;
      haughty eyes you bring low.[l]
29 You, LORD, give light to my lamp;
      my God brightens the darkness about me.[m]
30 With you I can rush an armed band,
      with my God to help I can leap a wall.
31 God's way is unerring;
      the LORD's promise is tried and true;
      he is a shield for all who trust in him.[n]

   IV
32 Truly, who is God except the LORD?
      Who but our God is the rock?[o]
33 This God who girded me with might,
      kept my way unerring,
34 Who made my feet swift as a deer's,
      set me safe on the heights,[p]
35 Who trained my hands for war,
      my arms to bend even a bow of bronze.[q]

   V
36 You have given me your protecting shield;
      your right hand has upheld me;
      you stooped to make me great.
37 You gave me room to stride;
      my feet never stumbled.[r]
38 I pursued my enemies and overtook them;
      I did not turn back till I destroyed them.
39 I struck them down; they could not rise;
      they fell dead at my feet.
40 You girded me with strength for war,
      subdued adversaries at my feet.
41 My foes you put to flight before me;
      those who hated me I destroyed.

---

[l] Jb 22, 29; Prv 3, 34.
[m] Pss 27, 1; 36, 10; 43, 3; 119, 105; Jb 29, 3; Mi 7, 8.
[n] Pss 12, 6; 77, 13; Prv 30, 5.
[o] Is 44, 8; 45, 21.
[p] Hb 3, 19.
[q] Ps 144, 1.
[r] Ps 17, 5.

18, 35: *Bow of bronze:* hyperbole for a bow difficult to bend and therefore capable of propelling an arrow with great force.

42 They cried for help, but no one saved them;
   cried to the LORD but got no answer.
43 I ground them fine as dust in the wind;
   like mud in the streets I trampled them down.
44 You rescued me from the strife of peoples;
   you made me head over nations.
   A people I had not known became my slaves;
45   as soon as they heard of me they obeyed.
   Foreigners cringed before me;
46   their courage failed;
   they came trembling from their fortresses.[s]

   VI
47 The LORD lives! Blessed be my rock![t]
   Exalted be God, my savior!
48 O God who granted me vindication,
   made peoples subject to me,[u]
49   and preserved me from my enemies,
   Truly you have exalted me above my adversaries,
   from the violent you have rescued me.
50 Thus I will proclaim you, LORD, among the nations;
   I will sing the praises of your name.[v]
51 You have given great victories to your king,
   and shown kindness to your anointed,
   to David and his posterity forever.[w]

Psalm 19
God's Glory in the Heavens and in the Law

1 *For the leader. A psalm of David.*

   I
2 The heavens declare the glory of God;
   the sky proclaims its builder's craft.[x]

---

[s] Mi 7, 17.
[t] Ps 144, 1.
[u] Ps 144, 2.
[v] Pss 7, 18; 30, 5; 57, 9; 135, 3; 146, 2; Rom 15, 9.
[w] Pss 89, 28-37; 144, 10; 1 Sm 2, 10.
[x] Pss 8, 1; 50, 6; 97, 6.

Ps 19: The heavenly elements of the world, now beautifully arranged, bespeak the power and wisdom of their creator (2-7). The creator's wisdom is available to human beings in the law (8-11), toward which the

3 One day to the next conveys that message;
    one night to the next imparts that knowledge.
4 There is no word or sound;
    no voice is heard;
5 Yet their report goes forth through all the earth,
    their message, to the ends of the world.
  God has pitched there a tent for the sun;
6   it comes forth like a bridegroom from his chamber,
    and like an athlete joyfully runs its course.
7 From one end of the heavens it comes forth;
    its course runs through to the other;
    nothing escapes its heat.

  II
8 The law of the LORD is perfect,
    refreshing the soul.
  The decree of the LORD is trustworthy,
    giving wisdom to the simple.[y]
9 The precepts of the LORD are right,
    rejoicing the heart.
  The command of the LORD is clear,
    enlightening the eye.
10 The fear of the LORD is pure,
    enduring forever.
  The statutes of the LORD are true,
    all of them just;
11 More desirable than gold,
    than a hoard of purest gold,
  Sweeter also than honey
    or drippings from the comb.[z]

---

[y] Pss 12, 7; 119.   [z] Sir 24, 19.

---

psalmist prays to be open (12-15). The themes of light and speech unify the poem.

19, 4: *No word or sound:* the regular functioning of the heavens and the alternation of day and night inform humans without words of the creator's power and wisdom.

19, 5: *The sun:* in other religious literature the sun is a judge and lawgiver since it sees all in its daily course; 5b-7 form a transition to the law in 8-11. The six synonyms for God's revelation (8-11) are applied to the sun in comparable literature.

12 By them your servant is instructed;
  obeying them brings much reward.

 III
13 Who can detect heedless failings?
  Cleanse me from my unknown faults.
14 But from willful sins keep your servant;
  let them never control me.
 Then shall I be blameless,
  innocent of grave sin.
15 Let the words of my mouth meet with your favor,
  keep the thoughts of my heart before you,
  LORD, my rock and my redeemer.

Psalm 20
Prayer for the King in Time of War

1 *For the leader. A psalm of David.*

 I
2 The LORD answer you in time of distress;
  the name of the God of Jacob defend you!
3 May God send you help from the temple,
  from Zion be your support.[a]
4 May God remember your every offering,
  graciously accept your holocaust,   *Selah*
5 Grant what is in your heart,
  fulfill your every plan.

---

a Pss 128, 5; 134, 3.

19, 12: *Instructed:* the Hebrew verb means both to shine and to teach. Cf Dn 12, 3.

Ps 20: The people pray for the king before battle. The people ask for divine help (2-6) and express confidence that such help will be given (7-10). A solemn assurance of divine help may well have been given between the two sections in the liturgy, something like the promises of Pss 12, 6 and 21, 9-13. The final verse (10) echoes the opening verse.

20, 4: *Remember:* God's remembering implies readiness to act. Cf Gn 8, 1; Ex 2, 24.

6 May we shout for joy at your victory,
　　　raise the banners in the name of our God.
　　The LORD grant your every prayer!

　II

7 Now I know victory is given
　　　to the anointed of the LORD.[b]
　God will answer him from the holy heavens
　　　with a strong arm that brings victory.

8 Some rely on chariots, others on horses,
　　　but we on the name of the LORD our God.[c]

9 They collapse and fall,
　　　but we stand strong and firm.[d]

10 LORD, grant victory to the king;
　　　answer when we call upon you.

Psalm 21
Thanksgiving and Assurances for the King

1 *For the leader. A psalm of David.*

　I

2 LORD, the king finds joy in your power;[e]
　　　in your victory how greatly he rejoices!

3 You have granted him his heart's desire;
　　　you did not refuse the prayer of his lips.　　　　*Selah*

4 For you welcomed him with goodly blessings;
　　　you placed on his head a crown of pure gold.

---

[b] Pss 18, 51; 144, 10; 1 Sm 2, 10.　　　[d] Is 40, 30.
[c] Ps 147, 10-11; 2 Chr 14, 10; Prv 21,　　[e] Ps 63, 12.
　31; 1 Sm 17, 45; Is 31, 1; 36, 9.

20, 6: *Victory:* the Hebrew root is often translated "salvation," "to save," but in military contexts it can have the specific meaning of "victory."

Ps 21: The first part of this royal psalm is a thanksgiving (2-8), and the second is a promise that the king will triumph over his enemies (9-14). The king's confident prayer (3. 5) and trust in God (8) enable him to receive the divine gifts of vitality, peace, and military success. V 14 reprises v 1. When kings ceased in Israel after the sixth century B.C., the psalm was sung of a future Davidic king.

5 He asked life of you;
       you gave it to him,
       length of days forever.[f]
6 Great is his glory in your victory;
       majesty and splendor you confer upon him.
7 You make him the pattern of blessings forever,
       you gladden him with the joy of your presence.
8 For the king trusts in the Lord,
       stands firm through the love of the Most High.

    II

9 Your hand will reach all your enemies;
       your right hand will reach your foes!
10 At the time of your coming
       you will drive them into a furnace.
    Then the Lord's anger will consume them,
       devour them with fire.
11 Even their descendants you will wipe out from the earth,
       their offspring from the human race.
12 Though they intend evil against you,
       devising plots, they will not succeed,
13 For you will put them to flight;
       you will aim at them with your bow.

    III

14 Arise, Lord, in your power![g]
    We will sing and chant the praise of your might.

Psalm 22
The Prayer of an Innocent Person

1 *For the leader; according to "The deer of the dawn." A psalm of David.*

    I

2 My God, my God, why have you abandoned me?
       Why so far from my call for help,

---

[f] 1 Kgs 3, 14.   [g] Nm 10, 35.

Ps 22: A lament unusual in structure and in intensity of feeling. The psalmist's present distress is contrasted with God's past mercy in vv 2-12. In vv 13-22 enemies surround the psalmist. The last third is an invitation

from my cries of anguish?[h]

3 My God, I call by day, but you do not answer;
     by night, but I have no relief.[i]

4 Yet you are enthroned as the Holy One;
     you are the glory of Israel.[j]

5 In you our ancestors trusted;
     they trusted and you rescued them.

6 To you they cried out and they escaped;
     in you they trusted and were not disappointed.[k]

7 But I am a worm, hardly human,
     scorned by everyone, despised by the people.[l]

8 All who see me mock me;
     they curl their lips and jeer;
     they shake their heads at me:[m]

9 "You relied on the LORD—let him deliver you;
     if he loves you, let him rescue you."[n]

10 Yet you drew me forth from the womb,
      made me safe at my mother's breast.

11 Upon you I was thrust from the womb;
      since birth you are my God.[o]

12 Do not stay far from me,
      for trouble is near,
      and there is no one to help.[p]

II

13 Many bulls surround me;
      fierce bulls of Bashan encircle me.

---

h Is 49, 14; 54, 7; Mt 27, 46; Mk 15, 34.
i Sir 2, 10.
j Is 6, 3.
k Ps 25, 3; Is 49, 23; Dn 3, 40.
l Is 53, 3.

m Ps 109, 25; Mt 27, 39; Mk 15, 29; Lk 23, 35.
n Ps 71, 11; Wis 2, 18-20; Mt 27, 43.
o Ps 71, 6; Is 44, 2; 46, 3.
p Pss 35, 22; 38, 22; 71, 12.

---

to praise God (23-27), becoming a universal chorus of praise (28-32). The psalm is important in the New Testament. Its opening words occur on the lips of the crucified Jesus (Mk 15, 34; Mt 27, 46), and several other verses are quoted, or at least alluded to, in the accounts of Jesus' passion (Mt 27, 35. 43; Jn 19, 24).

22, 1: *The deer of the dawn:* apparently the title of the melody.

22, 7: *I am a worm, hardly human:* the psalmist's sense of isolation and dehumanization, an important motif of Ps 22, is vividly portrayed here.

22, 13-14: *Bulls:* the enemies of the psalmist are also portrayed in less-

14 They open their mouths against me,
lions that rend and roar.[q]
15 Like water my life drains away;
all my bones grow soft.
My heart has become like wax,
it melts away within me.
16 As dry as a potsherd is my throat;
my tongue sticks to my palate;
you lay me in the dust of death.
17 Many dogs surround me;
a pack of evildoers closes in on me.
So wasted are my hands and feet
18 that I can count all my bones.[r]
They stare at me and gloat;
19 they divide my garments among them;
for my clothing they cast lots.[s]
20 But you, LORD, do not stay far off;
my strength, come quickly to help me.
21 Deliver me from the sword,
my forlorn life from the teeth of the dog.
22 Save me from the lion's mouth,
my poor life from the horns of wild bulls.[t]

III

23 Then I will proclaim your name to the assembly;
in the community I will praise you:[u]
24 "You who fear the LORD, give praise!
All descendants of Jacob, give honor;

---

[q] Ps 17, 12; Jb 4, 10; 1 Pt 5, 8.
[r] Ps 109, 24.
[s] Mt 27, 35; Mk 15, 24; Lk 23, 34; Jn 19, 24.
[t] Pss 7, 2-3; 17, 12; 35, 17; 57, 5; 58, 7; 2 Tm 4, 17.
[u] Pss 26, 12; 35, 18; 40, 10; 109, 30; 149, 1; 2 Sm 22, 50; Heb 2, 12.

---

than-human form, as wild animals (cf 17. 21-22). *Bashan:* a grazing land east of the Jordan, famed for its cattle. Cf Dt 32, 14; Ez 39, 18; Am 4, 1.

22, 16: *The dust of death:* the netherworld, the domain of the dead.

22, 23: *In the community I will praise you:* the person who offered a thanksgiving sacrifice in the temple recounted to the other worshipers the favor received from God and invited them to share in the sacrificial banquet. The final section (24-32) may be a summary or a citation of the psalmist's poem of praise.

show reverence, all descendants of Israel!

25 For God has not spurned or disdained
the misery of this poor wretch,
Did not turn away from me,
but heard me when I cried out.

26 I will offer praise in the great assembly;
my vows I will fulfill before those who fear him.

27 The poor will eat their fill;
those who seek the LORD will offer praise.
May your hearts enjoy life forever!"[v]

IV

28 All the ends of the earth
will worship and turn to the LORD;
All the families of nations
will bow low before you.[w]

29 For kingship belongs to the LORD,
the ruler over the nations.[x]

30 All who sleep in the earth
will bow low before God;
All who have gone down into the dust
will kneel in homage.

31 And I will live for the LORD;
my descendants will serve you.

32 The generation to come will be told of the Lord,
that they may proclaim to a people yet unborn
the deliverance you have brought.[y]

---

[v] Pss 23, 5; 69, 33.
[w] Ps 86, 9; Tb 13, 11; Is 45, 22; 52, 10; Zec 14, 16.
[x] Ps 103, 19; Ob 21; Zec 14, 9.
[y] Pss 48, 14-15; 71, 18; 78, 6; 102, 19; Is 53, 10.

22, 25: *Turn away:* literally, "hides his face from me," an important metaphor for God withdrawing from someone, e.g., Mi 3, 4; Is 8, 17; Pss 27, 9; 69, 18; 88, 15.

22, 27: *The poor:* originally the poor, who were dependent on God; the term *('anawim)* came to include the religious sense of "humble, pious, devout."

22, 30: Hebrew unclear. The translation assumes that all on earth (28-29) and under the earth (30) will worship God.

Psalm 23
The Lord, Shepherd and Host

1   *A psalm of David.*

I

The LORD is my shepherd;
    there is nothing I lack.[z]

2   In green pastures you let me graze;
    to safe waters you lead me;

3   you restore my strength.
You guide me along the right path
    for the sake of your name.[a]

4   Even when I walk through a dark valley,[b]
    I fear no harm for you are at my side;
    your rod and staff give me courage.

II

5   You set a table before me
    as my enemies watch;
You anoint my head with oil;[c]
    my cup overflows.[d]

6   Only goodness and love will pursue me
    all the days of my life;

---

[z] Pss 80, 2; 95, 7; 100, 3; Dt 2, 7.   [c] Ps 92, 11.
[a] Prv 4, 11.   [d] Ps 16, 5.
[b] Jb 10, 21-22; Is 50, 10.

Ps 23: God's loving care for the psalmist is portrayed under the figures of a shepherd for the flock (1-4) and a host's generosity toward a guest (5-6). The imagery of both sections is drawn from traditions of the exodus (Is 40, 11; 49, 10; Jer 31, 10).

23, 1: *My shepherd:* God as good shepherd is common in both the Old Testament and the New Testament (Ez 34, 11-16 and Jn 10, 11-18).

23, 3: *The right path:* connotes "right way" and "way of righteousness."

23, 4: *A dark valley:* a different division of the Hebrew consonants yields the translation "the valley of the shadow of death."

23, 5: *You set a table before me:* this expression occurs in an exodus context in Ps 78, 19. *As my enemies watch:* my enemies see that I am God's friend and guest. *Oil:* a perfumed ointment made from olive oil, used especially at banquets (Ps 104, 15; Mt 26, 7; Lk 7, 37. 46; Jn 12, 2).

23, 6: *Goodness and love:* the blessings of God's covenant with Israel.

I will dwell in the house of the LORD[e]
    for years to come.

Psalm 24
The Glory of God in Procession to Zion

1 *A psalm of David.*

I

The earth is the LORD's and all it holds,[f]
    the world and those who live there.
2 For God founded it on the seas,
    established it over the rivers.[g]

II

3 Who may go up the mountain of the LORD?[h]
    Who can stand in his holy place?
4 "The clean of hand and pure of heart,
    who are not devoted to idols,
    who have not sworn falsely.
5 They will receive blessings from the LORD,
    and justice from their saving God.
6 Such are the people that love the LORD,
    that seek the face of the God of Jacob."   *Selah*

III

7 Lift up your heads, O gates;
    rise up, you ancient portals,
    that the king of glory may enter.[i]

---

[e] Ps 27, 4.
[f] Pss 50, 12; 89; 12; Dt 10, 14; 1 Cor 10, 26.
[g] Ps 136, 6; Is 42, 5.
[h] Ps 15, 1.
[i] Ps 118, 19-20.

Ps 24: The psalm apparently accompanied a ceremony of the entry of God (invisibly enthroned upon the ark), followed by the people, into the temple. The temple commemorated the creation of the world (1-2). The people had to affirm their fidelity before being admitted into the sanctuary (3-6; cf Ps 15). A choir identifies the approaching God and invites the very temple gates to bow down in obeisance (7-10).

24, 4-5: Literally, "the one whose hands are clean." The singular is used for the entire class of worshipers, hence the plural translation.

24, 7. 9: *Lift up your heads, O gates . . . you ancient portals:* the literal meaning is impossible since the portcullis (a gate that moves up and

8   Who is this king of glory?
     The LORD, a mighty warrior,
     the LORD, mighty in battle.
9   Lift up your heads, O gates;
     rise up, you ancient portals,
     that the king of glory may enter.
10 Who is this king of glory?
     The LORD of hosts is the king of glory.   *Selah*

Psalm 25
Confident Prayer for Forgiveness and Guidance

1   *Of David.*

  I

  I wait for you, O LORD;
     I lift up my soul (2) to my God.[j]
  In you I trust; do not let me be disgraced;[k]
     do not let my enemies gloat over me.
3   No one is disgraced who waits for you,[l]
     but only those who lightly break faith.
4   Make known to me your ways, LORD;
     teach me your paths.[m]
5   Guide me in your truth and teach me,
     for you are God my savior.
  For you I wait all the long day,
     because of your goodness, LORD.

---

[j] Pss 86, 4; 143, 8.
[k] Ps 71, 1.
[l] Ps 22, 6; Is 49, 23; Dn 3, 40.

[m] Pss 27, 11; 86, 11; 119, 12. 35; 143, 8. 10.

---

down) was unknown in the ancient world. Extra-biblical parallels suggest a full personification of the circle of gate towers: they are like a council of elders, bowed down and anxious, awaiting the return of the army and the Great Warrior gone to battle.

Ps 25: A lament. Each verse begins with a successive letter of the Hebrew alphabet. Such acrostic psalms are often a series of statements only loosely connected. The psalmist mixes ardent pleas (1-2. 16-22) with expressions of confidence in God who forgives and guides.

25, 5: *Because of your goodness, LORD:* these words have been transposed from the end of 7 to preserve the pattern of two lines per letter of the Hebrew alphabet in the acrostic poem.

6   Remember your compassion and love, O LORD;
         for they are ages old.[n]
7   Remember no more the sins of my youth;[o]
         remember me only in light of your love.

   II
8   Good and upright is the LORD,
         who shows sinners the way,
9   Guides the humble rightly,
         and teaches the humble the way.
10 All the paths of the LORD are faithful love
         toward those who honor the covenant demands.
11 For the sake of your name, LORD,
         pardon my guilt, though it is great.
12 Who are those who fear the LORD?
         God shows them the way to choose.[p]
13 They live well and prosper,
         and their descendants inherit the land.[q]
14 The counsel of the LORD belongs to the faithful;
         the covenant instructs them.
15 My eyes are ever upon the LORD,
         who frees my feet from the snare.[r]

   III
16 Look upon me, have pity on me,
         for I am alone and afflicted.[s]
17 Relieve the troubles of my heart;
         bring me out of my distress.
18 Put an end to my affliction and suffering;
         take away all my sins.
19 See how many are my enemies,
         see how fiercely they hate me.
20 Preserve my life and rescue me;
         do not let me be disgraced, for I trust in you.
21 Let honesty and virtue preserve me;
         I wait for you, O LORD.

---

[n] Sir 51, 8.
[o] Jb 13, 26; Is 64, 8.
[p] Prv 19, 23.

[q] Ps 37, 9. 29.
[r] Pss 123, 1. 2; 141, 8.
[s] Pss 86, 16; 119, 132.

22 Redeem Israel, God,
       from all its distress!

Psalm 26
Prayer of Innocence

1 *Of David.*

   I
   Grant me justice, LORD!
       I have walked without blame.[t]
   In the LORD I have trusted;
       I have not faltered.
2 Test me, LORD, and try me;
       search my heart and mind.[u]
3 Your love is before my eyes;
       I walk guided by your faithfulness.[v]

   II
4 I do not sit with deceivers,
       nor with hypocrites do I mingle.
5 I hate the company of evildoers;
       with the wicked I do not sit.
6 I will wash my hands in innocence[w]
       and walk round your altar, LORD,
7 Lifting my voice in thanks,
       recounting all your wondrous deeds.

---

[t] Ps 7, 9.   [v] Ps 86, 11.
[u] Pss 17, 3; 139, 23.   [w] Ps 73, 13.

25, 22: A final verse beginning with the Hebrew letter *pe* is added to the normal 22-letter alphabet. Thus the letters *aleph, lamed,* and *pe* open the first, middle (v 11), and last lines of the psalm. Together, they spell *aleph,* the first letter of the alphabet.

Ps 26: Like a priest washing before approaching the altar (Ex 30, 17-21), the psalmist seeks God's protection upon entering the temple. 1-3, matched by 11-12, remind God of past integrity while asking for purification; 4-5, matched by 9-10, pray for inclusion among the just; 6-8, the center of the poem, express the joy in God at the heart of all ritual.

26, 6: *I will wash my hands:* the washing of hands was a liturgical act (Ex 30, 19. 21; 40, 31-32), symbolic of inner as well as outer cleanness. Cf Is 1, 16.

8 LORD, I love the house where you dwell,
      the tenting-place of your glory.[x]

III

9 Do not take me away with sinners,
      nor my life with the violent.[y]
10 Their hands carry out their schemes;
      their right hands are full of bribes.
11 But I walk without blame;[z]
      redeem me, be gracious to me![a]
12 My foot stands on level ground;
      in assemblies I will bless the LORD.[b]

Psalm 27
Trust in God

1 *Of David*

A

I

The LORD is my light and my salvation;[c]
   whom do I fear?
The LORD is my life's refuge;
   of whom am I afraid?
2 When evildoers come at me
      to devour my flesh,[d]

---

[x] Pss 29, 9; 63, 3; Ex 24, 16; 25, 8.
[y] Ps 28, 3.
[z] Ps 101, 6.
[a] Ps 25, 16.

[b] Pss 22, 23; 35, 18; 149, 1.
[c] Pss 18, 29; 36, 10; 43, 3; Is 10, 17;
   Mi 7, 8.
[d] Ps 14, 4.

26, 12: *On level ground:* in safety, where there is no danger of tripping and falling. *In assemblies:* at the temple. Having walked around the altar, the symbol of God's presence, the psalmist blesses God.

Ps 27: Tradition has handed down the two sections of the psalm (1-6 and 7-14) as one psalm, though each part could be understood as complete in itself. Asserting boundless hope that God will bring rescue (1-3), the psalmist longs for the presence of God in the temple, protection from all enemies (4-6). In part B there is a clear shift in tone (7-12); the climax of the poem comes with "I believe" (13), echoing "I trust" (3).

27, 2: *To devour my flesh:* the psalmist's enemies are rapacious beasts (Pss 7, 3; 17, 12; 22, 14. 17).

> These my enemies and foes
> > themselves stumble and fall.

3 Though an army encamp against me,
> > my heart does not fear;
> Though war be waged against me,
> > even then do I trust.

II

4 One thing I ask of the LORD;
> > this I seek:
> To dwell in the LORD's house
> > all the days of my life,
> To gaze on the LORD's beauty,
> > to visit his temple.[e]

5 For God will hide me in his shelter
> > in time of trouble,[f]
> Will conceal me in the cover of his tent;
> > and set me high upon a rock.

6 Even now my head is held high
> > above my enemies on every side!
> I will offer in his tent
> > sacrifices with shouts of joy;
> > I will sing and chant praise to the LORD.

B

I

7 Hear my voice, LORD, when I call;
> > have mercy on me and answer me.

8 "Come," says my heart, "seek God's face";
> > your face, LORD, do I seek![g]

9 Do not hide your face from me;
> > do not repel your servant in anger.
> You are my help; do not cast me off;
> > do not forsake me, God my savior!

---

e Pss 23, 6; 61, 5.   g Ps 24, 6; Hos 5, 15.
f Ps 31, 21.

27, 8: *Seek God's face* (literally: "to seek his face"): to commune with God in the temple. The idiom is derived from the practice of journeying to sacred places. Cf Hos 5, 15; 2 Sm 21, 1; Ps 24, 6.

10 Even if my father and mother forsake me,
    the LORD will take me in.[h]

    II

11 LORD, show me your way;
    lead me on a level path
    because of my enemies.[i]
12 Do not abandon me to the will of my foes;
    malicious and lying witnesses have risen against me.
13 But I believe I shall enjoy the LORD's goodness
    in the land of the living.[j]
14 Wait for the LORD, take courage;
    be stouthearted, wait for the LORD!

Psalm 28
Petition and Thanksgiving

1 *Of David.*

    I
    To you, LORD, I call;
    my Rock, do not be deaf to me.[k]
    If you fail to answer me,
    I will join those who go down to the pit.[l]
2 Hear the sound of my pleading when I cry to you,
    lifting my hands toward your holy place.[m]

---

h Is 49, 15.
i Pss 25, 4; 86, 11.
j Ps 116, 9; Is 38, 11.

k Ps 18, 2.
l Pss 30, 4; 88, 5; 143, 7; Prv 1, 12.
m Ps 134, 2.

27, 13: *In the land of the living:* or "in the land of life," an epithet of the Jerusalem Temple (Pss 52, 7; 116, 9; Is 38, 11), where the faithful had access to the life-giving presence of God.

Ps 28: A lament asking that the psalmist, who has taken refuge in the temple (2), not be punished with the wicked, who are headed inevitably toward destruction (1. 3-5). The statement of praise is exceptionally lengthy and vigorous (6-7). The psalm ends with a prayer (8-9).

28, 1: *The pit:* a synonym for Sheol, the shadowy place of the dead.

28, 2: *Your holy place:* the innermost part of the temple, the holy of holies, containing the ark. Cf 1 Kgs 6, 16. 19-23; 8, 6-8.

3 Do not drag me off with the wicked,
    with those who do wrong,[n]
  Who speak peace to their neighbors
    though evil is in their hearts.[o]
4 Repay them for their deeds,
    for the evil that they do.
  For the work of their hands repay them;
    give them what they deserve.[p]
5 They pay no heed to the LORD's works,
    to the deeds of God's hands.[q]
  God will tear them down,
    never to be rebuilt.

II

6 Blessed be the LORD,
    who has heard the sound of my pleading.
7 The LORD is my strength and my shield,
    in whom my heart trusted and found help.
  So my heart rejoices;
    with my song I praise my God.

III

8 LORD, you are the strength of your people,
    the saving refuge of your anointed king.
9 Save your people, bless your inheritance;
    feed and sustain them forever!

---

[n] Ps 26, 9.   [p] 2 Sm 3, 39.
[o] Pss 12, 2; 55, 22; 62, 5; Prv 26, 24-28.   [q] Is 5, 12.

28, 6: The psalmist shifts to fervent thanksgiving, probably responding to a priestly or prophetic oracle in 5cd (not usually transmitted) assuring the worshiper that the prayer has been heard.

28, 8: *Your people . . . your anointed king:* salvation is more than individual, affecting all the people and their God-given leader.

Psalm 29
The Lord of Majesty Acclaimed as King of the World

1 *A psalm of David.*

I
Give to the LORD, you heavenly beings,
    give to the LORD glory and might;
2 Give to the LORD the glory due God's name.
    Bow down before the LORD's holy splendor![r]

II
3 The voice of the LORD is over the waters;
    the God of glory thunders,
    the LORD, over the mighty waters.
4 The voice of the LORD is power;
    the voice of the LORD is splendor.[s]
5 The voice of the LORD cracks the cedars;
    the LORD splinters the cedars of Lebanon,
6 Makes Lebanon leap like a calf,
    and Sirion like a young bull.
7 The voice of the LORD strikes with fiery flame;

---

[r] Pss 68, 35; 96, 7-9.
[s] Pss 46, 7; 77, 18-19; Jb 37, 4; Is 30, 30.

Ps 29: The hymn invites the members of the heavenly court to acknowledge God's supremacy by ascribing glory and might to God alone (1-2a. 9b). Divine glory and might are dramatically visible in the storm (3-9a). The storm apparently comes from the Mediterranean onto the coast of Syria-Palestine and then moves inland. In 10 the divine beings acclaim God's eternal kingship. The psalm concludes with a prayer that God will impart the power just displayed to the Israelite king and through the king to Israel.

29,1: *You heavenly beings:* literally "sons of God," i.e., members of the heavenly court who served Israel's God in a variety of capacities.

29, 3: *The voice of the LORD:* the sevenfold repetition of the phrase imitates the sound of crashing thunder and may allude to God's primordial slaying of Leviathan, the seven-headed sea monster of Canaanite mythology.

29, 6: *Sirion:* the Phoenician name for Mount Hermon. Cf Dt 3, 9.

8   the voice of the LORD rocks the desert;
      the LORD rocks the desert of Kadesh.
9 The voice of the LORD twists the oaks
      and strips the forests bare.
      All in his palace say, "Glory!"

   III
10 The LORD sits enthroned above the flood!ᵗ
      The LORD reigns as king forever!
11 May the LORD give might to his people;
      may the LORD bless his people with peace!ᵘ

Psalm 30
Thanksgiving for Deliverance

1 *A psalm. A song for the dedication of the temple. Of David.*

   I
2 I praise you, LORD, for you raised me up
      and did not let my enemies rejoice over me.
3 O LORD, my God,
      I cried out to you and you healed me.

ᵗ Bar 3, 3.   ᵘ Ps 68, 36.

29, 8: *The desert of Kadesh:* probably north of Palestine in the neighborhood of Lebanon and Hermon.

29, 9b-10: Having witnessed God's supreme power (3-9a), the gods acknowledge the glory that befits the king of the divine and human world.

29, 10: *The flood:* God defeated the primordial waters and made them part of the universe. Cf Pss 89, 10-13 and 93, 3-4.

29,11: *His people:* God's people, Israel.

Ps 30: An individual thanksgiving in four parts: praise and thanks for deliverance and restoration (2-4); an invitation to others to join in (5-6); a flashback to the time before deliverance (7-11); a return to praise and thanks (12-13). Two sets of images recur: 1) going down, death, silence; 2) coming up, life, praising. God has delivered the psalmist from one state to the other.

30, 1: *For the dedication of the temple:* a later adaptation of the psalm to celebrate the purification of the temple in 164 B.C. during the Maccabean Revolt.

30, 3: *Healed:* for God as healer, see also Pss 103, 3; 107, 20; Hos 6, 1; 7, 1; 11, 3; 14, 5.

4 LORD, you brought me up from Sheol;
      you kept me from going down to the pit.[v]

  II
5 Sing praise to the LORD, you faithful;
      give thanks to God's holy name.
6 For divine anger lasts but a moment;
      divine favor lasts a lifetime.
   At dusk weeping comes for the night;
      but at dawn there is rejoicing.

  III
7 Complacent, I once said,
      "I shall never be shaken."
8 LORD, when you showed me favor
      I stood like the mighty mountains.
   But when you hid your face
      I was struck with terror.[w]
9 To you, LORD, I cried out;
      with the Lord I pleaded for mercy:
10 "What gain is there from my lifeblood,
      from my going down to the grave?
   Does dust give you thanks
      or declare your faithfulness?
11 Hear, O LORD, have mercy on me;
      LORD, be my helper."

  IV
12 You changed my mourning into dancing;
      you took off my sackcloth
      and clothed me with gladness.[x]

---

[v] Ps 28, 1; Jon 2, 7.   [x] Is 61, 3; Jer 31, 13.
[w] Ps 104, 29.

30, 4: *Sheol . . . pit:* the shadowy underworld residence of the spirits of the dead, here a metaphor for near death.

30, 7: *Complacent:* untroubled existence is often seen as a source of temptation to forget God. Cf Dt 8, 10-18; Hos 13, 6; Prv 30, 9.

30, 10: in the stillness of Sheol no one gives you praise; let me live and be among your worshipers. Cf Pss 6, 6; 88, 11-13; 115, 17; Is 38, 18.

13 With my whole being I sing
          endless praise to you.
     O LORD, my God,
          forever will I give you thanks.

Psalm 31
Prayer in Distress and Thanksgiving for Escape

1 *For the leader. A psalm of David.*

     I
2 In you, LORD, I take refuge;[y]
          let me never be put to shame.
     In your justice deliver me;
3   incline your ear to me;
          make haste to rescue me!
     Be my rock of refuge,
          a stronghold to save me.
4 You are my rock and my fortress;[z]
          for your name's sake lead and guide me.
5 Free me from the net they have set for me,
          for you are my refuge.
6 Into your hands I commend my spirit;[a]
          you will redeem me, LORD, faithful God.
7 You hate those who serve worthless idols,
          but I trust in the LORD.
8 I will rejoice and be glad in your love,
          once you have seen my misery,
          observed my distress.[b]

---

y 2-4: Ps 71, 1-3.   a Lk 23, 46; Acts 7, 59.
z Ps 18, 2.   b Ps 10, 14.

Ps 31: A lament (2-19) with a strong emphasis on trust (4. 6. 15-16), ending with an anticipatory thanksgiving (20-25). As is usual in laments, the affliction is couched in general terms. The psalmist feels overwhelmed by evil people but trusts in the "faithful God" (6).

31, 6: *Into your hands I commend my spirit:* in Lk 23, 46 Jesus breathes his last with this psalm verse. Stephen in Acts 7, 59 alludes to these words as he is attacked by enemies. The verse is used as an antiphon in the Divine Office at Compline, the last prayer of the day.

9   You will not abandon me into enemy hands,
>   but will set my feet in a free and open space.

>   II

10   Be gracious to me, LORD, for I am in distress;
>   with grief my eyes are wasted,
>   my soul and body spent.
11   My life is worn out by sorrow,
>   my years by sighing.
>   My strength fails in affliction;
>   my bones are consumed.[c]
12   To all my foes I am a thing of scorn,
>   to my neighbors, a dreaded sight,
>   a horror to my friends.
>   When they see me in the street,
>   they quickly shy away.[d]
13   I am forgotten, out of mind like the dead;
>   I am like a shattered dish.
14   I hear the whispers of the crowd;
>   terrors are all around me.
>   They conspire against me;
>   they plot to take my life.
15   But I trust in you, LORD;
>   I say, "You are my God."[e]
16   My times are in your hands;
>   rescue me from my enemies,
>   from the hands of my pursuers.
17   Let your face shine on your servant;[f]
>   save me in your kindness.
18   Do not let me be put to shame,
>   for I have called to you, LORD.
>   Put the wicked to shame;
>   reduce them to silence in Sheol.

---

[c] Pss 32, 3; 38, 10-11.   [e] Ps 140, 7; Is 25, 1.
[d] Jb 19, 13-19.   [f] Ps 67, 1; Nm 6, 24.

31, 13: *Like a shattered dish:* a common comparison for something ruined and useless. Cf Is 30, 14; Jer 19, 11; 22, 28.
31, 14: *Terrors are all around:* a cry used in inescapable danger. Cf Jer 6, 25; 20, 10; 46, 5; 49, 29.

19 Strike dumb their lying lips,
       proud lips that attack the just
       in contempt and scorn.^g

    III

20 How great is your goodness, Lord,
       stored up for those who fear you.
    You display it for those who trust you,
       in the sight of all the people.
21 You hide them in the shelter of your presence,
       safe from scheming enemies.
    You keep them in your abode,
       safe from plotting tongues.^h
22 Blessed be the Lord,
       who has shown me wondrous love,
       and been for me a city most secure.
23 Once I said in my anguish,
       "I am shut out from your sight."ⁱ
    Yet you heard my plea,
       when I cried out to you.
24 Love the Lord, all you faithful.
       The Lord protects the loyal,
       but repays the arrogant in full.
25 Be strong and take heart,
       all you who hope in the Lord.

Psalm 32
Remission of Sin

1 *Of David. A* maskil.

    I
    Happy the sinner whose fault is removed,
       whose sin is forgiven.^j

---

g Ps 12, 4.   i Jon 2, 5.
h Ps 27, 5.   j Is 1, 18; Ps 65, 3; Rom 4, 7-8.

Ps 32: An individual thanksgiving and the second of the seven Penitential Psalms (cf Ps 6). The opening declaration—the forgiven are blessed
(1-2)—arises from the psalmist's own experience. At one time the psalmist

2   Happy those to whom the LORD imputes no guilt,
        in whose spirit is no deceit.

    II

3   As long as I kept silent, my bones wasted away;
        I groaned all the day.[k]

4   For day and night your hand was heavy upon me;
        my strength withered as in dry summer heat.   *Selah*

5   Then I declared my sin to you;
        my guilt I did not hide.[l]
    I said, "I confess my faults to the LORD,"
        and you took away the guilt of my sin.   *Selah*

6   Thus should all your faithful pray
        in time of distress.
    Though flood waters threaten,
        they will never reach them.[m]

7   You are my shelter; from distress you keep me;
        with safety you ring me round.   *Selah*

    III

8   I will instruct you and show you the way you should walk,
        give you counsel and watch over you.

9   Do not be senseless like horses or mules;
        with bit and bridle their temper is curbed,
        else they will not come to you.

    IV

10 Many are the sorrows of the wicked,
        but love surrounds those who trust in the LORD.

11 Be glad in the LORD and rejoice, you just;
        exult, all you upright of heart.[n]

---

k Ps 31, 11.   m Ps 18, 5.
l Pss 38, 19; 51, 5.   n Ps 33, 1.

---

was stubborn and closed, a victim of sin's power (3-4), and then became open to the forgiving God (5-7). Sin here, as often in the Bible, is not only the personal act of rebellion against God but also the consequences of that act—frustration and waning of vitality. Having been rescued, the psalmist can teach others the joys of justice and the folly of sin (8-11).

32, 3: *I kept silent:* did not confess the sin before God.

32, 6: *Flood waters:* the untamed waters surrounding the earth, a metaphor for danger.

Psalm 33
Praise of God's Power and Providence

I

1 Rejoice, you just, in the LORD;
praise from the upright is fitting.[o]
2 Give thanks to the LORD on the harp;
on the ten-stringed lyre offer praise.[p]
3 Sing to God a new song;
skillfully play with joyful chant.
4 For the LORD's word is true;
all his works are trustworthy.
5 The LORD loves justice and right
and fills the earth with goodness.[q]

II

6 By the LORD's word the heavens were made;
by the breath of his mouth all their host.[r]
7 The waters of the sea were gathered as in a bowl;
in cellars the deep was confined.[s]

III

8 Let all the earth fear the LORD;
let all who dwell in the world show reverence.
9 For he spoke, and it came to be,
commanded, and it stood in place.[t]

---

[o] Pss 32, 11; 147, 1.
[p] Pss 92, 4; 144, 9.
[q] Ps 119, 64.
[r] Gn 2, 1.
[s] Ps 78, 13; Gn 1, 9-10; Ex 15, 8.
[t] Ps 148, 5; Gn 1, 3f; Jdt 16, 14.

Ps 33: A hymn in which the just are invited (1-3) to praise God, who by a mere word (4-5) created the three-tiered universe of the heavens, the cosmic waters, and the earth (6-9). Human words, in contrast, effect nothing (10-11). The greatness of human beings consists in God's choosing them as a special people and their faithful response (12-22).

33, 6: *All their host:* the stars of the sky are commonly viewed as a vast army, e.g., Neh 9, 6; Is 40, 26; 45, 12; Jer 33, 22.

33, 7: *The waters . . . as in a bowl:* ancients sometimes attributed the power keeping the seas from overwhelming land to a primordial victory of the storm-god over personified Sea. God confines the seas as easily as one puts water in a bowl.

10　The LORD foils the plan of nations,
　　　　frustrates the designs of peoples.
11　But the plan of the LORD stands forever,
　　　　wise designs through all generations.ᵘ
12　Happy the nation whose God is the LORD,
　　　　the people chosen as his very own.ᵛ

　　　IV
13　From heaven the LORD looks down
　　　　and observes the whole human race,ʷ
14　Surveying from the royal throne
　　　　all who dwell on earth.
15　The one who fashioned the hearts of them all
　　　　knows all their works.

　　　V
16　A king is not saved by a mighty army,
　　　　nor a warrior delivered by great strength.
17　Useless is the horse for safety;
　　　　its great strength, no sure escape.
18　But the LORD's eyes are upon the reverent,
　　　　upon those who hope for his gracious help,
19　Delivering them from death,
　　　　keeping them alive in times of famine.

　　　VI
20　Our soul waits for the LORD,
　　　　who is our help and shield.ˣ
21　For in God our hearts rejoice;
　　　　in your holy name we trust.
22　May your kindness, LORD, be upon us;
　　　　we have put our hope in you.

ᵘ Prv 19, 21; Is 40, 8.　　　　　19.
ᵛ Ps 144, 15; Ex 19, 6; Dt 7, 6.　　ˣ Ps 115, 9.
ʷ Jb 34, 21; Sir 15, 19; Jer 16, 17; 32,

Psalm 34
Thanksgiving to God Who Delivers the Just

1 *Of David, when he feigned madness before Abimelech, who forced him to depart.*

I

2 I will bless the LORD at all times;
  praise shall be always in my mouth.[y]

3 My soul will glory in the LORD
  that the poor may hear and be glad.

4 Magnify the LORD with me;
  let us exalt his name together.

II

5 I sought the LORD, who answered me,
  delivered me from all my fears.

6 Look to God that you may be radiant with joy
  and your faces may not blush for shame.

7 In my misfortune I called,
  the LORD heard and saved me from all distress.

8 The angel of the LORD, who encamps with them,
  delivers all who fear God.[z]

9 Learn to savor how good the LORD is;
  happy are those who take refuge in him.[a]

10 Fear the LORD, you holy ones;
  nothing is lacking to those who fear him.[b]

11 The powerful grow poor and hungry,
  but those who seek the LORD lack no good thing.

---

[y] Ps 145, 2.   [a] Ps 2, 12.
[z] Ex 14, 19.   [b] Prv 3, 7.

Ps 34: A thanksgiving in acrostic form, each line beginning with a successive letter of the Hebrew alphabet. In this psalm one letter is missing and two are in reverse order. The psalmist, fresh from the experience of being rescued (5. 7), can teach the "poor," those who are defenseless, to trust in God alone (4. 12). God will make them powerful (5-11) and give them protection (12-23).

34, 1: *Abimelech:* a scribal error for Achish. In 1 Sm 21, 13-16, David feigned madness before Achish, not Abimelech.

34, 11: *The powerful:* literally, "lions." Fierce animals were sometimes metaphors for influential people.

III

12 Come, children, listen to me;[c]
    I will teach you the fear of the LORD.
13 Who among you loves life,[d]
    takes delight in prosperous days?
14 Keep your tongue from evil,
    your lips from speaking lies.
15 Turn from evil and do good;[e]
    seek peace and pursue it.
16 The LORD has eyes for the just[f]
    and ears for their cry.
17 The LORD's face is against evildoers
    to wipe out their memory from the earth.
18 When the just cry out, the LORD hears
    and rescues them from all distress.
19 The LORD is close to the brokenhearted,
    saves those whose spirit is crushed.
20 Many are the troubles of the just,
    but the LORD delivers from them all.
21 God watches over all their bones;
    not a one shall be broken.[g]
22 Evil will slay the wicked;
    those who hate the just are condemned.
23 The LORD redeems loyal servants;
    no one is condemned whose refuge is God.

Psalm 35
Prayer for Help against Unjust Enemies

1 *Of David.*

I

Oppose, LORD, those who oppose me;
    war upon those who make war upon me.

---

[c] Prv 1, 8; 4, 1.
[d] 13-17: 1 Pt 3, 10-12.
[e] Ps 37, 27.

[f] Ps 33, 18.
[g] Jn 19, 36.

34, 12: *Children:* the customary term for students in Wisdom literature.
Ps 35: A lament of a person betrayed by friends. The psalmist prays that the evildoers be publicly exposed as unjust (1-8), and gives thanks

2 Take up the shield and buckler;
    rise up in my defense.
3 Brandish lance and battle-ax
    against my pursuers.
  Say to my heart,
    "I am your salvation."
4 Let those who seek my life
    be put to shame and disgrace.
  Let those who plot evil against me[h]
    be turned back and confounded.
5 Make them like chaff before the wind,[i]
    with the angel of the LORD driving them on.
6 Make their way slippery and dark,
    with the angel of the LORD pursuing them.

  II
7 Without cause they set their snare for me;
    without cause they dug a pit for me.
8 Let ruin overtake them unawares;
    let the snare they have set catch them;
    let them fall into the pit they have dug.[j]
9 Then I will rejoice in the LORD,
    exult in God's salvation.
10 My very bones shall say,
    "O LORD, who is like you,[k]
  Who rescue the afflicted from the powerful,
    the afflicted and needy from the despoiler?"

---

[h] Pss 40, 15; 71, 13.
[i] Pss 1, 4; 83, 14; Jb 21, 18.
[j] Pss 7, 16; 9, 16; 57, 7; Prv 26, 27; Eccl 10, 8; Sir 27, 26.
[k] Ps 86, 8; 89, 7. 9; Ex 15, 11.

---

in anticipation of vindication (9-10). Old friends are the enemies (11-16). May their punishment come quickly (17- 21)! The last part (22-26) echoes the opening in praying for the destruction of the psalmist's persecutors. The psalm may appear vindictive, but one must keep in mind that the psalmist is praying for *public* redress now of a *public* injustice. There is at this time no belief in an afterlife in which justice will be redressed.

35, 1-6: The mixture of judicial, martial, and hunting images shows that the language is figurative. The actual injustice is false accusation of serious crimes (11. 15. 20-21). The psalmist seeks lost honor through a trial before God.

III

11 Malicious witnesses come forward,
       accuse me of things I do not know.
12 They repay me evil for good
       and I am all alone.[l]
13 Yet I, when they were ill, put on sackcloth,
       afflicted myself with fasting,
       sobbed my prayers upon my bosom.
14 I went about in grief as for my brother,
       bent in mourning as for my mother.
15 Yet when I stumbled they gathered with glee,
       gathered against me like strangers.
    They slandered me without ceasing;
16   without respect they mocked me,
       gnashed their teeth against me.

IV

17 Lord, how long will you look on?
       Save me from roaring beasts,
       my precious life from lions![m]
18 Then I will thank you in the great assembly;
       I will praise you before the mighty throng.[n]
19 Do not let lying foes smirk at me,
       my undeserved enemies wink knowingly.[o]
20 They speak no words of peace,
       but against the quiet in the land
       they fashion deceitful speech.[p]
21 They open wide their mouths against me.
       They say, "Aha! Good!
       Our eyes relish the sight!"[q]
22 You see this, LORD; do not be silent;[r]
       Lord, do not withdraw from me.

---

[l] Pss 27, 12; 38, 20-21; 109, 5; Jer 18, 20.
[m] Pss 17, 12; 22, 22; 58, 7.
[n] Pss 22, 23; 26, 12; 35, 18; 40, 10; 149, 1.
[o] Ps 38, 17.
[p] Ps 120, 6-7.
[q] Ps 40, 16; Lam 2, 16.
[r] Pss 22, 12; 38, 21; 109, 1.

35, 13. 15-17: The Hebrew is obscure.

23 Awake, be vigilant in my defense,
     in my cause, my God and my Lord.
24 Defend me because you are just, LORD;
     my God, do not let them gloat over me.
25 Do not let them say in their hearts,
     "Aha! Just what we wanted!"
    Do not let them say,
     "We have devoured that one!"
26 Put to shame and confound
     all who relish my misfortune.
    Clothe with shame and disgrace
     those who lord it over me.
27 But let those who favor my just cause
     shout for joy and be glad.
    May they ever say, "Exalted be the LORD
     who delights in the peace of his loyal servant."
28 Then my tongue shall recount your justice,
     declare your praise, all the day long.[s]

Psalm 36
Human Wickedness and Divine Providence

1 *For the leader. Of David, the servant of the LORD.*

   I
2 Sin directs the heart of the wicked;
     their eyes are closed to the fear of God.[t]
3 For they live with the delusion:
     their guilt will not be known and hated.
4 Empty and false are the words of their mouth;
     they have ceased to be wise and do good.

---

[s] Ps 71, 15-16.   [t] Rom 3, 18.

Ps 36: A psalm with elements of wisdom (2-5), the hymn (6-10), and the lament (11-13). The rule of sin over the wicked (2-5) is contrasted with the rule of divine love and mercy over God's friends (6-10). The psalm ends with a prayer that God's guidance never cease (11-13).
    36, 3: *Hated:* punished by God.

5 In their beds they hatch plots;
      they set out on a wicked way;
      they do not reject evil.[u]

II

6 LORD, your love reaches to heaven;
      your fidelity, to the clouds.[v]
7 Your justice is like the highest mountains;
      your judgments, like the mighty deep;
      all living creatures you sustain, LORD.
8 How precious is your love, O God!
      We take refuge in the shadow of your wings.[w]
9 We feast on the rich food of your house;
      from your delightful stream[x] you give us drink.
10 For with you is the fountain of life,[y]
      and in your light we see light.[z]
11 Continue your kindness toward your friends,
      your just defense of the honest heart.
12 Do not let the foot of the proud overtake me,
      nor the hand of the wicked disturb me.
13 There make the evildoers fall;
      thrust them down, never to rise.

Psalm 37
The Fate of Sinners and the Reward of the Just

1 *Of David.*

Aleph

Do not be provoked by evildoers;
      do not envy those who do wrong.[a]

---

[u] Mi 2, 1.
[v] Pss 57, 11; 71, 19.
[w] Ps 17, 8.
[x] Gn 2, 8. 10.

[y] Is 55, 1; Jn 4, 14.
[z] Ps 80, 4. 8. 20.
[a] Prv 3, 31; 23, 17; 24, 1. 19.

36, 6-7: *Love . . . judgments:* God actively controls the entire world.
    36, 8: *The shadow of your wings:* metaphor for divine protection. It probably refers to the winged cherubim in the holy of holies in the temple. Cf 1 Kgs 6, 23-28. 32; 2 Chr 3, 10-13; Ez 1, 4-9.
    Ps 37: The psalm responds to the problem of evil, which the Old Testament often expresses as a question: why do the wicked prosper and the

2 Like grass they wither quickly;
    like green plants they wilt away.[b]

Beth

3 Trust in the LORD and do good
    that you may dwell in the land and live secure.[c]

4 Find your delight in the LORD
    who will give you your heart's desire.[d]

Gimel

5 Commit your way to the LORD;
    trust that God will act[e]

6 And make your integrity shine like the dawn,
    your vindication like noonday.[f]

Daleth

7 Be still before the LORD;
    wait for God.

   Do not be provoked by the prosperous,
    nor by malicious schemers.

He

8 Give up your anger, abandon your wrath;
      do not be provoked; it brings only harm.

9 Those who do evil will be cut off,
    but those who wait for the LORD will possess the land.[g]

Waw

10 Wait a little, and the wicked will be no more;
    look for them and they will not be there.

---

[b] Pss 90, 5-6; 102, 12; 103, 15-16; Jb 14, 2; Is 40, 7.
[c] Ps 128, 2.
[d] Prv 10, 24.
[e] Ps 55, 23; Prv 3, 5; 16, 3.
[f] Wis 5, 6; Is 58, 10.
[g] Ps 25, 13; Prv 2, 21; Is 57, 13.

---

good suffer? The psalm answers that the situation is only temporary. God will reverse things, rewarding the good and punishing the wicked here on earth. The perspective is concrete and earthbound: people's very actions place them among the ranks of the good or wicked. Each group or "way" has its own inherent dynamism—eventual frustration for the wicked, eventual reward for the just. The psalm is an acrostic, i.e., each section begins with a successive letter of the Hebrew alphabet. Each section has its own imagery and logic.

37, 3. 9. 11. 22. 27. 29. 34: *The land:* the promised land, Israel, which became for later interpreters a type or figure of heaven. Cf Heb 11, 9-10.

11 But the poor will possess the land,[h]
       will delight in great prosperity.
                              Zayin
12 The wicked plot against the just
       and grind their teeth at them;
13 But the LORD laughs at them,[i]
       knowing their day is coming.
                              Heth
14 The wicked draw their swords;
       they string their bows
    To fell the poor and oppressed,
       to slaughter those whose way is honest.[j]
15 Their swords will pierce their own hearts;
       their bows will be broken.
                              Teth
16 Better the poverty of the just
       than the great wealth of the wicked.[k]
17 The arms of the wicked will be broken;
       the LORD will sustain the just.
                              Yodh
18 The LORD watches over the days of the blameless;
       their heritage lasts forever.
19 They will not be disgraced when times are hard;
       in days of famine they will have plenty.
                              Kaph
20 The wicked perish,
       the enemies of the LORD;
    Like the beauty of meadows they vanish;
       like smoke they disappear.[l]
                              Lamedh
21 The wicked borrow but do not repay;
       the just are generous in giving.

---

h Mt 5, 4.   k Prv 15, 16; 16, 8.
i Pss 2, 4; 59, 9; Wis 4, 18.   l Wis 5, 14.
j Pss 11, 2; 57, 5; 64, 4.

13-16. The New Testament Beatitudes (Mt 5, 3-12; Lk 6, 20-26) have been influenced by the psalm, especially their total reversal of the present and their interpretation of the happy future as possession of the land.

22 For those blessed by the Lord will possess the land,
  but those accursed will be cut off.

Mem

23 Those whose steps are guided by the LORD;[m]
  whose way God approves,

24 May stumble, but they will never fall,
  for the LORD holds their hand.

Nun

25 Neither in my youth, nor now in old age
  have I ever seen the just abandoned[n]
  or their children begging bread.

26 The just always lend generously,
  and their children become a blessing.

Samekh

27 Turn from evil and do good,
  that you may inhabit the land forever.[o]

28 For the LORD loves justice
  and does not abandon the faithful.

Ayin

When the unjust are destroyed,
  and the children of the wicked cut off,

29 The just will possess the land
  and live in it forever.[p]

Pe

30 The mouths of the just utter wisdom;[q]
  their tongues speak what is right.

31 God's teaching is in their hearts;[r]
  their steps do not falter.

Sadhe

32 The wicked spy on the just
  and seek to kill them.

33 But the LORD does not leave the just in their power,
  nor let them be condemned when tried.

---

[m] Prv 20, 24.
[n] Jb 4, 7; Sir 2, 10.
[o] Ps 34, 14-15; Am 5, 14.
[p] Ps 25, 13; Prv 2, 21; Is 57, 13.
[q] Prv 10, 31.
[r] Ps 40, 9; Dt 6, 6; Is 51, 7; Jer 31, 33.

Qoph

34 Wait eagerly for the Lord,
    and keep to the way;[s]
God will raise you to possess the land;
    you will gloat when the wicked are cut off.

Resh

35 I have seen ruthless scoundrels,
    strong as flourishing cedars.[t]
36 When I passed by again, they were gone;
    though I searched, they could not be found.

Shin

37 Observe the honest, mark the upright;
    those at peace with God have a future.[u]
38 But all sinners will be destroyed;
    the future of the wicked will be cut off.

Taw

39 The salvation of the just is from the Lord,
    their refuge in time of distress.[v]
40 The Lord helps and rescues them,
    rescues and saves them from the wicked,
    because in God they take refuge.

Psalm 38
Prayer of an Afflicted Sinner

1 *A psalm of David. For remembrance.*

I

2 Lord, punish me no more in your anger;
    in your wrath do not chastise me![w]
3 Your arrows have sunk deep in me;[x]
    your hand has come down upon me.

---

s Ps 31, 24.
t Ps 92, 8-9; Is 2, 13; Ez 31, 10-11.
u Prv 23, 18; 24, 14.

v Ps 9, 10; Is 25, 4.
w Ps 6, 2.
x Jb 6, 4; Lam 3, 12; Pss 31, 11; 64, 7.

Ps 38: In this lament, one of the Penitential Psalms (cf Ps 6), the psalmist acknowledges the sin that has brought physical and mental sickness and social ostracism. There is no one to turn to for help; only God can undo the past and restore the psalmist.

4 My flesh is afflicted because of your anger;
    my frame aches because of my sin.[y]
5 My iniquities overwhelm me,
    a burden beyond my strength.[z]

II

6 Foul and festering are my sores
    because of my folly.
7 I am stooped and deeply bowed;[a]
    all day I go about mourning.
8 My loins burn with fever;
    my flesh is afflicted.
9 I am numb and utterly crushed;
    I wail with anguish of heart.[b]
10 My Lord, my deepest yearning is before you;
    my groaning is not hidden from you.
11 My heart shudders, my strength forsakes me;
    the very light of my eyes has failed.[c]
12 Friends and companions shun my pain;
    my neighbors stand far off.
13 Those who seek my life lay snares for me;
    they seek my misfortune, they speak of ruin;
    they plot treachery all the day.

III

14 But I am like the deaf, hearing nothing,
    like the dumb, saying nothing,
15 Like someone who does not hear,
    who has no answer ready.
16 LORD, I wait for you;
    O Lord, my God, answer me.[d]
17 For I fear they will gloat,
    exult over me if I stumble.

IV

18 I am very near to falling;
    my pain is with me always.

---

[y] Is 1, 5-6.
[z] Ps 40, 13; Ezr 9, 6.
[a] Ps 35, 14.
[b] Ps 102, 4-6.
[c] Pss 6, 8; 31, 10.
[d] Ps 13, 4.

19 I acknowledge my guilt
        and grieve over my sin.ᵉ
20 But many are my foes without cause,
        a multitude of enemies without reason,
21 Repaying me evil for good,
        harassing me for pursuing good.ᶠ
22 Forsake me not, O LORD;
        my God, be not far from me!ᵍ
23 Come quickly to help me,ʰ
        my Lord and my salvation!

Psalm 39
The Vanity of Life

1 *For the leader, for Jeduthun.ⁱ A psalm of David.*

    I

2 I said, "I will watch my ways,
        lest I sin with my tongue;
        I will set a curb on my mouth."
3 Dumb and silent before the wicked,
        I refrained from any speech.
    But my sorrow increased;
4   my heart smoldered within me.ʲ
    In my thoughts a fire blazed up,
        and I broke into speech:

    II

5 LORD, let me know my end, the number of my days,
        that I may learn how frail I am.

ᵉ Pss 32, 5; 51, 5.   ʰ Ps 40, 14.
ᶠ Ps 109, 5.   ⁱ 1 Chr 16, 41; Pss 62,˙1; 77, 1.
ᵍ Pss 22, 2. 12. 20; 35, 22.   ʲ Jer 20, 9.

Ps 39: The lament of a mortally ill person who at first had resolved
to remain silently submissive (2-4). But the grief was too much and now
the psalmist laments the brevity and vanity of life (5-7), yet remaining
hopeful (8-10). The psalmist continues to express both acceptance of the
illness and hope for healing in 11-14.

6 You have given my days a very short span;
    my life is as nothing before you.
    All mortals are but a breath.[k]   *Selah*
7 Mere phantoms, we go our way;
    mere vapor, our restless pursuits;
    we heap up stores without knowing for whom.
8 And now, Lord, what future do I have?
    You are my only hope.
9 From all my sins deliver me;
    let me not be the taunt of fools.

   III

10 I was silent and did not open my mouth
    because you were the one who did this.
11 Take your plague away from me;
    I am ravaged by the touch of your hand.
12 You rebuke our guilt and chasten us;
    you dissolve all we prize like a cobweb.
    All mortals are but a breath.   *Selah*
13 Listen to my prayer, LORD, hear my cry;
    do not be deaf to my weeping!
  I sojourn with you like a passing stranger,
    a guest, like all my ancestors.[l]
14 Turn your gaze from me, that I may find peace
    before I depart to be no more.

Psalm 40
Gratitude and Prayer for Help

1 *For the leader. A psalm of David.*

A

   I

2 I waited, waited for the LORD;
    who bent down and heard my cry,[m]

---

[k] Pss 62, 10; 90, 9-10; 144, 4; Jb 7, 6.   [Pt] 2, 11.
  16; 14, 1. 5; Eccl 6, 12; Wis 2, 5.   [m] Lam 3, 25.
[l] Ps 119, 19; Gn 23, 4; Heb 11, 13; 1

Ps 40: A thanksgiving (2-13) has been combined with a lament (14-18), that appears also in Ps 70. The psalmist describes the rescue in spa-

3 Drew me out of the pit of destruction,
out of the mud of the swamp,[n]
Set my feet upon rock,
steadied my steps,
4 And put a new song in my mouth,[o]
a hymn to our God.
Many shall look on in awe
and they shall trust in the LORD.

II
5 Happy those whose trust is the LORD,
who turn not to idolatry
or to those who stray after falsehood.[p]
6 How numerous, O LORD, my God,
you have made your wondrous deeds!
And in your plans for us
there is none to equal you.[q]
Should I wish to declare or tell them,
too many are they to recount.[r]

III
7 Sacrifice and offering you do not want;[s]
but ears open to obedience you gave me.
Holocausts and sin-offerings you do not require;
8 so I said, "Here I am;
your commands for me are written in the scroll.

---

[n] Pss 28, 1; 30, 4; 69, 3. 15-16; 88, 5; Prv 1, 12; Jon 2, 7.
[o] Ps 33, 3.
[p] Ps 1, 1; Prv 16, 20; Jer 17, 7.
[q] Ps 35, 10.
[r] Pss 71, 15; 139, 17-18.
[s] 7-9: Heb 10, 5-7; Ps 51, 18-19; Am 5, 22; Hos 6, 6; Is 1, 11-15.

---

tial terms—being raised up from the swampy underworld to firm earth where one can praise God (2-4). All who trust God will experience like protection (5-6)! The psalm stipulates the precise mode of thanksgiving: not animal sacrifice but open and enthusiastic proclamation of the salvation just experienced (7-11). A prayer for protection concludes (12-18).

40, 4: *A new song:* a song in response to the new action of God (cf Pss 33, 3; 96, 1; 144, 9; 149, 1; Is 42, 10). Giving thanks is not purely a human response but is itself a divine gift.

40, 7-9: Obedience is better than sacrifice (cf 1 Sm 15, 22; Is 1, 10-20; Hos 6, 6; Am 5, 22-25; Mi 6, 6-8; Acts 7, 42-43 [quoting Am 5, 25-26 LXX]).

9 To do your will is my delight;
        my God, your law is in my heart!"[t]

10 I announced your deed to a great assembly;
        I did not restrain my lips;
        you, LORD, are my witness.[u]

11 Your deed I did not hide within my heart;
        your loyal deliverance I have proclaimed.
    I made no secret of your enduring kindness
        to a great assembly.

B

I

12 LORD, do not withhold your compassion from me;
        may your enduring kindness ever preserve me.[v]

13 For all about me are evils beyond count;
        my sins so overcome me I cannot see.
    They are more than the hairs of my head;
        my courage fails me.[w]

II

14 LORD, graciously rescue me![x]
        Come quickly to help me, LORD!

15 Put to shame and confound
        all who seek to take my life.
    Turn back in disgrace
        those who desire my ruin.[y]

16 Let those who say "Aha!"[z]
        know dismay and shame.

17 But may all who seek you
        rejoice and be glad in you.
    May those who long for your help
        always say, "The LORD be glorified."[a]

18 Though I am afflicted and poor,
        the Lord keeps me in mind.

---

[t] Ps 37, 31.   [x] 14-18: Pss 70, 2-6; 71, 12.
[u] Pss 22, 23; 26, 12; 35, 18; 149, 1. [y] Ps 35, 4. 26.
[v] Ps 89, 34.   [z] Ps 35, 21. 25.
[w] Ps 38, 5. 11; Ezr 9, 6.   [a] Ps 35, 27.

Heb 10, 5-9 quotes the somewhat different Greek version and interprets it as Christ's self-oblation.

You are my help and deliverer;
my God, do not delay!

Psalm 41
Thanksgiving after Sickness

1 *For the leader. A psalm of David.*

I

2 Happy those concerned for the lowly and poor;
when misfortune strikes, the LORD delivers them.[b]
3 The LORD keeps and preserves them,
makes them happy in the land,
and does not betray them to their enemies.
4 The LORD sustains them on their sickbed,
allays the malady when they are ill.

II

5 Once I prayed, "LORD, have mercy on me;
heal me, I have sinned against you.
6 My enemies say the worst of me:
'When will that one die and be forgotten?'
7 When people come to visit me,
they speak without sincerity.
Their hearts store up malice;
they leave and spread their vicious lies.[c]
8 My foes all whisper against me;
they imagine the worst about me:

---

b Tb 4, 7-11.   13-19; Jer 20, 10.
c Pss 31, 12; 38, 12-13; 88, 8; Jb 19,

Ps 41: A thanksgiving for rescue from illness (4. 5. 9). Many people,
even friends, have interpreted the illness as a divine punishment for sin
and have ostracized the psalmist (5-11). The healing shows the return
of God's favor and rebukes the psalmist's detractors (12-13).

41, 2: *Happy those concerned for the lowly and poor:* other psalms use
the same formula ("Happy those") for those whom God favors. Cf Pss
32, 1-2; 34, 9; 40, 5; 65, 5. The psalmist's statement about God's love
of the poor is based on the experience of being rescued (1-3).

9　I have a deadly disease, they say;
　　　　I will never rise from my sickbed.
10　Even the friend who had my trust,
　　　　who shared my table, has scorned me.[d]
11　But you, LORD, have mercy and raise me up
　　　　that I may repay them as they deserve.''

　　III
12　By this I know you are pleased with me,
　　　　that my enemy no longer jeers at me.
13　For my integrity you have supported me
　　　　and let me stand in your presence forever.

　　　　　　　* * *

14　Blessed be the LORD, the God of Israel,
　　　　from all eternity and forever.
　　　　Amen. Amen.[e]

---

[d] Ps 55, 14-15; Jn 13, 18.　　　　　　[e] Neh 9, 5.

41, 10: *Even the friend . . . has scorned me:* Jn 13, 18 cites this verse to characterize Judas as a false friend. *Scorned me:* an interpretation of the unclear Hebrew, ''made great the heel against me.''

41, 11: *That I may repay them as they deserve:* the healing itself is an act of judgment through which God decides for the psalmist and against the false friends. The prayer is not necessarily for strength to punish enemies.

41, 14: The doxology, not part of the psalm, marks the end of the first of the five books of the Psalter. Compare Pss 72, 18-20; 89, 53; 106, 48.

SECOND BOOK—PSALMS 42-72

Psalms 42–43
Longing for God's Presence in the Temple

1 *For the leader. A* maskil *of the Korahites.*

I

2 As the deer longs for streams of water,[f]
    so my soul longs for you, O God.

3 My being thirsts for God, the living God.
    When can I go and see the face of God?[g]

4 My tears have been my food day and night,[h]
    as they ask daily, "Where is your God?"[i]

5 Those times I recall
    as I pour out my soul,[j]
When I went in procession with the crowd,
    I went with them to the house of God,
Amid loud cries of thanksgiving,
    with the multitude keeping festival.[k]

6 Why are you downcast, my soul;
    why do you groan within me?
Wait for God, whom I shall praise again,
    my savior and my God.

---

[f] 2-3: Pss 63, 2; 84, 3; 143, 6; Is 26, 9.
[g] Ps 27, 4.
[h] Pss 80, 6; 102, 10.
[i] Ps 79, 10; Jl 2, 17.
[j] Lam 3, 20.
[k] Ps 122, 5.

Pss 42–43: Pss 42–43 form a single lament of three sections, each section ending in an identical refrain (42, 6. 12; 43, 5). The psalmist is in the extreme north of Israel, far from Jerusalem, and longs for the divine presence that Israel experienced in the temple liturgy. Despite sadness, the psalmist hopes once again to join the worshiping crowds.

42, 1: *The Korahites:* a major guild of temple singers (2 Chr 20, 19) whose name appears in the superscriptions of Pss 42; 44-49; 84-85; 87-88.

42, 3: *See the face of God:* "face" designates a personal presence (Gn 33, 10; Ex 10, 28-29; 2 Sm 17, 11). The expressions "see God/God's face" occur elsewhere (Pss 11, 7; 17, 15; 63, 3; cf Ex 24, 10; 33, 7-11; Jb 33, 26) for the presence of God in the temple.

II

7 My soul is downcast within me;
        therefore I will remember you
    From the land of the Jordan and Hermon,
        from the land of Mount Mizar.[l]
8 Here deep calls to deep in the roar of your torrents.
        All your waves and breakers sweep over me.[m]
9 At dawn may the LORD bestow faithful love
        that I may sing praise through the night,
        praise to the God of my life.
10 I say to God, "My rock,
        why do you forget me?[n]
    Why must I go about mourning
        with the enemy oppressing me?"
11 It shatters my bones, when my adversaries reproach me.
        They say to me daily: "Where is your God?"
12 Why are you downcast, my soul,
        why do you groan within me?
    Wait for God, whom I shall praise again,
        my savior and my God.

III

1 Grant me justice, God;
        defend me from a faithless people;
        from the deceitful and unjust rescue me.[o]
2 You, God, are my strength.
        Why then do you spurn me?
    Why must I go about mourning,
        with the enemy oppressing me?

---

[l] Ps 43, 3.   [n] Pss 18, 2; 31, 3-4.
[m] Pss 18, 5; 32, 6; 69, 2; 88, 8; Jon 2, 4.   [o] Ps 119, 154.

42, 7: *From the land of the Jordan:* the sources of the Jordan are in the foothills of Mount Hermon in present-day southern Lebanon. Mount Mizar is presumed to be a mountain in the same range.

42, 8: *Here deep calls to deep:* to the psalmist, the waters arising in the north are overwhelming and far from God's presence, like the waters of chaos (Pss 18, 5; 69, 2-3. 15; Jon 2, 3-6).

3   Send your light and fidelity,
  that they may be my guide[p]
  And bring me to your holy mountain,
   to the place of your dwelling,[q]
4   That I may come to the altar of God,
  to God, my joy, my delight.
  Then I will praise you with the harp,
   O God, my God.
5   Why are you downcast, my soul?
  Why do you groan within me?
  Wait for God, whom I shall praise again,
   my savior and my God.

Psalm 44
God's Past Favor and Israel's Present Need

1   *For the leader. A* maskil *of the Korahites.*

 I

2   O God, we have heard with our own ears;
  our ancestors have told us[r]
  The deeds you did in their days,
   with your own hand in days of old:
3   You rooted out nations to plant them,[s]
  crushed peoples to make room for them.
4   Not with their own swords did they conquer the land,[t]
  nor did their own arms bring victory;

---

p Pss 18, 29; 27, 1; 36, 10; Mi 7, 8.   s Pss 78, 55; 80, 9f.
q Ps 122, 1.   t Dt 8, 17f; Jos 24, 12.
r Ps 78, 3.

43, 3: *Your light and fidelity:* a pair of divine attributes personified as guides for the pilgrimage. The psalmist seeks divine protection for the journey to Jerusalem.

Ps 44: In this lament the community reminds God of past favors which it has always acknowledged (2-9). But now God has abandoned Israel to defeat and humiliation (10-17), though the people are not conscious of any sin against the covenant (18-23). They struggle with being God's special people amid divine silence; yet they continue to pray (24-27).

It was your right hand, your own arm,
 the light of your face, for you favored them.[u]

5 You are my king and my God,[v]
 who bestows victories on Jacob.

6 Through you we batter our foes;
 through your name, trample our adversaries.

7 Not in my bow do I trust,
 nor does my sword bring me victory.

8 You have brought us victory over our enemies,
 shamed those who hate us.

9 In God we have boasted all the day long;
 your name we will praise forever.   *Selah*

 II

10 But now you have rejected and disgraced us;[w]
 you do not march out with our armies.[x]

11 You make us retreat before the foe;
 those who hate us plunder us at will.[y]

12 You hand us over like sheep to be slaughtered,
 scatter us among the nations.[z]

13 You sell your people for nothing;
 you make no profit from their sale.[a]

14 You make us the reproach of our neighbors,[b]
 the mockery and scorn of those around us.

15 You make us a byword among the nations;
 the peoples shake their heads at us.

16 All day long my disgrace is before me;
 shame has covered my face

17 At the sound of those who taunt and revile,
 at the sight of the spiteful enemy.

---

[u] Pss 4, 7; 31, 17; 67, 2; 80, 4; Nm 6, 25; Dn 9, 17.
[v] Ps 145, 1.
[w] 10-27: Ps 89, 39-52.
[x] Ps 60, 12.
[y] Lv 26, 17; Dt 28, 25.
[z] Lv 26, 33; Dt 28, 64.
[a] Dt 32, 30; Is 52, 3.
[b] 14-17: Pss 79, 4; 80, 7; 123, 3-4; Jb 12, 4; Dn 9, 16.

44, 11: *You make us retreat:* the corollary of v 4. Defeat, like victory, is God's doing; neither Israel nor its enemies can claim credit (23).

III

18 All this has come upon us,
    though we have not forgotten you,
    nor been disloyal to your covenant.
19 Our hearts have not turned back,
    nor have our steps strayed from your path.
20 Yet you have left us crushed,
    desolate in a place of jackals;ᶜ
    you have covered us with darkness.
21 If we had forgotten the name of our God,
    stretched out our hands to another god,
22 Would not God have discovered this,
    God who knows the secrets of the heart?
23 For you we are slain all the day long,
    considered only as sheep to be slaughtered.ᵈ

    IV

24 Awake! Why do you sleep, O Lord?
    Rise up! Do not reject us forever!ᵉ
25 Why do you hide your face;ᶠ
    why forget our pain and misery?
26 We are bowed down to the ground;ᵍ
    our bodies are pressed to the earth.
27 Rise up, help us!
    Redeem us as your love demands.

ᶜ Jer 9, 10. ᶠ Pss 10, 11; 89, 47; Jb 13, 24.
ᵈ Rom 8, 36. ᵍ Ps 119, 25.
ᵉ Pss 10, 1; 74, 1; 77, 8; 79, 5; 83, 2.

44, 19: *Our hearts have not turned back:* Israel's defeat was not caused by its lack of fidelity.

44, 20: *A place of jackals:* following Israel's defeat and exile (11-12), the land lies desolate, inhabited only by jackals. Cf Is 13, 22; Jer 9, 10; 10, 22. Others take *tannim* as "sea monster" (cf Ez 29, 3; 32, 2) and render: "you crushed us as you did the sea monster."

Psalm 45
Song for a Royal Wedding

1 *For the leader; according to "Lilies." A* maskil *of the Korahites. A love song.*

I

2 My heart is stirred by a noble theme,
    as I sing my ode to the king.
    My tongue is the pen of a nimble scribe.

II

3 You are the most handsome of men;
    fair speech has graced your lips,
    for God has blessed you forever.[h]
4 Gird your sword upon your hip, mighty warrior!
    In splendor and majesty ride on triumphant![i]
5 In the cause of truth and justice
    may your right hand show you wondrous deeds.
6 Your arrows are sharp;
    peoples will cower at your feet;
    the king's enemies will lose heart.
7 Your throne, O god, stands forever;[j]
    your royal scepter is a scepter for justice.
8 You love justice and hate wrongdoing;
    therefore God, your God, has anointed you
    with the oil of gladness above your fellow kings.

---

h Song 5, 10-16.   j 7-8: Heb 1, 8-9.
i Ps 21, 5.

Ps 45: A song for the Davidic king's marriage to a foreign princess from Tyre in Phoenicia. The court poet sings (2. 18) of God's choice of the king (3. 8), of his role in establishing divine rule (4-8), and of his splendor as he waits for his bride (9-10). The woman is to forget her own house when she becomes wife to the king (11-13). Her majestic beauty today is a sign of the future prosperity of the royal house (14-18). The psalm was retained in the collection when there was no reigning king, and came to be applied to the king who was to come, the messiah.

45, 7: *O god:* the king, in courtly language, is called "god," i.e., more than human, representing God to the people. Heb 1, 8-9 applies 7-8 to Christ.

9   With myrrh, aloes, and cassia
        your robes are fragrant.
    From ivory-paneled palaces
        stringed instruments bring you joy.
10 Daughters of kings are your lovely wives;
        a princess arrayed in Ophir's gold
        comes to stand at your right hand.

    III
11 Listen, my daughter, and understand;
        pay me careful heed.
    Forget your people and your father's house,
12   that the king might desire your beauty.
    He is your lord;
13   honor him, daughter of Tyre.
    Then the richest of the people
        will seek your favor with gifts.[k]
14 All glorious is the king's daughter as she enters,[l]
        her raiment threaded with gold;
15 In embroidered apparel she is led to the king.
        The maids of her train are presented to the king.
16 They are led in with glad and joyous acclaim;
        they enter the palace of the king.

    IV
17 The throne of your fathers your sons will have;
        you shall make them princes through all the land.[m]
18 I will make your name renowned through all generations;
        thus nations shall praise you forever.[n]

---

[k] Ps 72, 10-11; Is 60, 5f.   [m] Gn 17, 6.
[l] 14-16: Ez 16, 10-13.   [n] Is 60, 15.

45, 9: *Ivory-paneled palaces:* literally, "palaces of ivory." Ivory panel-ing and furniture decoration have been found in Samaria and other an-cient Near Eastern cities. Cf Am 3, 15.

45, 10: *Ophir's gold:* uncertain location, possibly a region on the coast of southern Arabia or eastern Africa, famous for its gold. Cf 1 Kgs 9, 28; 10, 11; Jb 22, 24.

45, 11: *Forget your people and your father's house:* the bride should no longer consider herself a daughter of her father's house, but the wife of the king—the queen.

Psalm 46
God, the Protector of Zion

1 *For the leader. A song of the Korahites. According to* alamoth.

I

2 God is our refuge and our strength,
an ever-present help in distress.[o]
3 Thus we do not fear, though earth be shaken
and mountains quake to the depths of the sea,
4 Though its waters rage and foam
and mountains totter at its surging.[p]
The LORD of hosts is with us;
our stronghold is the God of Jacob. *Selah*

II

5 Streams of the river gladden the city of God,
the holy dwelling of the Most High.[q]
6 God is in its midst; it shall not be shaken;
God will help it at break of day.[r]
7 Though nations rage and kingdoms totter,
God's voice thunders and the earth trembles.[s]

---

[o] Ps 48, 4; Is 33, 2.
[p] Ps 93, 3-4; Jb 9, 5-6; Is 24, 18-20; 54, 10.
[q] Pss 48, 2-3; 76, 3.
[r] Is 7, 14.
[s] Pss 2, 1-5; 48, 5-8; 76, 7-9; Is 17, 12-14.

Ps 46: A song of confidence in God's protection of Zion with close parallels to Ps 48. The dominant note in Ps 46 is sounded by the refrain, *The LORD of hosts is with us* (4. 8. 12). The first strophe (2-4) sings of the security of God's presence even in utter chaos; the second (5-8), of divine protection of the city from its enemies; the third (9-12), of God's imposition of imperial peace.

46, 1: *Alamoth:* the melody of the psalm, now lost.

46, 3-4: Figurative ancient Near Eastern language to describe social and political upheavals.

46, 4b: The first line of the refrain is similar in structure and meaning to Isaiah's name for the royal child, Immanuel, *With us is God* (Is 7, 14; 8, 8. 10).

46, 5: Jerusalem is not situated on a river. This description derives from mythological descriptions of the divine abode and symbolizes the divine presence as the source of all life (cf Is 33, 21; Ez 47, 1-12; Jl 4, 18; Zec 14, 8; Rv 22, 1-2).

8 The LORD of hosts is with us;
    our stronghold is the God of Jacob.   *Selah*

III

9 Come and see the works of the LORD,
    who has done fearsome deeds on earth;[t]
10 Who stops wars to the ends of the earth,
    breaks the bow, splinters the spear,
    and burns the shields with fire;[u]
11 Who says:
    "Be still and confess that I am God!
    I am exalted among the nations,
    exalted on the earth."[v]
12 The LORD of hosts is with us;
    our stronghold is the God of Jacob.   *Selah*

Psalm 47
The Ruler of All the Nations

1 *For the leader. A psalm of the Korahites.*

I

2 All you peoples, clap your hands;
    shout to God with joyful cries.[w]
3 For the LORD, the Most High, inspires awe,
    the great king over all the earth,[x]
4 Who made people subject to us,
    brought nations under our feet,[y]
5 Who chose a land for our heritage,
    the glory of Jacob, the beloved.[z]   *Selah*

---

[t] Ps 48, 9-10.
[u] Ps 76, 4.
[v] Ps 48, 11.
[w] Ps 89, 16; Zep 3, 14.

[x] Ps 95, 3; Ex 15, 18; Is 24, 23; 52, 7.
[y] Ps 2, 8.
[z] Is 58, 14.

Ps 47: A hymn calling on the nations to acknowledge the universal rule of Israel's God (2-5) who is enthroned as king over Israel and the nations (6-10).

47, 5: *Our heritage . . . the glory:* the land of Israel (cf Is 58, 14), which God has given Israel in an act of sovereignty.

II

6 God mounts the throne amid shouts of joy;
      the LORD, amid trumpet blasts.[a]

7 Sing praise to God, sing praise;
      sing praise to our king, sing praise.

III

8 God is king over all the earth;[b]
      sing hymns of praise.

9 God rules over the nations;
      God sits upon his holy throne.

10 The princes of the peoples assemble
       with the people of the God of Abraham.

   For the rulers of the earth belong to God,
      who is enthroned on high.[c]

Psalm 48
The Splendor of the Invincible City

1 *A psalm of the Korahites. A song.*

I

2 Great is the LORD and highly praised
      in the city of our God:[d]

   The holy mountain, (3) fairest of heights,
      the joy of all the earth,[e]

---

[a] Pss 24, 8. 10; 68, 18-19; 98, 6.
[b] 8-9: Pss 72, 11; 93, 1; 96, 10; 97, 1;
   99, 1; Jer 10, 7.
[c] Ps 89, 19; Ex 3, 6; Is 2, 2-4.
[d] Pss 96, 4; 145, 3.
[e] Ps 50, 2; Lam 2, 15.

47, 6: *God mounts the throne:* "has gone up to the throne," according to the context (9). Christian liturgical tradition has applied the verse to the ascension of Christ.

Ps 48: A Zion hymn, praising the holy city as the invincible dwelling place of God. Unconquerable, it is an apt symbol of God who has defeated all enemies. After seven epithets describing the city (2-3), the psalm describes the victory by the Divine Warrior over hostile kings (4-8). The second half proclaims the dominion of the God of Zion over all the earth (9-12) and invites pilgrims to announce that God is eternally invincible like Zion itself (13-15).

48, 1: *Korahites:* see note on Ps 42, 1.

48, 3: *The heights of Zaphon:* the mountain abode of the Canaanite

Mount Zion, the heights of Zaphon,[f]
    the city of the great king.

II

4 God is its citadel,
    renowned as a stronghold.
5 See! The kings assembled,
    together they invaded.
6 When they looked they were astounded;
    terrified, they were put to flight![g]
7 Trembling seized them there,
    anguish, like a woman's labor,[h]
8 As when the east wind wrecks
    the ships of Tarshish!

III

9 What we had heard we now see
    in the city of the Lord of hosts,
  In the city of our God,
    founded to last forever.   *Selah*
10 O God, within your temple
    we ponder your steadfast love.
11 Like your name, O God,
    your praise reaches the ends of the earth.[i]

---

[f] Is 14, 13.   [h] Ex 15, 14; Jer 4, 31.
[g] Jgs 5, 19.   [i] Mal 1, 11.

storm-god Baal in comparable texts. To speak of Zion as if it were Zaphon was to claim for Israel's God what Canaanites claimed for Baal. Though topographically speaking Zion is only a hill, viewed religiously it towers over other mountains as the home of the supreme God (cf Ps 68, 16-17).

48, 6: *When they looked:* the kings are stunned by the sight of Zion, touched by divine splendor. The language is that of holy war, in which the enemy panics and flees at the sight of divine glory.

48, 8: *The ships of Tarshish:* large ships, named after the distant land or port of Tarshish, probably ancient Tartessus in southern Spain, although other identifications have been proposed. Cf Is 2, 16; 60, 9; Jon 1, 3.

48, 9: *What we had heard we now see:* the glorious things that new pilgrims had heard about the holy cityits beauty and awesomenessthey now see with their own eyes. The seeing here contrasts with the seeing of the hostile kings in 6.

Your right hand is fully victorious.
12   Mount Zion is glad!
The cities of Judah rejoice
      because of your saving deeds!ʲ

IV

13 Go about Zion, walk all around it,
      note the number of its towers.
14 Consider the ramparts, examine its citadels,
      that you may tell future generations:ᵏ
15 "Yes, so mighty is God,
      our God who leads us always!"

Psalm 49
Confidence in God rather than in Riches

1 *For the leader. A psalm of the Korahites.*

2 Hear this, all you peoples!
      Give ear, all who inhabit the world,
3 You of lowly birth or high estate,
      rich and poor alike.
4 My mouth shall speak wisdom,
      my heart shall offer insight.ˡ
5 I will turn my attention to a problem,
      expound my question to the music of a lyre.

ʲ Ps 97, 8.   ˡ Ps 78, 2; Mt 13, 35.
ᵏ Pss 22, 31-32; 71, 18.

48, 15: *So mighty is God:* Israel's God is like Zion in being eternal and invincible. The holy city is therefore a kind of "sacrament" of God.

Ps 49: The psalm affirms confidence in God (cf Pss 23; 27, 1-6; 62) in the face of the apparent good fortune of the unjust rich. Cf Pss 37; 73. Reliance on wealth is misplaced (8-10) for it is of no avail in the face of death (18-20). After inviting all to listen to this axiom of faith (2-5), the psalmist depicts the self-delusion of the ungodly (6-13), whose destiny is to die like ignorant beasts (13. 18; cf Prv 7, 21-23). Their wealth should occasion no alarm, for they will come to nought, whereas God will save the just (14-21).

49,1: *Korahites:* see note on Ps 42, 1.

49, 5: *Problem:* the psalmist's personal solution to the perennial biblical problem of the prosperity of the wicked. *Question:* parallel in mean-

I

6　Why should I fear in evil days,
　　　　when my wicked pursuers ring me round,
7　Those who trust in their wealth
　　　　and boast of their abundant riches?[m]
8　One cannot redeem oneself,
　　　　pay to God a ransom.[n]
9　Too high the price to redeem a life;
　　　　one would never have enough
10　To stay alive forever
　　　　and never see the pit.
11　Anyone can see that the wisest die,
　　　　the fool and the senseless pass away too,[o]
　　　　and must leave their wealth to others.[p]
12　Tombs are their homes forever,
　　　　their dwellings through all generations,
　　　　though they gave their names to their lands.
13　For all their riches
　　　　mortals do not abide;
　　　　they perish like the beasts.[q]

II

14　This is the destiny of those who trust in folly,
　　　　the end of those so pleased with their wealth.　　*Selah*
15　Like sheep they are herded into Sheol,
　　　　where death will be their shepherd.
　　Straight to the grave they descend,
　　　　where their form will waste away,
　　　　Sheol will be their palace.

---

[m] Jb 31, 24.　　　　　　　　　　　[p] Ps 39, 7; Sir 11, 18-19.
[n] Prv 10, 15; 11, 4; Ez 7, 19; Mt 16, 26.　　[q] Eccl 3, 18-21.
[o] Eccl 2, 16.

---

ing to *problem;* in Wisdom literature it means the mysterious way of how the world works.

49, 8: *One cannot redeem oneself:* an axiom. For the practice of redemption, cf Jb 6, 21-23. A play on the first Hebrew word of v 8 and v 16 relates the two verses.

16 But God will redeem my life,   *Selah*
    will take me from the power of Sheol.ʳ
17 Do not fear when others become rich,
    when the wealth of their houses grows great.
18 When they die they will take nothing with them,
    their wealth will not follow them down.ˢ
19 When living, they congratulate themselves and say:
    "All praise you, you do so well."
20 But they will join the company of their forebears,
    never again to see the light.ᵗ
21 For all their riches,
    if mortals do not have wisdom,
    they perish like the beasts.

Psalm 50
The Acceptable Sacrifice

1 *A psalm of Asaph.*

I
The LORD, the God of gods,
    has spoken and summoned the earth
    from the rising of the sun to its setting.ᵘ
2 From Zion God shines forth,ᵛ
    perfect in beauty.
3 Our God comes and will not be silent!
    Devouring fire precedes,
    storming fiercely round about.ʷ

ʳ Pss 16, 10; 86, 13; 103, 4; 116, 8.   ᵘ Dt 10, 17; Jos 22, 22.
ˢ Sir 11, 18-19; Eccl 5, 15; 1 Tm 6, 7.   ᵛ Ps 48, 2.
ᵗ Jb 10, 21-22.   ʷ Ps 97, 3; Dn 7, 10.

49, 16: *Will take me:* the same Hebrew verb is used of God "taking up" a favored servant: Enoch in Gn 5, 24; Elijah in 2 Kgs 2, 11-12; the righteous person in Ps 73, 24. The verse apparently states the hope that God will rescue the faithful psalmist in the same manner.

Ps 50: A covenant lawsuit stating that the sacrifice God really wants is the sacrifice of praise accompanied by genuine obedience (cf Mi 6, 1-8). It begins with a theophany and the summoning of the court (1-6). Then in direct address God explains what is required of the faithful (7-15), rebukes the hypocritical worshiper (16-21), and concludes with a threat and a promise (22-23; cf Is 1, 19-20).

4   God summons the heavens above
      and the earth to the judgment of his people:
5   "Gather my faithful ones before me,
      those who made a covenant with me by sacrifice."
6   The heavens proclaim divine justice,
      for God alone is the judge.[x]   *Selah*

    II
7   "Listen, my people, I will speak;
      Israel, I will testify against you;
      God, your God, am I.
8   Not for your sacrifices do I rebuke you,
      nor for your holocausts, set before me daily.
9   I need no bullock from your house,
      no goats from your fold.[y]
10   For every animal of the forest is mine,
      beasts by the thousands on my mountains.
11   I know every bird of the heavens;
      the creatures of the field belong to me.
12   Were I hungry, I would not tell you,
      for mine is the world and all that fills it.[z]
13   Do I eat the flesh of bulls
      or drink the blood of goats?
14   Offer praise as your sacrifice to God;[a]
      fulfill your vows to the Most High.
15   Then call on me in time of distress;[b]
      I will rescue you, and you shall honor me."

    III
16   But to the wicked God says:
      "Why do you recite my commandments
      and profess my covenant with your lips?
17   You hate discipline;
      you cast my words behind you!
18   When you see thieves, you befriend them;
      with adulterers you throw in your lot.

---

[x] Pss 19, 2; 97, 6.
[y] Ps 69, 32; Am 5, 21-22.
[z] Pss 24, 1; 89, 12; Dt 10, 14; 1 Cor 10, 26.
[a] Heb 13, 15.
[b] Ps 77, 3.

19 You give your mouth free rein for evil;
     you harness your tongue to deceit.
20 You sit maligning your own kin,
     slandering the child of your own mother.
21 When you do these things should I be silent?
     Or do you think that I am like you?
     I accuse you, I lay the charge before you.

    IV
22 "Understand this, you who forget God,
     lest I attack you with no one to rescue.
23 Those who offer praise as a sacrifice honor me;
     to the obedient I will show the salvation of God."[c]

Psalm 51
The Miserere: Prayer of Repentance

1 *For the leader. A psalm of David, (2) when Nathan the prophet came to him after his affair with Bathsheba.*[d]

    I
3 Have mercy on me, God, in your goodness;
     in your abundant compassion blot out my offense.
4 Wash away all my guilt;
     from my sin cleanse me.

---

[c] Ps 91, 16.   [d] 2 Sm 12.

Ps 51: A lament, the most famous of the seven Penitential Psalms, prays for the removal of the personal and social disorders that sin has brought. The poem has two parts of approximately equal length: 3-10 and 11-19, and a conclusion in 20-21. The two parts interlock by repetition of "blot out" in the first verse of each section (3. 11), of "wash (away)" just after the first verse of each section (4) and just before the last verse (9) of the first section, and of "heart," "God," and "spirit" in 12 and 19. The first part (3-10) asks deliverance from sin, which is not just a past act but its emotional, physical, and social consequences. The second part (11-19) seeks something more profound than wiping the slate clean: nearness to God, living by the spirit of God (12-13), like the relation between God and people described in Jer 31, 33-34. Nearness to God brings joy and the authority to teach sinners (15-16). Such proclamation is better than offering sacrifice (17-19). The last two verses ask for the rebuilding of Jerusalem (20-21).

5 For I know my offense;
    my sin is always before me.[e]
6 Against you alone have I sinned;
    I have done such evil in your sight
That you are just in your sentence,
    blameless when you condemn.[f]
7 True, I was born guilty,
    a sinner, even as my mother conceived me.[g]
8 Still, you insist on sincerity of heart;
    in my inmost being teach me wisdom.
9 Cleanse me with hyssop, that I may be pure;
    wash me, make me whiter than snow.[h]
10 Let me hear sounds of joy and gladness;
    let the bones you have crushed rejoice.

II
11 Turn away your face from my sins;
    blot out all my guilt.
12 A clean heart create for me, God;
    renew in me a steadfast spirit.[i]
13 Do not drive me from your presence,
    nor take from me your holy spirit.[j]
14 Restore my joy in your salvation;
    sustain in me a willing spirit.
15 I will teach the wicked your ways,
    that sinners may return to you.
16 Rescue me from death, God, my saving God,
    that my tongue may praise your healing power.[k]

---

[e] Pss 32, 5; 38, 19; Is 59, 12.
[f] Rom 3, 4.
[g] Jb 14, 4.
[h] Jb 9, 30; Is 1, 18; Ez 36, 25.
[i] Ez 11, 19.
[j] Wis 1, 5; 9, 17; Is 63, 11; Hg 2, 5; Rom 8, 9.
[k] Ps 30, 10.

51, 7: *A sinner, even as my mother conceived me:* literally, "In iniquity was I conceived," an instance of hyperbole: at no time was the psalmist ever without sin. Cf Ps 88, 16, "I am mortally afflicted since youth," i.e., I have always been afflicted. The verse does not imply that the sexual act of conception is sinful.

51, 9: *Hyssop:* a small bush whose many woody twigs make a natural sprinkler. It was prescribed in the Mosaic law as an instrument for sprinkling sacrificial blood or lustral water for cleansing. Cf Ex 12, 22; Lv 14, 4; Nm 19, 18.

17 Lord, open my lips;
        my mouth will proclaim your praise.
18 For you do not desire sacrifice;
        a burnt offering you would not accept.[l]
19 My sacrifice, God, is a broken spirit;
        God, do not spurn a broken, humbled heart.

    III
20 Make Zion prosper in your good pleasure;
        rebuild the walls of Jerusalem.[m]
21 Then you will be pleased with proper sacrifice,
        burnt offerings and holocausts;
        then bullocks will be offered on your altar.

Psalm 52
The Deceitful Tongue

1   *For the leader. A* maskil *of David, (2) when Doeg the Edomite went and
    told Saul, "David went to the house of Ahimelech."*[n]

    I
3   Why do you glory in evil,
        you scandalous liar?
    All day long (4) you plot destruction;
        your tongue is like a sharpened razor,
        you skillful deceiver.[o]
5   You love evil rather than good,
        lies rather than honest speech.[p]   *Selah*

---

l Ps 40, 7; 50, 8; Am 5, 21-22; Hos 6,   n 1 Sm 21, 8; 22, 6ff.
  6; Is 1, 11-15; Heb 10, 5-7.   o Pss 12, 3; 59, 8; 120, 2-3; Sir 51, 3.
m Jer 31, 4; Ez 36, 33.   p Jer 4, 22; Jn 3, 19-20.

51, 18: *For you do not desire sacrifice:* the mere offering of the ritual
sacrifice apart from good dispositions is not acceptable to God. Cf Ps 50.

51, 20-21: Most scholars think that these verses were added to the
psalm some time after the destruction of the temple in 587 B.C. The
verses assume that the rebuilt temple will be an ideal site for national
reconciliation.

Ps 52: A condemnation of the powerful and arrogant (3-6), who bring
down upon themselves God's judgment (7). The just, those who trust in
God alone, are gladdened and strengthened by the downfall of their traditional enemies (8-11).

6 You love any word that destroys,
    you deceitful tongue.q

    II

7 Now God will strike you down,
    leave you crushed forever,
  Pluck you from your tent,
    uproot you from the land of the living.r   *Selah*

8 The righteous will look on with awe;
    they will jeer and say:s

9 "That one did not take God as a refuge,
    but trusted in great wealth,
    relied on devious plots."t

    III

10 But I, like an olive tree in the house of God,u
    trust in God's faithful love forever.

11 I will praise you always
    for what you have done.
  I will proclaim before the faithfulv
    that your name is good.

Psalm 53
A Lament over Widespread Corruption

1 *For the leader; according to* Mahalath. *A* maskil *of David.*

    I

2 Fools say in their hearts,w
    "There is no God."x
  Their deeds are loathsome and corrupt;
    not one does what is right.

---

q Jer 9, 4.
r Pss 27, 13; 28, 5; 56, 14; Jb 18, 14; Prv 2, 22; Is 38, 11.
s Pss 44, 14; 64, 9.
t Jb 31, 24; Prv 11, 28.
u Pss 1, 3; 92, 12-14; Jer 11, 16; 17, 8.
v Pss 22, 23; 26, 12; 35, 18; 149, 1.
w 2-6a: Ps 14, 1-5a.
x Pss 10, 4; 36, 2; Is 32, 6; Jer 5, 12.

52, 10: *Like a green olive tree:* the righteous will flourish in the house of God like a well-watered olive tree. Cf Pss 92, 14; 128, 3.

Ps 53: A lament of an individual, duplicated in Ps 14, except that "God" is used for "the LORD," and v 6 is different. See under Ps 14.

3 God looks down from heaven
    upon the human race,[y]
  To see if even one is wise,[z]
    if even one seeks God.
4 All have gone astray;
    all alike are perverse.
  Not one does what is right, not even one.[a]

II

5 Will these evildoers never learn?
    They devour my people as they devour bread;[b]
    they do not call upon God.[c]
6 They have good reason to fear,
    though now they do not fear.
  For God will certainly scatter
    the bones of the godless.
  They will surely be put to shame,
    for God has rejected them.

III

7 Oh, that from Zion might come
    the deliverance of Israel,
  That Jacob may rejoice and Israel be glad[d]
    when God restores the people!

Psalm 54
Confident Prayer in Great Peril

1 *For the leader. On stringed instruments. A* maskil *of David,* (2) *when the Ziphites came and said to Saul, "David is hiding among us."*[e]

I

3 O God, by your name save me.
    By your strength defend my cause.

---

[y] Pss 11, 4; 102, 20.
[z] 2b-3: Rom 3, 11-12.
[a] Ps 12, 2.
[b] Ps 27, 2; Is 9, 11.
[c] Ps 79, 6.
[d] Ps 85, 2.
[e] 1 Sm 23, 19; 26, 1.

Ps 54: A lament in which the person under attack calls directly upon God for help (3-5). Refusing to despair, the psalmist hopes in God, who is active in history and just (6-7). The psalm ends with a serene promise to return thanks (8-9).

4 O God, hear my prayer.
        Listen to the words of my mouth.
5 The arrogant have risen against me;
        the ruthless seek my life;
        they do not keep God before them.^f   *Selah*

II
6 God is present as my helper;^g
        the Lord sustains my life.
7 Turn back the evil upon my foes;
        in your faithfulness, destroy them.^h
8 Then I will offer you generous sacrifice
        and praise your gracious name, LORD,
9 Because it has rescued me from every trouble,
        and my eyes look down on my foes.^i

Psalm 55
A Lament over Betrayal

1 For the leader. On stringed instruments. A maskil *of David.*

I
2 Listen, God, to my prayer;^j
        do not hide from my pleading;
3   hear me and give answer.

---

f Ps 86, 14.	i Pss 59, 11; 91, 8; 92, 12.
g Ps 118, 7.	j 2-3: Pss 5, 2-3; 55, 2-3; 86, 6; 130, 1-2;
h Ps 143, 12.	Lam 3, 56; Jon 2, 3.

54, 3: *By your name:* one is present in one's name, hence God as revealed to humans.

Ps 55: The psalmist, betrayed by intimate friends (14-15, 21-22), prays that God punish those oath breakers and thus be acknowledged as the protector of the wronged. The sufferings of the psalmist include both ostracism (4) and mental turmoil (5-6), culminating in the wish to flee society (7-9). The wish for a sudden death for one's enemies (16) occurs elsewhere in the psalms; an example of such a death is the earth opening under the wicked Dathan and Abiram (Nm 16, 31-32). The psalmist, confident of vindication, exhorts others to a like trust in the God of justice (23-24). The psalm is not so much for personal vengeance as for a public vindication of God's righteousness now. There was no belief in an afterlife where such vindication could take place.

I rock with grief; I groan
4   at the uproar of the enemy,
          the clamor of the wicked.
   They heap trouble upon me,
          savagely accuse me.
5 My heart pounds within me;
          death's terrors fall upon me.
6 Fear and trembling overwhelm me;
          shuddering sweeps over me.
7 I say, "If only I had wings like a dove
          that I might fly away and find rest.[k]
8 Far away I would flee;
          I would stay in the desert.[l]   *Selah*
9 I would soon find a shelter
          from the raging wind and storm."

   II

10 Lord, check and confuse their scheming.
          I see violence and strife in the city
11   making rounds on its walls day and night.
   Within are mischief and evil;
12   treachery is there as well;
          oppression and fraud never leave its streets.[m]
13 If an enemy had reviled me,
          that I could bear;
   If my foe had viewed me with contempt,
          from that I could hide.
14 But it was you, my other self,
          my comrade and friend,[n]
15 You, whose company I enjoyed,
          at whose side I walked
          in procession in the house of God.

   III

16 Let death take them by surprise;
          let them go down alive to Sheol,[o]
          for evil is in their homes and hearts.

---

[k] Ps 11, 1.
[l] Jer 9, 1; Rv 12, 6.
[m] Jer 5, 1; 6, 6; Ez 22, 2; Hb 1, 3; Zep 3, 1.

[n] Ps 41, 10; Jer 9, 3; Mt 26, 21-24 par.
[o] Ps 49, 15; Nm 16, 33; Prv 1, 2; Is 5, 14.

17 But I will call upon God,
and the LORD will save me.
18 At dusk, dawn, and noon
I will grieve and complain,
and my prayer will be heard.[p]
19 God will give me freedom and peace
from those who war against me,
though there are many who oppose me.
20 God, who sits enthroned forever,[q]
will hear me and humble them.
For they will not mend their ways;
they have no fear of God.
21 They strike out at friends
and go back on their promises.
22 Softer than butter is their speech,
but war is in their hearts.
Smoother than oil are their words,
but they are unsheathed swords.[r]
23 Cast your care upon the LORD,
who will give you support.
God will never allow
the righteous to stumble.[s]
24 But you, God, will bring them down
to the pit of destruction.[t]
These bloodthirsty liars
will not live half their days,
but I put my trust in you.[u]

[p] Dn 6, 11.
[q] Pss 29, 10; 93, 2; Bar 3, 3.
[r] Pss 12, 3; 28, 3; 57, 5; 62, 5; 64, 4; Prv 26, 24-28; Jer 9, 7.
[s] Ps 37, 5; Prv 3, 5; 16, 3; 1 Pt 5, 7.
[t] Pss 28, 1; 30, 4; 40, 3; 88, 5; 143, 7; Prv 1, 12; Jon 2, 7.
[u] Pss 25, 2; 56, 4; 130, 5.

Psalm 56
Trust in God

1 *For the director. According to* Yonath elem rehoqim. *A* miktam *of David, when the Philistines seized him at Gath.*[v]

I

2 Have mercy on me, God,
      for I am treated harshly;
      attackers press me all the day.
3 My foes treat me harshly all the day;
      yes, many are my attackers.
   O Most High, (4) when I am afraid,
      in you I place my trust.
5 God, I praise your promise;
      in you I trust, I do not fear.[w]
      What can mere flesh do to me?[x]

II

6 All the day they foil my plans;
      their every thought is of evil against me.
7 They hide together in ambush;
      they watch my every step;
      they lie in wait for my life.[y]
8 They are evil; watch them, God!
      Cast the nations down in your anger!
9 My wanderings you have noted;
      are my tears not stored in your vial,
      recorded in your book?[z]

---

[v] 1 Sm 21, 10.
[w] Ps 130, 5.
[x] Ps 118, 6; Heb 13, 6.
[y] Ps 140, 5-6.
[z] Ps 10, 14; 2 Kgs 20, 5; Is 25, 8; Rv 7, 17.

Ps 56: Beset physically (2-3) and psychologically (6-7), the psalmist maintains a firm confidence in God (5. 9-10). Nothing will prevent the psalmist from keeping the vow to give thanks for God's gift of life (13-14). A refrain (5. 11-12) divides the psalm in two equal parts.

56, 1: *Yonath elem rehoqim:* Hebrew words probably designating the melody to which the psalm was to be sung.

56, 9: *Are my tears not stored in your vial:* a unique saying in the Old Testament. The context suggests that the tears are saved because they are precious; God puts a high value on each of the psalmist's troubles.

10 My foes turn back when I call on you.
      This I know: God is on my side.
11 God, I praise your promise;
12   in you I trust, I do not fear.
      What can mere mortals do to me?

III

13 I have made vows to you, God;
      with offerings I will fulfill them,[a]
14 Once you have snatched me from death,
      kept my feet from stumbling,
That I may walk before God
      in the light of the living.

Psalm 57
Confident Prayer for Deliverance

1 *For the director. Do not destroy. A miktam of David, when he fled from Saul into a cave.*[b]

I

2 Have mercy on me, God,
      have mercy on me.
      In you I seek shelter.
In the shadow of your wings I seek shelter
      till harm pass by.[c]
3 I call to God Most High,
      to God who provides for me.
4 May God send help from heaven to save me,
      shame those who trample upon me.

---

a Nm 30, 3.   c Pss 17, 8; 36, 8.
b 1 Sm 22, 1.

Ps 57: Each of the two equal strophes contains a prayer for rescue from enemies, accompanied by joyful trust in God (2-5, 7-11). The refrain prays that God be manifested as saving (6, 12). Ps 108 is nearly identical to part of this psalm (57, 8-12 = 108, 2-6).

57, 1: *Do not destroy:* probably the title of the melody to which the psalm was to be sung.

57, 2: *The shadow of your wings:* probably refers to the wings of the cherubim (powerful winged animals) whose wings spread over the ark in the inner chamber of the temple (1 Kgs 6, 23-28).

May God send fidelity and love.   *Selah*

5   I must lie down in the midst of lions
        hungry for human prey.ᵈ
    Their teeth are spears and arrows;
        their tongue, a sharpened sword.ᵉ
6   Show yourself over the heavens, God;
        may your glory appear above all the earth.ᶠ

    II
7   They have set a trap for my feet;
        my soul is bowed down;
    They have dug a pit before me.
        May they fall into it themselves!ᵍ   *Selah*
8   My heart is steadfast, God,
        my heart is steadfast.
    I will sing and chant praise.ʰ
9   Awake, my soul;
        awake, lyre and harp!
    I will wake the dawn.ⁱ
10 I will praise you among the peoples, Lord;
        I will chant your praise among the nations.ʲ
11 For your love towers to the heavens;
        your faithfulness, to the skies.ᵏ
12 Show yourself over the heavens, God;
        may your glory appear above all the earth.

Psalm 58
The Dethroning of Unjust Rulers

1   *For the leader. Do not destroy. A* miktam *of David.*

    I
2   Do you indeed pronounce justice, O gods;
        do you judge mortals fairly?ˡ

ᵈ Pss 17, 11-12; 22, 22; 58, 7.
ᵉ Pss 11, 2; 64, 4.
ᶠ Ps 72, 19; Nm 14, 21.
ᵍ Pss 7, 15; 140, 5-6.
ʰ Ps 108, 2.
ⁱ Jb 38, 12.
ʲ Pss 9, 12; 18, 50.
ᵏ Pss 36, 6; 71, 19.
ˡ Ps 82, 2; Dt 16, 19.

57, 9: *I will wake the dawn:* by a bold figure the psalmist imagines the sound of music and singing will waken a new day.

Ps 58: A lament expressing trust in God's power to dethrone all powers obstructing divine rule of the world. First condemned are "the gods,"

3 No, you freely engage in crime;
   your hands dispense violence to the earth.

II

4 The wicked have been corrupt since birth;
   liars from the womb, they have gone astray.
5 Their poison is like the poison of a snake,
   like that of a serpent stopping its ears,[m]
6 So as not to hear the voice of the charmer
   who casts such cunning spells.

III

7 O God, smash the teeth in their mouths;
   break the jaw-teeth of these lions, LORD![n]
8 Make them vanish like water flowing away;[o]
   trodden down, let them wither like grass.[p]
9 Let them dissolve like a snail that oozes away,
   like an untimely birth that never sees the sun.[q]
10 Suddenly, like brambles or thistles,
   have the whirlwind snatch them away.[r]
11 Then the just shall rejoice to see the vengeance
   and bathe their feet in the blood of the wicked.[s]
12 Then it will be said:
   "Truly there is a reward for the just;
   there is a God who is judge on earth!"

---

[m] Pss 64, 4; 140, 3; Rom 3, 13.
[n] Ps 3, 7.
[o] Wis 16, 29.
[p] Ps 37, 2.
[q] Jb 3, 16.
[r] Jb 21, 18; Hos 13, 3; Na 1, 10.
[s] Ps 68, 24; Is 63, 1-6.

---

the powers that were popularly imagined to control human destinies (2-3), then "the wicked," the human instruments of these forces (4-6). The psalmist prays God to prevent them from harming the just (7-10). The manifestation of justice will gladden the just; they will see that their God is with them (11-12). The psalm is less concerned with personal vengeance than with public vindication of God's justice now.

58, 1: *Do not destroy:* probably the title of the melody to which the psalm was to be sung.

58, 2: *Gods:* the Bible sometimes understands pagan gods to be lesser divine beings who are assigned by Israel's God to rule the foreign nations. Here they are accused of injustice, permitting the human judges under their patronage to abuse the righteous. Cf Ps 82.

58, 5-6: The image is that of a poisonous snake that is controlled by the voice or piping of its trainer.

58, 9: *A snail that oozes away:* empty shells suggested to ancients that snails melted away as they left a slimy trail.

Psalm 59
Complaint against Bloodthirsty Enemies

1 *For the director. Do not destroy. A* miktam *of David, when Saul sent people to watch his house and kill him.*[t]

I

2 Rescue me from my enemies, my God;
 lift me out of reach of my foes.
3 Deliver me from evildoers;
 from the bloodthirsty save me.
4 They have set an ambush for my life;
 the powerful conspire against me.
For no offense or misdeed of mine, LORD,
5 for no fault they hurry to take up arms.
Come near and see my plight!
6 You, LORD of hosts, are the God of Israel!
Awake! Punish all the nations.
 Have no mercy on these worthless traitors.   *Selah*
7 Each evening they return,
 growling like dogs, prowling the city.[u]
8 Their mouths pour out insult;
 sharp words are on their lips.
They say: "Who is there to hear?"
9 You, LORD, laugh at them;
 you deride all the nations.[v]
10 My strength, for you I watch;
 you, God, are my fortress, (11) my loving God.

II

May God go before me,
 and show me my fallen foes.

---

[t] 1 Sm 19, 11.
[u] Ps 55, 11.

[v] Pss 2, 4; 37, 13; Wis 4, 18.

Ps 59: A lament in two parts (2-9, 11b-17), each ending in a refrain (10, 18). Both parts alternate prayer for vindication (2-3, 5b-6; 11b-14) with vivid depictions of the psalmist's enemies (4-5a. 7-8. 15-16). The near curse in 12-13 is not a crude desire for revenge but a wish that God's just rule over human affairs be recognized now.

59, 1: *Do not destroy:* probably the title of the melody to which the psalm was to be sung.

59, 8: *Who is there to hear?:* a sample of the enemies' godless reflection. The answer is that God hears their blasphemies.

12 Slay them, God,
        lest they deceive my people.
    Shake them by your power;
        Lord, our shield, bring them down.
13 For the sinful words of their mouths and lips
        let them be caught in their pride.
    For the lies they have told under oath[w]
14   destroy them in anger,
        destroy till they are no more.
    Then people will know God rules over Jacob,
        yes, even to the ends of the earth.[x]   *Selah*
15 Each evening they return,
        growling like dogs, prowling the city.
16 They roam about as scavengers;
        if they are not filled, they howl.

    III
17 But I shall sing of your strength,
        extol your love at dawn,
    For you are my fortress,
        my refuge in time of trouble.
18 My strength, your praise I will sing;
        you, God, are my fortress, my loving God.

Psalm 60
Lament after Defeat in Battle

1   *For the leader; according to "The Lily of . . . . " A* mitkam *of David
    (for teaching),* (2) *when he fought against Aram-Naharaim and Aram-
    Zobah; and Joab, coming back, killed twelve thousand Edomites in the
    Valley of Salt.*[y]

    I
3   O God, you rejected us, broke our defenses;
        you were angry but now revive us.

---

w Prv 12, 13; 18, 7.   y 2 Sm 8, 2. 3. 13; 1 Chr 18, 2. 3. 12.
x Ps 83, 18-19; Ez 5, 13.

Ps 60: The community complains that God has let the enemy win the
battle (3-5) and asks for an assurance of victory (6-7). In the oracle God
affirms ownership of the land; the invasion of other nations is not perma-
nent and will be reversed ultimately (8-10). With renewed confidence, the
community resolves to fight again (11). The opening lament is picked up
again (12-14), but this time with new awareness of God's power and
human limitation.

4   You rocked the earth, split it open;[z]
        repair the cracks for it totters.
5   You made your people go through hardship,
        made us stagger from the wine you gave us.[a]
6   Raise up a flag for those who revere you,
        a refuge for them out of bowshot.   *Selah*
7   Help with your right hand and answer us
        that your loved ones may escape.

    II

8   In the sanctuary God promised:
        "I will exult, will apportion Shechem;
        the valley of Succoth I will measure out.
9   Gilead is mine, mine is Manasseh;
        Ephraim is the helmet for my head,
        Judah, my own scepter.
10 Moab is my washbowl;
        upon Edom I cast my sandal.[b]
    I will triumph over Philistia."

    III

11 Who will bring me to the fortified city?
        Who will lead me into Edom?
12 Was it not you who rejected us, God?
        Do you no longer march with our armies?[c]
13 Give us aid against the foe;
        worthless is human help.
14 We will triumph with the help of God,
        who will trample down our foes.

---

z Ps 75, 4; Is 24, 19.   b Ru 4, 7-8.
a Ps 75, 9; Is 51, 17. 21-22; Jer 25, 15.   c Ps 44, 10.

60, 7-14: These verses occur again as the second half of Ps 108.

60, 8: *I will apportion . . . measure out:* God lays claim to these places. *The valley of Succoth:* probably the lower stretch of the Jabbok valley.

60, 9: *Judah, my own scepter:* an allusion to the Testament of Jacob, Gn 49, 10.

60, 10: *Moab is my washbowl:* Moab borders the Dead Sea, hence a metaphor for the country. *Upon Edom I cast my sandal:* an ancient legal gesture of taking possession of land.

60, 11: *The fortified city:* perhaps Bozrah, the fortified capital of Edom. Cf Is 34, 6; 63, 1; Am 1, 12.

Psalm 61
Prayer of the King in Time of Danger

1   *For the leader; with stringed instruments. Of David.*

    I

2   Hear my cry, O God,
       listen to my prayer!
3   From the brink of Sheol I call;
       my heart grows faint.
    Raise me up, set me on a rock,
4   for you are my refuge,
       a tower of strength against the foe.[d]
5   Then I will ever dwell in your tent,
       take refuge in the shelter of your wings.[e]   *Selah*

    II

6   O God, when you accept my vows
       and hear the plea of those
       who revere your name in prayer:
7   "Add to the days of the king's life;
       may his years be many generations;[f]
8   May he reign before God forever;[g]
       may your love and fidelity preserve him"—[h]
9   Then I will sing your name forever,
       fulfill my vows day after day.

---

[d] Ps 46, 2.   [g] Pss 72, 5; 89, 5. 30. 37.
[e] Pss 17, 8; 36, 8; 57, 2.   [h] Pss 85, 11; 89, 15. 25; Prv 20, 28.
[f] Ps 21, 5.

Ps 61: A lament of the king who feels himself at the brink of death (3) and cries out for the strong and saving presence of God (3b-5). The king cites the prayer being made for him (7-8), and promises to give thanks to God.

61, 3: *Brink of Sheol:* literally, "edge of the earth," "earth" being taken in its occasional meaning "the underworld." Cf Jon 2, 3.

61, 6: *In prayer:* added for sense. Vv 7-8 express *the plea* of v 6.

61, 9: *Then:* Hebrew "just as," i.e., in accord with the vows referred to in v 6.

Psalm 62
Trust in God Alone

1   *For the leader;* 'al Jeduthun. *A psalm of David.*

I

2   My soul rests in God alone,[i]
       from whom comes my salvation.
3   God alone is my rock and salvation,
       my secure height; I shall never fall.
4   How long will you set upon people,
       all of you beating them down,
    As though they were a sagging fence
       or a battered wall?
5   Even from my place on high
       they plot to dislodge me.
    They delight in lies;
       they bless with their mouths,
       but inwardly they curse.[j]   *Selah*

II

6   My soul, be at rest in God alone,
       from whom comes my hope.
7   God alone is my rock and my salvation,
       my secure height; I shall not fall.
8   My safety and glory are with God,[k]
       my strong rock and refuge.
9   Trust God at all times, my people!
       Pour out your hearts to God our refuge!   *Selah*

III

10 Mortals are a mere breath,
       the powerful but an illusion;[l]

---

[i] 2-3. 6-7: Pss 18, 3; 31, 3-4; 42, 10;
   118, 8; 146, 3.
[j] Pss 12, 3; 28, 3; 55, 22; Prv 26, 24-25.
[k] Ps 3, 3; Is 26, 4; 60, 19.
[l] Pss 39, 6-7; 144, 4; Jb 7, 16; Wis 2, 5.

Ps 62: A song of trust displaying serenity from experiencing God's power (the refrains of 2-3 and 6-7) and anger toward unjust enemies (4-5). From the experience of being rescued, the psalmist can teach others to trust in God (10-13).

62, 1: *'Al Jeduthun:* apparently the Hebrew name for the melody.

62, 10: *On a balance they rise:* precious objects were weighed by balancing two pans suspended from a beam. The lighter pan rises.

On a balance they rise;
together they are lighter than air.
11 Do not trust in extortion;
in plunder put no empty hope.
Though wealth increase,
do not set your heart upon it.[m]
12 One thing God has said;
two things I have heard:[n]
Power belongs to God;
13 so too, Lord, does kindness,
And you render to each of us
according to our deeds.[o]

Psalm 63
Ardent Longing for God

1 *A psalm of David, when he was in the wilderness of Judah.*[p]

I

2 O God, you are my God—
for you I long!
For you my body yearns;
for you my soul thirsts,
Like a land parched, lifeless,
and without water.[q]
3 So I look to you in the sanctuary
to see your power and glory.

---

[m] Jb 31, 25; Eccl 5, 9; Jer 17, 11; Mt 6, 19-21. 24.
[n] Jb 40, 5.
[o] Pss 28, 4; 31, 24; 2 Sm 3, 39; Jb 34, 11; Jer 17, 10; Mt 16, 27; Rom 2, 6; 2 Tm 4, 14.
[p] 1 Sm 24.
[q] Pss 42, 2; 143, 6; Is 26, 9.

62, 12: *One thing . . . two things:* parallelism of numbers for the sake of variation, a common device in Semitic poetry. One should not literally add up the numbers. Cf Am 1, 3; Prv 6, 16-19; 30, 15. 18. 21.

Ps 63: A psalm expressing the intimate relationship between God and the worshiper. Separated from God (2), the psalmist longs for the divine life given in the temple (3-6), which is based on a close relationship with God (7-9). May all my enemies be destroyed and God's true worshipers continue in giving praise (10-12)!

111

4 For your love is better than life;
      my lips offer you worship!

   II

5 I will bless you as long as I live;
      I will lift up my hands, calling on your name.
6 My soul shall savor the rich banquet of praise,
      with joyous lips my mouth shall honor you!
7 When I think of you upon my bed,
      through the night watches I will recall
8 That you indeed are my help,
      and in the shadow of your wings I shout for joy.[r]
9 My soul clings fast to you;
      your right hand upholds me.

   III

10 But those who seek my life will come to ruin;
      they shall go down to the depths of the earth!
11 They shall be handed over to the sword
      and become the prey of jackals!
12 But the king shall rejoice in God;
      all who swear by the Lord shall exult,
      for the mouths of liars will be shut![s]

Psalm 64
Treacherous Conspirators Punished by God

1 *For the leader. A psalm of David.*

   I

2 O God, hear my anguished voice;
      from the foes I dread protect my life.

---

[r] Pss 17, 8; 36, 8.   [s] Ps 107, 42.

63, 4: *For your love is better than life:* only here in the Old Testament is anything prized above life—in this case God's love.

63, 12: *All who swear by the Lord:* to swear by a particular god meant that one was a worshiper of that god (Is 45, 23; 48, 1; Zep 1, 5).

Ps 64: A lament of a person overwhelmed by the malice of the wicked who are depicted in the psalms as the enemies of the righteous (2-7). When people see God bringing upon the wicked the evil they intended

3 Hide me from the malicious crowd,
>   the mob of evildoers.
4 They sharpen their tongues like swords,
>   ready their bows for arrows of poison words.[t]
5 They shoot at the innocent from ambush,
>   shoot without risk, catch them unawares.
6 They resolve on their wicked plan;
>   they conspire to set snares;
>   they say: "Who will see us?"
7 They devise wicked schemes,
>   conceal the schemes they devise;
>   the designs of their hearts are hidden.[u]

II

8 But God will shoot arrows at them
>   and strike them unawares.[v]
9 They will be brought down by their own tongues;
>   all who see them will shake their heads.[w]
10 Then all will fear and proclaim God's deed,
>   pondering what has been done.
11 The just will rejoice and take refuge in the LORD;
>   all the upright will glory in their God.[x]

Psalm 65
Thanksgiving for God's Blessings

1 *For the leader. A psalm of David. A song.*

I

2 To you we owe our hymn of praise,
>   O God on Zion;

---

[t] Pss 11, 2; 37, 14; 55, 22; 57, 5.   [w] Pss 5, 11; 44, 14; 52, 6.
[u] Ps 140, 3; Prv 6, 14.   [x] Pss 36, 8; 57, 2.
[v] Pss 7, 13-14; 38, 3; Dt 32, 42.

---

against others, they will know who is the true ruler of the world (8-10).
The final verse is a vow of praise (11).
   64, 5: *Catch them unawares:* literally, "suddenly," i.e., "unexpectedly."
   Ps 65: The community, aware of its unworthiness (3-4), gives thanks
for divine bounty (5), a bounty resulting from God's creation victory (6-9).
At God's touch the earth comes alive with vegetation and flocks (10-14).
   65, 2: *Vows:* the Israelites were accustomed to promising sacrifices
in the temple if their prayers were heard.

To you our vows must be fulfilled,
3   you who hear our prayers.
To you all flesh must come[y]
4   with its burden of wicked deeds.
We are overcome by our sins;
     only you can pardon them.[z]
5 Happy the chosen ones you bring
     to dwell in your courts.
May we be filled with the good things of your house,
     the blessings of your holy temple!

II

6 You answer us with awesome deeds of justice,
     O God our savior,
The hope of all the ends of the earth
     and of far distant islands.[a]
7 You are robed in power,
     you set up the mountains by your might.
8 You still the roaring of the seas,[b]
     the roaring of their waves,
     the tumult of the peoples.[c]
9 Distant peoples stand in awe of your marvels;
     east and west you make resound with joy.
10 You visit the earth and water it,
     make it abundantly fertile.[d]
God's stream is filled with water;
     with it you supply the world with grain.
Thus do you prepare the earth:

---

[y] Is 66, 23.
[z] Pss 32, 1-2; 78, 38; Is 1, 18.
[a] Is 66, 19.
[b] Pss 89, 10; 107, 29; Jb 38, 11; Mt 8,
26.
[c] Is 17, 12.
[d] Lv 26, 4; Is 30, 23. 25; Jl 2, 22-23.

65, 3: *To you all flesh must come:* all must have recourse to God's mercy.

65, 6: *Awesome deeds:* the acts of creating—installing mountains, taming seas, restraining nations (7-8)—that are visible worldwide (6. 9).

65, 10-14: Apparently a description of the agricultural year, beginning with the first fall rains that soften the hard sun-baked soil (10-11).

65, 10: *God's stream:* the fertile waters of the earth derive from God's fertile waters in the heavenly world.

11　　　you drench plowed furrows,
　　　　　and level their ridges.
　　　With showers you keep the ground soft,
　　　　　blessing its young sprouts.
12　You adorn the year with your bounty;
　　　　　your paths drip with fruitful rain.
13　The untilled meadows also drip;
　　　　　the hills are robed with joy.
14　The pastures are clothed with flocks,
　　　　　the valleys blanketed with grain;
　　　　　they cheer and sing for joy.[e]

Psalm 66
Praise of God, Israel's Deliverer

1　*For the leader. A song; a psalm.*

　　I
　　Shout joyfully to God, all you on earth;
2　　　sing of his glorious name;
　　　　give him glorious praise.[f]
3　Say to God: "How awesome your deeds!
　　　　Before your great strength your enemies cringe.
4　All on earth fall in worship before you;[g]
　　　　they sing of you, sing of your name!"　　　　　*Selah*

　　II
5　Come and see the works of God,
　　　　awesome in the deeds done for us.

---

e Is 44, 23.　　　　　　　　　g 3-4: Ps 18, 45; Mi 7, 17.
f Ps 65, 14; Is 44, 23.

65, 12: *Paths:* probably the tracks of God's storm chariot dropping rain upon earth.

Ps 66: In the first part (1-12), the community praises God for powerful acts for Israel, both in the past (the exodus from Egypt and the entry into the land [6]) and in the present (deliverance from a recent but unspecified calamity [8-12]). In the second part (13-20), an individual from the rescued community fulfills a vow to offer a sacrifice of thanksgiving. As often in thanksgivings, the rescued person steps forward to teach the community what God has done (16-20).

66, 5-6: Cf the events described in Ex 14, 1-15, 21; Jos 3, 11-4, 24, and Ps 114.

115

6 He changed the sea to dry land;
    through the river they passed on foot.[h]
  Therefore let us rejoice in him,
7   who rules by might forever,
  Whose eyes are fixed upon the nations.
    Let no rebel rise to challenge!   *Selah*
8 Bless our God, you peoples;
    loudly sound his praise,
9 Who has kept us alive
    and not allowed our feet to slip.[i]
10 You tested us, O God,
    tried us as silver tried by fire.[j]
11 You led us into a snare;
    you bound us at the waist as captives.
12 You let captors set foot on our neck;
    we went through fire and water;
    then you led us out to freedom.[k]

  III
13 I will bring holocausts to your house;
    to you I will fulfill my vows,
14 The vows my lips pronounced
    and my mouth spoke in distress.
15 Holocausts of fatlings I will offer you
    and burnt offerings of rams;
    I will sacrifice oxen and goats.   *Selah*
16 Come and hear, all you who fear God,
    while I recount what has been done for me.

---

[h] Pss 74, 15; 114, 3; Ex 14, 21f; Jos 3,   23.
  14ff; Is 44, 27; 50, 2.   [j] Is 48, 10.
[i] Pss 91, 12; 121, 3; 1 Sm 2, 9; Prv 3,   [k] Is 43, 2.

66, 12: *You let captors set foot on our neck:* literally, "you let men mount our head." Conquerors placed their feet on the neck of their enemies as a sign of complete defeat. Cf Jos 10, 24. A ceremonial footstool of the Egyptian king Tutankhamen portrays bound and prostrate bodies of enemies ready for the king's feet on their heads, and one of Tutankhamen's ceremonial chariots depicts the king as a sphinx standing with paw atop the neck of an enemy.

66, 13: *Holocausts:* wholly burnt offerings. Cf Lv 1, 3-13; 6, 1-4; 22, 17-20.

17 I called to the Lord with my mouth;
    praise was upon my tongue.
18 Had I cherished evil in my heart,
    the Lord would not have heard.
19 But God did hear
    and listened to my voice in prayer.
20 Blessed be God, who did not refuse me
    the kindness I sought in prayer.

Psalm 67
Harvest Thanks and Petition

1 *For the leader; with stringed instruments. A psalm; a song.*

I

2 May God be gracious to us and bless us;
    may God's face shine upon us.[l]   *Selah*
3 So shall your rule be known upon the earth,
    your saving power among all the nations.[m]
4 May the peoples praise you, God;
    may all the peoples praise you!

II

5 May the nations be glad and shout for joy;
    for you govern the peoples justly,
    you guide the nations upon the earth.[n]   *Selah*
6 May the peoples praise you, God;
    may all the peoples praise you!

III

7 The earth has yielded its harvest;
    God, our God, blesses us.[o]
8 May God bless us still;
    that the ends of the earth may revere our God.

---

[l] Pss 4, 7; 31, 17; 44, 4; 80, 4; Dn 9, 17.
[m] Jer 33, 9.
[n] Ps 98, 9.
[o] Ps 85, 13; Lv 26, 4; Ez 34, 27; Hos 2, 23-24.

Ps 67: A petition for a bountiful harvest (7), made in the awareness that Israel's prosperity will persuade the nations to worship its God.

67, 2: *May God be gracious to us:* the people's petition echoes the blessing pronounced upon them by the priests. Cf Nm 6, 22-27.

Psalm 68
The Exodus and Conquest, Pledge of Future Help

1 *For the leader. A psalm of David; a song.*

I

2 God will arise for battle;
the enemy will be scattered;
those who hate God will flee.[p]
3 The wind will disperse them like smoke;
as wax is melted by fire,
so the wicked will perish before God.[q]
4 Then the just will be glad;
they will rejoice before God;
they will celebrate with great joy.

II

5 Sing to God, praise the divine name;
exalt the rider of the clouds.

---

[p] Nm 10, 35. [q] Ps 97, 5; Jdt 16, 15; Wis 5, 14; Mi 1, 4.

Ps 68: The psalm is extremely difficult because the Hebrew text is badly preserved and the ceremony that it describes is uncertain. The translation assumes the psalm accompanied the early autumn Feast of Tabernacles (Sukkoth), which included a procession of the tribes (25-28). Israel was being oppressed by a foreign power, perhaps Egypt (31-32)—unless Egypt stands for any oppressor. The psalm may have been composed from segments of ancient poems, which would explain why the transitions are implied rather than explicitly stated. At any rate, v 2 is based on Nm 10, 35-36, and vv 8-9 are derived from Jgs 5, 4-5.

The argument develops in nine stanzas (each of three to five poetic lines): 1. confidence that God will destroy Israel's enemies (2-4); 2. call to praise God as savior (5-7); 3. God's initial rescue of Israel from Egypt (8), the Sinai encounter (9), and the settlement in Canaan (10-11); 4. the defeat of the Canaanite kings (12-15); 5. the taking of Jerusalem, where Israel's God will rule the world (16-19); 6. praise for God's past help and for the future interventions that will be modeled on the ancient exodus-conquest (20-24); 7. procession at the Feast of Tabernacles (25-28); 8. prayer that the defeated enemies bring tribute to the temple (29-32); 9. invitation for all kingdoms to praise Israel's God (33-36).

68, 2: The opening line alluding to Nm 10, 35 makes clear that God's assistance in the period of the exodus and conquest is the model and assurance of all future divine help.

68, 5: *Exalt the rider of the clouds:* God's intervention is in the imagery of Canaanite myth in which the storm-god mounted the storm clouds to

Rejoice before this God
    whose name is the LORD.[r]

6 Father of the fatherless, defender of widows[s]—
    this is the God whose abode is holy,

7 Who gives a home to the forsaken,
    who leads prisoners out to prosperity,
    while rebels live in the desert.

III

8 God, when you went forth before your people,[t]
    when you marched through the desert,   *Selah*

9 The earth quaked, the heavens shook,
    before God, the One of Sinai,
    before God, the God of Israel.

10 You claimed a land as your own, O God;
11   your people settled there.
There you poured abundant rains, God,
    graciously given to the poor in their need.

IV

12a The Lord announced the news of victory:
13a   "The kings and their armies are in desperate flight.[u]
12b All you people so numerous,
14a   will you stay by the sheepfolds?[v]
13b   Every household will share the booty,
14b   perhaps a dove sheathed with silver,
14c   its wings covered with yellow gold."

---

[r] Pss 18, 10; 104, 3; Dt 33, 26; Is 19, 1.   Heb 12, 26.
[s] 6-7: Pss 103, 6; 146, 7. 9; Ex 22,   [u] Jgs 5, 19. 22.
    20-22; Bar 6, 37.   [v] Jgs 5, 16.
[t] 8-9: Pss 44, 10; 114, 4. 7; Jgs 5, 4-5;

---

ride to battle. Such theophanies occur throughout the psalm: 2-3. 8-10. 12-15. 18-19. 22-24. 29-32. 34-35. See Dt 33, 26; Ps 18, 8-16; Is 19, 1.

68, 7: *While rebels live in the desert:* rebels must live in the arid desert, whereas God's people will live in the well-watered land (vv 8-11).

68, 12-15: The Hebrew text upon which the translation is based has apparently suffered dislocation and has been substantially rearranged for sense. The version of the defeat of the kings differs from that in the Book of Joshua, where the people play a significant role. Here God alone is responsible for the victory (though the actual battle is not described); Israel only gathers the spoils. God alone is the source of Israel's success; human effort is not important.

119

15 When the Almighty routed the kings there,
        the spoils were scattered like snow on Zalmon.

    V

16 You high mountains of Bashan,
        you rugged mountains of Bashan,
17 You rugged mountains, why look with envy
        at the mountain where God has chosen to dwell,
        where the LORD resides forever?[w]
18 God's chariots were myriad, thousands upon thousands;
        from Sinai the Lord entered the holy place.
19 You went up to its lofty height;
        you took captives, received slaves as tribute.[x]
        No rebels can live in the presence of God.

    VI

20 Blessed be the Lord day by day,
        God, our salvation, who carries us.[y]   *Selah*
21 Our God is a God who saves;
        escape from death is in the LORD God's hands.
22 God will crush the skulls of the enemy,
        the hairy heads of those who walk in sin.[z]
23 The Lord has said:
        "Even from Bashan I will fetch them,
        fetch them even from the depths of the sea.
24 You will wash your feet in your enemy's blood;
        the tongues of your dogs will lap it up."[a]

    VII

25 Your procession comes into view, O God,
        your procession into the holy place, my God and king.

---

[w] Ps 132, 13-14; Ez 43, 7.   [z] Dt 32, 42.
[x] Ps 47, 8; Eph 4, 8-10.   [a] Ps 58, 11; 1 Kgs 21, 19; 22, 38; Is 63,
[y] Pss 34, 2; 145, 2; Is 46, 3-4; 63, 9.   1-6.

68, 15: *Zalmon:* generally taken as the name of a mountain where snow is visible in winter, perhaps to be located in the Golan Heights or in the mountains of Bashan or Hauran east of the Sea of Galilee.

68, 17: *The mountain:* Mount Zion, the site of the temple.

68, 23: *Even from Bashan . . . from the depths of the sea:* the heights and the depths, the farthest places where enemies might flee.

68, 25-28: *Your procession:* the procession renews God's original taking up of residence on Zion, described in 16-19.

26　The singers go first, the harpists follow;
　　　in their midst girls sound the timbrels.[b]
27　In your choirs, bless God;
　　　bless the LORD, you from Israel's assemblies.
28　In the lead is Benjamin, few in number;
　　　there the princes of Judah, a large throng,
　　　the princes of Zebulun, the princes of Naphtali, too.[c]

VIII
29　Summon again, O God, your power,
　　　the divine power you once showed for us.
30　Show it from your temple on behalf of Jerusalem,
　　　that kings may bring you tribute.
31　Roar at the wild beast of the reeds,
　　　the herd of mighty bulls, the lords of nations;
　　　scatter the nations that delight in war.
32　Exact rich tribute from lower Egypt,[d]
　　　from upper Egypt, gold and silver;
　　　make Ethiopia extend its hands to God.[e]

IX
33　You kingdoms of the earth, sing to God;[f]
　　　chant the praises of the Lord,　　　　　　　　　*Selah*
34　Who rides the heights of the ancient heavens,
　　　whose voice is thunder, mighty thunder.
35　Confess the power of God,
　　　whose majesty protects Israel,
　　　whose power is in the sky.
36　Awesome is God in his holy place,
　　　the God of Israel,
　　　who gives power and strength to his people.[g]
　　　Blessed be God!

---

[b] Pss 81, 2-3; 87, 7; 149, 3; 150, 3-5;　　[e] Is 18, 7; 45, 14.
　　2 Sm 6, 5.　　　　　　　　　　　　　　[f] Ps 138, 4.
[c] Is 8, 23.　　　　　　　　　　　　　　[g] Pss 28, 8; 29, 11.
[d] Ez 29, 2ff.

68, 31: *The wild beast of the reeds:* probably the Nile crocodile, a symbol for Egypt; see 32 and Ez 29, 2-5.

68, 31-32: *Lower Egypt* is the delta area north of Cairo. *Upper Egypt* is the Nile Valley from Cairo to Aswan. *Ethiopia* is still further south.

121

Psalm 69
A Cry of Anguish in Great Distress

1 *For the leader; according to "Lilies." Of David.*

I

2 Save me, God,
    for the waters have reached my neck.[h]
3 I have sunk into the mire of the deep,
    where there is no foothold.
I have gone down to the watery depths;
    the flood overwhelms me.[i]
4 I am weary with crying out;
    my throat is parched.
My eyes have failed,
    looking for my God.[j]
5 More numerous than the hairs of my head
    are those who hate me without cause.[k]
Too many for my strength
    are my treacherous enemies.

---

[h] Pss 18, 5; 93, 3-4; Jb 22, 11.   Is 38, 14.
[i] Pss 40, 2; 124, 4-5.   [k] Ps 40, 13; Lam 3, 52; Jn 15, 25.
[j] Pss 25, 15; 119, 82; 123, 2; 141, 8;

Ps 69: A lament complaining of suffering in language both metaphorical (2-3 and 15-16, the waters of chaos) and literal (4. 5. 9. 11-13, exhaustion, alienation from family and community, false accusation). In the second part the psalmist prays with special emphasis that the enemies be punished for all to see (23-29). Despite the pain, the psalmist does not lose hope that all be set right, and promises public praise (30-37). The psalm, which depicts the suffering of the innocent just person vividly, is cited often by the New Testament especially in the passion accounts, e.g., v 5 in Jn 15, 25; v 22 in Mk 15, 23. 36 and parallels and in Jn 19, 29. The psalm prays not so much for personal vengeance as for public vindication of God's justice. There was, at this time, no belief in an afterlife where such vindication could take place. Redress had to take place now, in the sight of all.

69, 1: *"Lilies":* apparently the name of the melody.

69, 2: *Waters:* the waters of chaos from which God created the world are a common metaphor for extreme distress. Cf Pss 18, 5; 42, 8; 88, 8; Jon 2, 3-6.

69, 5: *What I did not steal:* the psalmist, falsely accused of theft, is being forced to make restitution.

Must I now restore
    what I did not steal?

II

6 God, you know my folly;
    my faults are not hidden from you.
7 Let those who wait for you, LORD of hosts,
    not be shamed through me.
  Let those who seek you, God of Israel,[l]
    not be disgraced through me
8 For your sake I bear insult,
    shame covers my face.[m]
9 I have become an outcast to my kin,
    a stranger to my mother's children.[n]
10 Because zeal for your house consumes me,
    I am scorned by those who scorn you.[o]
11 I have wept and fasted,[p]
    but this led only to scorn.
12 I clothed myself in sackcloth;
    I became a byword for them.
13 They who sit at the gate gossip about me;
    drunkards make me the butt of their songs.

III

14 But I pray to you, LORD,
    for the time of your favor.
  God, in your great kindness answer me
    with your constant help.[q]
15 Rescue me from the mire;[r]
    do not let me sink.
  Rescue me from my enemies
    and from the watery depths.

---

[l] Ps 40, 17.
[m] Jer 15, 15.
[n] Jb 19, 13-15.
[o] Ps 119, 139; Jn 2, 17; Rom 15, 3.
[p] 11-13: Ps 109, 24-25; Jb 30, 9; Lam 3, 14.
[q] Is 49, 8.
[r] 15-16: Pss 28, 1; 30, 4; 32, 6; 40, 3; 88, 5; Prv 1, 12.

69, 10: *Zeal for your house consumes me:* the psalmist's commitment to God's cause brings only opposition. Cf Jn 2, 17. *I am scorned by those who scorn you:* Rom 15, 3 uses the verse as an example of Jesus' unselfishness.

16 Do not let the floodwaters overwhelm me,
      nor the deep swallow me,
      nor the mouth of the pit close over me.
17 Answer me, LORD, in your generous love;
      in your great mercy turn to me.
18 Do not hide your face from your servant;
      in my distress hasten to answer me.[s]
19 Come and ransom my life;
      because of my enemies redeem me.
20 You know my reproach, my shame, my disgrace;
      before you stand all my foes.
21 Insult has broken my heart, and I am weak;
      I looked for compassion, but there was none,
      for comforters, but found none.[t]
22 Instead they put gall in my food;
      for my thirst they gave me vinegar.[u]

    IV
23 Make their own table a snare for them,
      a trap for their friends.[v]
24 Make their eyes so dim they cannot see;
      keep their backs ever feeble.
25 Pour out your wrath upon them;
      let the fury of your anger overtake them.
26 Make their camp desolate,
      with none to dwell in their tents.[w]
27 For they pursued the one you struck,
      added to the pain of the one you wounded.
28 Add that to their crimes;
      let them not attain to your reward.
29 Strike them from the book of the living;
      do not count them among the just![x]

    V
30 But I am afflicted and in pain;
      let your saving help protect me, God,

---

s Pss 102, 3; 143, 7.
t Lam 1, 2.
u Lam 3, 15; Mt 27, 34. 48; Mk 15, 23.
v Rom 11, 9-10.
w Acts 1, 20.
x Ps 139, 16; Ex 32, 32; Is 4, 3; Dn 12, 1; Mal 3, 16; Rv 3, 5.

31 That I may praise God's name in song
    and glorify it with thanksgiving.
32 My song will please the LORD more than oxen,
    more than bullocks with horns and hooves:[y]
33 "See, you lowly ones, and be glad;
    you who seek God, take heart![z]
34 For the LORD hears the poor,
    does not spurn those in bondage.
35 Let the heavens and the earth sing praise,
    the seas and whatever moves in them!"

VI

36 God will rescue Zion,
    rebuild the cities of Judah.[a]
   God's servants shall dwell in the land and possess it;
37   it shall be the heritage of their descendants;
    those who love God's name shall dwell there.[b]

Psalm 70
Prayer for Divine Help

1 *For the leader; of David. For remembrance.*

2 Graciously rescue me, God![c]
    Come quickly to help me, LORD![d]
3 Confound and put to shame
    those who seek my life.[e]
   Turn back in disgrace
    those who desire my ruin.
4 Let those who say "Aha!"[f]
    turn back in their shame.

---

[y] Pss 40, 7; 50, 8-9. 14; 51, 18; Is 1, 11-15; Hos 6, 6; Am 5, 21-22; Heb 10, 5-8.
[z] Pss 22, 27; 35, 27; 70, 5.
[a] Is 44, 26; Ez 36, 10.

[b] Ps 102, 29; Is 65, 9.
[c] 2-6: Ps 40, 14-18.
[d] Ps 71, 12.
[e] Ps 35, 4. 26.
[f] Ps 35, 21. 25.

69, 31: *That I may praise God's name in song:* the actual song is cited in 33-35, the word "praise" in 35 referring back to "praise" in 31.

Ps 70: A lament of a poor and afflicted person (6) who has no resource except God, and who cries out to be saved from the enemy. The psalm is almost identical to Ps 40, 14-18.

5 But may all who seek you
   rejoice and be glad in you.
   May those who long for your help
   always say, "God be glorified!"[g]
6 Here I am, afflicted and poor.
   God, come quickly!
   You are my help and deliverer.
   LORD, do not delay!

Psalm 71
Prayer in Time of Old Age

I

1 In you, LORD, I take refuge;[h]
   let me never be put to shame.[i]
2 In your justice rescue and deliver me;
   listen to me and save me!
3 Be my rock and refuge,
   my secure stronghold;
   for you are my rock and fortress.[j]
4 My God, rescue me from the power of the wicked,
   from the clutches of the violent.[k]
5 You are my hope, Lord;
   my trust, GOD, from my youth.
6 On you I depend since birth;
   from my mother's womb you are my strength;[l]
   my hope in you never wavers.
7 I have become a portent to many,
   but you are my strong refuge!

---

g Ps 35, 27.
h 1-3: Ps 31, 2-4.
i Ps 25, 2.
j Ps 18, 3.
k Ps 140, 2.
l Ps 22, 11.

Ps 71: A lament of an old person (9. 18) whose afflictions are interpreted by enemies as a divine judgment (11). The first part of the psalm pleads for help (1-4) on the basis of a hope learned from a lifetime's experience of God; the second part describes the menace (9-13) yet remains buoyant (14-16); the third develops the theme of hope and praise.

71, 7: *A portent to many:* the afflictions of the sufferer are taken as a manifestation of God's anger. Cf Dt 28, 46; Ps 31, 12.

8   My mouth shall be filled with your praise,
        shall sing your glory every day.

    II

9   Do not cast me aside in my old age;
        as my strength fails, do not forsake me.
10 For my enemies speak against me;
        they watch and plot against me.[m]
11 They say, "God has abandoned that one
        Pursue, seize the wretch!
        No one will come to the rescue!"
12 God, do not stand far from me;
        my God, hasten to help me.[n]
13 Bring to a shameful end
        those who attack me;
    Cover with contempt and scorn
        those who seek my ruin.[o]
14 I will always hope in you
        and add to all your praise.
15 My mouth shall proclaim your just deeds,
        day after day your acts of deliverance,
        though I cannot number them all.[p]
16 I will speak of the mighty works of the Lord;
        O GOD, I will tell of your singular justice.

    III

17 God, you have taught me from my youth;
        to this day I proclaim your wondrous deeds.
18 Now that I am old and gray,[q]
        do not forsake me, God,
    That I may proclaim your might
        to all generations yet to come,[r]
    Your power (19) and justice, God,
        to the highest heaven.
    You have done great things;[s]
        O God, who is your equal?[t]

---

[m] Pss 3, 2; 22, 8.
[n] Ps 22, 20.
[o] Pss 35, 4; 40, 15; 70, 3.
[p] Ps 35, 28.

[q] Is 46, 3-4.
[r] Pss 22, 31-32; 48, 14-15; 145, 4.
[s] Ps 72, 18.
[t] Ps 86, 8.

127

20 You have sent me many bitter afflictions,
>   but once more revive me.
>   From the watery depths of the earth
>   once more raise me up.
21 Restore my honor;
>   turn and comfort me,
22 That I may praise you with the lyre
>   for your faithfulness, my God,
>   And sing to you with the harp,
>   O Holy One of Israel!
23 My lips will shout for joy as I sing your praise;
>   my soul, too, which you have redeemed.
24 Yes, my tongue shall recount
>   your justice day by day.
>   For those who sought my ruin
>   will have been shamed and disgraced.

Psalm 72
A Prayer for the King

1 *Of Solomon.*

I

O God, give your judgment to the king;
>   your justice to the son of kings;[u]
2 That he may govern your people with justice,
>   your oppressed with right judgment,[v]
3 That the mountains may yield their bounty for the people,
>   and the hills great abundance,[w]
4 That he may defend the oppressed among the people,
>   save the poor and crush the oppressor.

---

[u] Ps 99, 4; Jer 23, 5.   [w] Is 52, 7; 55, 12.
[v] Prv 31, 8-9.

Ps 72: A royal psalm in which the Israelite king, as the representative of God, is the instrument of divine justice (1-4. 12-14) and blessing (5-7. 15-17) for the whole world. The king is human, giving only what he has received from God. Hence intercession must be made for him. The extravagant language is typical of oriental royal courts.

72, 1: *The king . . . the son of kings:* the crown prince is the king's son; the prayer envisages the dynasty.

II

5 May he live as long as the sun endures,
       like the moon, through all generations.[x]

6 May he be like rain coming down upon the fields,
       like showers watering the earth,[y]

7 That abundance may flourish in his days,
       great bounty, till the moon be no more.

III

8 May he rule from sea to sea,
       from the river to the ends of the earth.[z]

9 May his foes kneel before him,
       his enemies lick the dust.[a]

10 May the kings of Tarshish and the islands bring tribute,
       the kings of Arabia and Seba offer gifts.[b]

11 May all kings bow before him,
       all nations serve him.[c]

12 For he rescues the poor when they cry out,
       the oppressed who have no one to help.

13 He shows pity to the needy and the poor[d]
       and saves the lives of the poor.

14 From extortion and violence he frees them,
       for precious is their blood in his sight.

IV

15 Long may he live, receiving gold from Arabia,
       prayed for without cease, blessed day by day.

---

[x] Ps 89, 37-38; Jer 31, 35.
[y] Dt 32, 2; Is 45, 8; Hos 6, 3.
[z] Dt 11, 24; Zec 9, 10.
[a] Is 49, 23; Mi 7, 17.

[b] Ps 68, 30; Is 60, 5-6; 1 Kgs 10, 1ff.
[c] Ps 47, 8.
[d] Prv 31, 9.

72, 8: *From sea to sea . . . the ends of the earth:* the boundaries of the civilized world known at the time: from the Mediterranean Sea (the western sea) to the Persian Gulf (the eastern sea), and from the Euphrates (the river) to the islands and lands of southwestern Europe, "the ends of the earth." The words may also have a mythic nuance—the earth surrounded by cosmic waters, hence everywhere.

72, 10: *Tarshish and the islands:* the far west (Ps 48, 6); *Arabia and Seba:* the far south (1 Kgs 10, 1).

72, 14: *Their blood:* cf Ps 116, 15.

16 May wheat abound in the land,
flourish even on the mountain heights.
May his fruit increase like Lebanon's,
his wheat like the grasses of the land.[e]
17 May his name be blessed forever;
as long as the sun, may his name endure.[f]
May the tribes of the earth give blessings with his name;
may all the nations regard him as favored.[g]

* * *

18 Blessed be the LORD, the God of Israel,
who alone does wonderful deeds.[h]
19 Blessed be his glorious name forever;
may all the earth be filled with the LORD's glory.[i]
Amen and amen.
20 The end of the psalms of David, son of Jesse.

THIRD BOOK—PSALMS 73–89

Psalm 73
The Trial of the Just

1 *A psalm of Asaph.*

How good God is to the upright,
the Lord, to those who are clean of heart!

---

[e] Is 27, 6; Hos 14, 6-8; Am 9, 13.
[f] Ps 21, 7.
[g] Gn 12, 3; Zec 8, 13.
[h] Pss 41, 14; 89, 53; 106, 48; 136, 4.
[i] Ps 57, 5; Nm 14, 21.

72, 16: The translation of the difficult Hebrew is tentative.

72, 17: *May the tribes of the earth give blessing with his name:* an echo of the promise to the ancestors (Gn 12, 3; 26, 4; 28, 14), suggesting that the monarchy in Israel fulfilled the promise to Abraham, Isaac, and Jacob.

72, 18-19: A doxology marking the end of Book II of the Psalter.

Ps 73: The opening verse of this probing poem (cf Pss 37, 49) is actually the psalmist's hard-won conclusion from personal experience: God is just and good! The psalmist describes near loss of faith (2-3), occasioned by observing the wicked who blasphemed God with seeming impunity (4-12). Feeling abandoned despite personal righteousness, the psalmist could not bear the injustice until an experience of God's near-

I

2 But, as for me, I lost my balance;
      my feet all but slipped,

3 Because I was envious of the arrogant
      when I saw the prosperity of the wicked.[j]

4 For they suffer no pain;
      their bodies are healthy and sleek.

5 They are free of the burdens of life;
      they are not afflicted like others.

6 Thus pride adorns them as a necklace;
      violence clothes them as a robe.

7 Out of their stupidity comes sin;
      evil thoughts flood their hearts.[k]

8 They scoff and spout their malice;
      from on high they utter threats.[l]

9 They set their mouths against the heavens,
      their tongues roam the earth.

10 So my people turn to them
      and drink deeply of their words.

11 They say, "Does God really know?"
      "Does the Most High have any knowledge?"[m]

12 Such, then, are the wicked,
      always carefree, increasing their wealth.

II

13 Is it in vain that I have kept my heart clean,
      washed my hands in innocence?[n]

14 For I am afflicted day after day,
      chastised every morning.

---

[j] Ps 37, 1; Jb 21, 13.   [m] Ps 10, 11; Jb 22, 13.
[k] Jb 15, 27.   [n] Ps 26, 6; Mal 3, 14.
[l] Ps 17, 10.

---

ness in the temple made clear how deluded the wicked were. Their sudden destruction shows their impermanence (13-20). The just can thus be confident, for, as the psalmist now knows, their security is from God (1. 23-28).

73, 9: *They set their mouths against the heavens:* in an image probably derived from mythic stories of half-divine giants, the monstrous speech of the wicked is likened to enormous jaws gaping wide, devouring everything in sight.

73, 10: The Hebrew is obscure.

15 Had I thought, "I will speak as they do,"
    I would have betrayed your people.
16 Though I tried to understand all this,
    it was too difficult for me,
17 Till I entered the sanctuary of God
    and came to understand their end.

III
18 You set them, indeed, on a slippery road;
    you hurl them down to ruin.
19 How suddenly they are devastated;
    undone by disasters forever!
20 They are like a dream after waking, Lord,
    dismissed like shadows when you arise.°

IV
21 Since my heart was embittered
    and my soul deeply wounded,
22 I was stupid and could not understand;
    I was like a brute beast in your presence.
23 Yet I am always with you;
    you take hold of my right hand.ᴾ
24 With your counsel you guide me,
    and at the end receive me with honor.
25 Whom else have I in the heavens?
    None beside you delights me on earth.
26 Though my flesh and my heart fail,
    God is the rock of my heart, my portion forever.

° Jb 20, 8.   ᴾ Ps 121, 5.

73, 17: *And came to understand their end:* the psalmist receives a double revelation in the temple: 1) the end of the wicked comes unexpectedly (18-20); 2) God is with me.

73, 24: *And at the end receive me with honor:* a perhaps deliberately enigmatic verse. It is understood by some commentators as reception into heavenly glory, hence the traditional translation, "receive me into glory." The Hebrew verb can indeed refer to mysterious divine elevation of a righteous person into God's domain: Enoch in Gn 5, 24; Elijah in 2 Kgs 2, 11- 12; the righteous psalmist in Ps 49, 16. Personal resurrection in the Old Testament, however, is clearly attested only in the second century B.C. The verse is perhaps best left unspecified as a reference to God's nearness and protection.

27 But those who are far from you perish;
       you destroy those unfaithful to you.
28 As for me, to be near God is my good,
       to make the Lord God my refuge.
   I shall declare all your works
       in the gates of daughter Zion.

Psalm 74
Prayer at the Destruction of the Temple

1 *A* maskil *of Asaph.*

   I

   Why, God, have you cast us off forever?[q]
       Why does your anger burn against the sheep of your
         pasture?[r]
2 Remember your flock that you gathered of old,
       the tribe you redeemed as your very own.
   Remember Mount Zion where you dwell.[s]
3 Turn your steps toward the utter ruins,
       toward the sanctuary devastated by the enemy.
4 Your foes roared triumphantly in your shrine;
       they set up their own tokens of victory.
5 They hacked away like foresters gathering boughs,
       swinging their axes in a thicket of trees.
6 They smashed all your engraved work,
       pounded it with hammer and pick.

---

[q] Pss 10, 1; 44, 24; 77, 8.   [s] Pss 68, 17; 132, 13; Ex 15, 17; Jer 10,
[r] Ps 80, 5.   16; 51, 19.

Ps 74: A communal lament sung when the enemy invaded the temple;
it would be especially appropriate at the destruction of Jerusalem in 587
B.C. Israel's God is urged to look upon the ruined sanctuary and remember the congregation who worshiped there (1-11). People and sanctuary
are bound together; an attack on Zion is an attack on Israel. In the second half of the poem, the community brings before God the story of their
origins—their creation (12-17)—in order to move God to reenact that deed
of creation now. Will God allow a lesser power to destroy the divine pro-
ject (18-23)?
   74, 1: *Forever:* the word implies that the disaster is already of long duration. Cf 74, 9 and note.

133

7 They set your sanctuary on fire;
     the abode of your name they razed and profaned.[t]
8 They said in their hearts, "Destroy them all!
     Burn all the shrines of God in the land!"
9 Now we see no signs,
     we have no prophets,[u]
     no one who knows how long.
10 How long, O God, shall the enemy jeer?[v]
     Shall the foe revile your name forever?
11 Why draw back your right hand,
     why keep it idle beneath your cloak?

II

12 Yet you, God, are my king from of old,
     winning victories throughout the earth.
13 You stirred up the sea in your might;[w]
     you smashed the heads of the dragons on the waters.[x]
14 You crushed the heads of Leviathan,[y]
     tossed him for food to the sharks.
15 You opened up springs and torrents,
     brought dry land out of the primeval waters.
16 Yours the day and yours the night;
     you set the moon and sun in place.
17 You fixed all the limits of the earth;
     summer and winter you made.[z]

---

[t] Is 64, 10; Ps 79, 1.
[u] Lam 2, 9.
[v] Ps 89, 47.
[w] Ps 89, 10.

[x] Is 51, 9-10.
[y] Jb 3, 8; 40, 25; Is 27, 1.
[z] 16-17: Gn 1.

74, 9: *Now we see no signs:* ancients often asked prophets to say for how long a divine punishment was to last. Cf 2 Sm 24, 13. Here no prophet has arisen to indicate the duration.

74, 12-17: Comparable Canaanite literature describes the storm-god's victory over all-encompassing Sea and its allies (dragons and Leviathan) and the subsequent peaceful arrangement of the universe, sometimes through the placement of paired cosmic elements (day and night, sun and moon). Cf Ps 89, 12-13. The psalm apparently equates the enemies attacking the temple with the destructive cosmic forces already tamed by God. Why then are those forces now raging untamed against your own people?

18 Remember how the enemy has jeered, O Lᴏʀᴅ,
      how a foolish people has reviled your name.
19 Do not surrender to beasts those who praise you;
      do not forget forever the life of your afflicted.
20 Look to your covenant,
      for the land is filled with gloom;
      the pastures, with violence.
21 Let not the oppressed turn back in shame;
      may the poor and needy praise your name.
22 Arise, God, defend your cause;
      remember the constant jeers of the fools.
23 Do not ignore the clamor of your foes,
      the unceasing uproar of your enemies.

Psalm 75
God the Judge of the World

1 *For the leader. Do not destroy! A psalm of Asaph; a song.*

I

2 We thank you, God, we give thanks;
      we call upon your name,
      declare your wonderful deeds.
    You said:
3 "I will choose the time;
      I will judge fairly.
4 The earth and all its inhabitants will quake,
      but I have firmly set its pillars."[a]   *Selah*

II

5 So I say to the boastful: "Do not boast!"[b]
      to the wicked: "Do not raise your horns!

---

[a] Pss 46, 3; 60, 4; 93, 1; 96, 10; 104,   [b] 1 Sm 2, 3; Zec 2, 1-4.
  5; 1 Sm 2, 8; Is 24, 19.

Ps 75: The psalmist gives thanks and rejoices (2. 10) for the direct intervention of God, which is promised in two oracles (3-4. 11). Expecting that divine intervention, the psalmist warns evildoers to repent (5-9).

75, 2: *You said:* supplied for clarity here and in v 11. The translation assumes in both places that the psalmist is citing an oracle of God.

75, 5: *Do not raise your horns!:* the horn is the symbol of strength; to raise one's horn is to exalt one's own power as v 6 explains.

6 Do not raise your horns against heaven!
        Do not speak arrogantly against the Rock!"[c]
7 For judgment comes not from east or from west,
        not from the desert or from the mountains,[d]
8 But from God who decides,
        who brings some low and raises others high.[e]
9 Yes, a cup is in the LORD's hand,
        foaming wine, fully spiced.
    When God pours it out,
        they will drain it even to the dregs;
        all the wicked of the earth must drink.[f]
10 But I will rejoice forever;
        I will sing praise to the God of Jacob,
11 Who has said:
    "I will break off all the horns of the wicked,
        but the horns of the just shall be lifted up."[g]

Psalm 76
God Defends Zion

1 *For the leader; a psalm with stringed instruments. A song of Asaph.*

    I
2 Renowned in Judah is God,[h]
        whose name is great in Israel.

---

[c] Jb 15, 25.
[d] Mt 24, 23-27.
[e] Jb 5, 11; 1 Sm 2, 7.
[f] Ps 60, 5; Jb 21, 20; Is 51, 17. 21-22;

Jer 25, 15ff.; Hb 2, 16.
[g] Ps 92, 11.
[h] Hb 3, 2.

75, 9: *A cup:* "the cup of God's wrath" is the punishment inflicted on the wicked. Cf Is 51, 17; Jer 25, 15-29; 49, 12; Ez 23, 31-33. *Spiced:* literally, "a mixed drink"; spices or drugs were added to wine. Cf Prv 9, 2. 5.

Ps 76: A song glorifying Zion, the mountain of Jerusalem where God destroyed Israel's enemies. Zion is thus the appropriate site to celebrate the victory (3-4), a victory described in parallel scenes (5-7. 8-11). Israel is invited to worship its powerful patron deity (12-13).

3 On Salem is God's tent, a shelter on Zion.
4   There the flashing arrows were shattered,
        shield, sword, and weapons of war.[i]   *Selah*

   II
5 Terrible and awesome are you,
        stronger than the ancient mountains.
6 Despoiled are the bold warriors;
        they sleep their final sleep;
        the hands of all the mighty have failed.[j]
7 At your roar, O God of Jacob,
        chariots and steeds lay still.
8 So terrible and awesome are you;
        who can stand before you and your great anger?[k]
9 From the heavens you pronounced sentence;
        the earth was terrified and reduced to silence,
10 When you arose, O God, for judgment
        to deliver the afflicted of the land.   *Selah*
11 Even wrathful Edom praises you;
        the remnant of Hamath keeps your feast.

   III
12 Make and keep vows to the LORD your God.[l]
        May all present bring gifts to this awesome God,
13 Who checks the pride of princes,
        inspires awe among the kings of earth.

---

[i] Pss 46, 10; 122, 6-9.   [k] Dt 7, 21; 1 Sm 6, 20; Na 1, 6; Mal 3, 2.
[j] 2 Kgs 19, 35; Jer 51, 39; Na 3, 18.   [l] Nm 30, 3.

76, 3: *Salem:* an ancient name for Jerusalem, used here perhaps on account of its allusion to the Hebrew word for peace, *shalom.* Cf Gn 14, 18; Heb 7, 1-3.

76, 5: *Ancient mountains:* conjectural translation of a difficult Hebrew phrase on the basis of Gn 49, 26. The mountains are part of the structure of the universe (Ps 89, 12-13).

76, 11: *Edom . . . Hamath:* conjectural translation. Israel's neighbors to the southeast and north.

Psalm 77
Confidence in God during National Distress

1 *For the leader;* 'al Jeduthun. *A psalm of Asaph.*

   I
2 I cry aloud to God,
       cry to God to hear me.
3 On the day of my distress I seek the Lord;
       by night my hands are raised unceasingly;[m]
       I refuse to be consoled.
4 When I think of God, I groan;
       as I ponder, my spirit grows faint.[n]   *Selah*
5 My eyes cannot close in sleep;
       I am troubled and cannot speak.
6 I consider the days of old;
       the years long past (7) I remember.[o]
   In the night I meditate in my heart;
       I ponder and my spirit broods:
8 "Will the Lord reject us forever,[p]
       never again show favor?
9 Has God's love ceased forever?
       Has the promise failed for all ages?
10 Has God forgotten mercy,
       in anger withheld compassion?"   *Selah*
11 I conclude: "My sorrow is this,
       the right hand of the Most High has left us."[q]

---

[m] Pss 50, 15; 88, 2.
[n] Jon 2, 8.
[o] Ps 143, 5; Dt 32, 7.

[p] 8-10: Pss 13, 2; 44, 24; 74, 1; 80, 5;
   89, 47; Lam 3, 31.
[q] Ex 15, 6. 12; Pss 17, 7; 18, 36.

Ps 77: A community lament in which the speaker ("I") describes the anguish of Israel at God's silence when its very existence is at stake (2-11). In response the speaker recites the story of how God brought the people into existence (12-21). The question is thus posed to God: Will you allow the people you created to be destroyed?

77, 11: *I conclude:* literally, "I said." The psalmist, after pondering the present distress and God's promises to Israel, has decided that God has forgotten the people.

II

12 I will remember the deeds of the LORD;
      yes, your wonders of old I will remember.ʳ
13 I will recite all your works;
      your exploits I will tell.
14 Your way, O God, is holy;
      what god is as great as our God?ˢ
15 You alone are the God who did wonders;
      among the peoples you revealed your might.ᵗ
16 With your arm you redeemed your people,
      the descendants of Jacob and Joseph.ᵘ   *Selah*
17 The waters saw you, God;
      the waters saw you and lashed about,
      trembled even to their depths.ᵛ
18 The clouds poured down their rains;
      the thunderheads rumbled;
      your arrows flashed back and forth.ʷ
19 The thunder of your chariot wheels resounded;
      your lightning lit up the world;
      the earth trembled and quaked.ˣ
20 Through the sea was your path;
      your way, through the mighty waters,
      though your footsteps were unseen.ʸ
21 You led your people like a flock
      under the care of Moses and Aaron.ᶻ

ʳ Ps 143, 5.
ˢ Ps 18, 31; Ex 15, 11.
ᵗ Pss 86, 10; 89, 6.
ᵘ Gn 46, 26-27; Neh 1, 10.
ᵛ Pss 18, 16; 114, 3; Na 1, 4.
ʷ Pss 18, 14-15; 29; 144, 6; Jb 37, 3-4; Wis 5, 21; Hb 3, 10-11; Zec 9, 14.

ˣ Pss 18, 8; 97, 4; 99, 1; Ex 19, 16; Jgs 5, 4-5.
ʸ Neh 9, 11; Wis 14, 3; Is 51, 10; Hb 3, 15.
ᶻ Ps 78, 52; Is 63, 11-14; Hos 12, 14; Mi 6, 4.

77, 12: *I will remember:* the verb sometimes means to make present the great deeds of Israel's past by reciting them. Cf Pss 78, 42; 105, 5; 106, 7.

Psalm 78
A New Beginning in Zion and David

1   *A* maskil *of Asaph.*

I
Attend, my people, to my teaching;
    listen to the words of my mouth.
2   I will open my mouth in story,
    drawing lessons from of old.[a]
3   We have heard them, we know them;
    our ancestors have recited them to us.[b]
4   We do not keep them from our children;
    we recite them to the next generation,
The praiseworthy and mighty deeds of the LORD,
    the wonders that he performed.[c]
5   God set up a decree in Jacob,
    established a law in Israel:[d]
What he commanded our ancestors,
    they were to teach their children;
6   That the next generation might come to know,
    children yet to be born.[e]

---

[a] Ps 49, 5; Mt 13, 35.
[b] Ps 44, 2.
[c] Ex 10, 2; Dt 4, 9; Jb 8, 8.
[d] Ps 147, 19; Dt 33, 4.
[e] Ps 22, 31-32; Dt 4, 9; 6, 7.

Ps 78: A recital of history to show that past generations did not respond to God's gracious deeds and were punished by God making the gift into a punishment. Will Israel now fail to appreciate God's new act—the choosing of Zion and of David? The tripartite introduction invites Israel to learn the lessons hidden in its traditions (1-4. 5-7. 8-11); each section ends with the mention of God's acts. There are two distinct narratives of approximately equal length: the wilderness events (12-39) and the movement from Egypt to Canaan (40-72). The structure of both is parallel: gracious act (12-16. 40-55), rebellion (17-20. 56-58), divine punishment (21-31. 59-64), God's readiness to forgive and begin anew (32-39. 65-72). The psalm may reflect the reunification program of either King Hezekiah (late eighth century) or King Josiah (late seventh century) in that the Northern Kingdom (Ephraim, Joseph) is especially invited to accept Zion and the Davidic king.

78, 2: *Story:* Hebrew *mashal* literally means "comparison" and can signify a story with a hidden meaning. Mt 13, 35 cites the verse to explain Jesus' use of parables.

In turn they were to recite them to their children,
7   that they too might put their trust in God,
And not forget the works of God,
       keeping his commandments.
8   They were not to be like their ancestors,
       a rebellious and defiant generation,[f]
A generation whose heart was not constant,[g]
       whose spirit was not faithful to God,
9   Like the ranks of Ephraimite archers,
       who retreated on the day of battle.
10 They did not keep God's covenant;
       they refused to walk by his law.
11 They forgot his works,
       the wondrous deeds he had shown them.

II

A

12 In the sight of their ancestors God did wonders,
       in the land of Egypt, the plain of Zoan.[h]
13 He split the sea and led them across,[i]
       piling up the waters rigid as walls.[j]
14 God led them with a cloud by day,
       all night with the light of fire.[k]
15 He split rock in the desert,
       gave water to drink, abounding as the deep.[l]
16 He made streams flow from crags,
       drew out rivers of water.

B

17 But they went on sinning against him,
       rebelling against the Most High in the desert.[m]

---

[f] Dt 31, 27; 32, 5.
[g] Ps 95, 10.
[h] Ps 106, 7.
[i] 13-14: Ex 14-15; Ps 136, 13.
[j] Ex 14, 22; 15, 8.
[k] Ps 105, 39; Ex 13, 21; Wis 18, 3.
[l] Pss 105, 41; 114, 8; Ex 17, 1-7; Nm 20, 2-13; Dt 8, 15; Wis 11, 4; Is 48, 21.
[m] Dt 9, 7; Ez 20, 13.

78, 9: *Ephraimite archers:* Ephraim was the most important tribe of the Northern Kingdom. Its military defeat (here unspecified) demonstrates its infidelity to God, who otherwise would have protected it.
78, 12. 43: *Zoan:* a city on the arm of the Nile, a former capital of Egypt.

18 They tested God in their hearts,
  demanding the food they craved.[n]
19 They spoke against God, and said,
  "Can God spread a table in the desert?[o]
20 True, when he struck the rock,
  water gushed forth,
  the wadis flooded.
But can he also provide bread,
  give meat to his people?"

C

21 The LORD heard and grew angry;[p]
  fire blazed up against Jacob;
  anger flared up against Israel.
22 For they did not believe in God,
  did not trust in his saving power.
23 So he commanded the skies above;
  the doors of heaven he opened.
24 God rained manna upon them for food;
  bread from heaven he gave them.[q]
25 All ate a meal fit for heroes;
  food he sent in abundance.
26 He stirred up the east wind in the heavens;
  by his power God brought on the south wind.
27 He rained meat upon them like dust,
  winged fowl like the sands of the sea,
28 Brought them down in the midst of the camp,
  round about their tents.
29 They ate and were well filled;
  he gave them what they had craved.
30 But while they still wanted more,
  and the food was still in their mouths,
31 God's anger attacked them,
  killed their best warriors,

---

n Ps 106, 14; Ex 16, 2-36.
o Ps 23, 5.
p 21f: Nm 11; Dt 32, 22.

q Ps 105, 40; Ex 16, 4. 14; Dt 8, 3; Wis 16, 20; Jn 6, 31.

78, 23-31: On the manna and the quail, see Ex 16 and Nm 11. Unlike Ex 16, here both manna and quail are instruments of punishment, showing that a divine gift can become deadly because of Israel's apostasy.

laid low the youth of Israel.[r]

32 In spite of all this they went on sinning,
    they did not believe in his wonders.

D

33 God ended their days abruptly,
    their years in sudden death.
34 When he slew them, they began to seek him;
    they again inquired of their God.[s]
35 They remembered that God was their rock,
    God Most High, their redeemer.
36 But they deceived him with their mouths,
    lied to him with their tongues.
37 Their hearts were not constant toward him;
    they were not faithful to his covenant.[t]
38 But God is merciful and forgave their sin;
    he did not utterly destroy them.
    Time and again he turned back his anger,
    unwilling to unleash all his rage.[u]
39 He was mindful that they were flesh,
    a breath that passes and does not return.

III

A

40 How often they rebelled against God in the desert,
    grieved him in the wasteland.
41 Again and again they tested God,
    provoked the Holy One of Israel.
42 They did not remember his power,
    the day he redeemed them from the foe,[v]
43 When he displayed his wonders in Egypt,
    his marvels in the plain of Zoan.[w]

---

[r] Nm 14, 29.
[s] Dt 32, 15. 18; Is 26, 16.
[t] Ps 95, 10; Is 29, 13.
[u] Ps 85, 4; Ex 32, 14; Is 48, 9; Ez 20, 22.

[v] Ps 106, 21.
[w] 43f: Pss 105, 27-36; 135, 9; Ex 7, 14-11, 10; 12, 29-36; Wis 16-18.

78, 35: *Remembered:* invoked God publicly in worship. Their words were insincere (36).

78, 38: God is always ready to forgive and begin anew, as in choosing Zion and David (65-72).

44 God changed their rivers to blood;
        their streams they could not drink.
45 He sent insects that devoured them,[x]
        frogs that destroyed them.
46 He gave their harvest to the caterpillar,
        the fruits of their labor to the locust.
47 He killed their vines with hail,[y]
        their sycamores with frost.
48 He exposed their flocks to deadly hail,
        their cattle to lightning.[z]
49 He unleashed against them his fiery breath,
        roar, fury, and distress,
        storming messengers of death.
50 He cleared a path for his anger;
        he did not spare them from death;
        he delivered their beasts to the plague.
51 He struck all the firstborn of Egypt,[a]
        love's first child in the tents of Ham.
52 God led forth his people like sheep;
        he guided them through the desert like a flock.[b]
53 He led them on secure and unafraid,
        but the sea enveloped their enemies.[c]
54 He brought them to his holy land,
        the mountain his right hand had won.[d]
55 God drove out the nations before them,
        apportioned them a heritage by lot,
        settled the tribes of Israel in their tents.

B

56 But they tested, rebelled against God Most High,
        his decres they did not observe.
57 They turned back, deceitful like their ancestors;
        they proved false like a bow with no tension.

---

[x] Ex 8, 17.   [b] Ps 77, 21.
[y] Wis 16, 16.   [c] Ex 14, 26-28.
[z] Ex 9, 3.   [d] Ex 15, 17.
[a] Pss 105, 36; 136, 10; Ex 12, 29.

78, 43-55: Ex 7-12 records ten plagues. Here there are six divine attacks upon Egypt; the seventh climactic act is God's bringing Israel to the holy land.

58 They enraged him with their high places;
      with their idols they goaded him.ᵉ

                              C
59 God heard and grew angry;
      he rejected Israel completely.
60 He forsook the shrine at Shiloh,ᶠ
      the tent where he dwelt with humans.
61 He gave up his might into captivity,
      his glorious ark into the hands of the foe.ᵍ
62 God abandoned his people to the sword;
      he was enraged against his heritage.
63 Fire consumed their young men;
      their young women heard no wedding songs.ʰ
64 Their priests fell by the sword;
      their widows made no lamentation.

                              D
65 Then the Lord awoke as from sleep,
      like a warrior from the effects of wine.
66 He put his enemies to flight;
      everlasting shame he dealt them.
67 He rejected the tent of Joseph,
      chose not the tribe of Ephraim.
68 God chose the tribe of Judah,
      Mount Zion which he favored.ⁱ
69 He built his shrine like the heavens,
      like the earth which he founded forever.
70 He chose David his servant,
      took him from the sheepfold.ʲ
71 From tending sheep God brought him,
      to shepherd Jacob, his people,
      Israel, his heritage.ᵏ

ᵉ Dt 32, 16. 21.
ᶠ Jos 18, 1; 1 Sm 1, 3; Jer 7, 12; 26, 6.
ᵍ 1 Sm 4, 11. 22.
ʰ Dt 32, 25; Jer 7, 34.
ⁱ Pss 48, 2; 50, 2; Lam 2, 15.
ʲ Ps 89, 21; Ez 34, 23; 37, 24; 2 Chr 6, 6.
ᵏ 1 Sm 16, 11-13; 2 Sm 7, 8.

78, 60: *Shiloh:* an important shrine in the north prior to Jerusalem. Despite its holy status, it was destroyed (60-64; cf Jer 7, 12. 14).

78, 68. 70: God's ultimate offer of mercy to the sinful helpless people is Zion and the Davidic king.

72 He shepherded them with a pure heart;
with skilled hands he guided them.

Psalm 79
A Prayer for Jerusalem

1 *A psalm of Asaph.*

I

O God, the nations have invaded your heritage;
they have defiled your holy temple,
have laid Jerusalem in ruins.[l]
2 They have left the corpses of your servants
as food for the birds of the heavens,
the flesh of your faithful for the beasts of the earth.[m]
3 They have spilled their blood like water
all around Jerusalem,
and no one is left to bury them.[n]
4 We have become the reproach of our neighbors,
the scorn and derision of those around us.[o]

II

5 How long, LORD? Will you be angry forever?
Will your rage keep burning like fire?[p]
6 Pour out your wrath on nations that reject you,
on kingdoms that do not call on your name,[q]
7 For they have devoured Jacob,
laid waste his home.

---

[l] 2 Kgs 25, 9-10; Lam 1, 10. Dn 9, 16; Zep 2, 8.
[m] Jer 7, 33. [p] Pss 13, 2; 44, 24; 89, 47; Dt 4, 24.
[n] 1 Mc 7, 17; Jer 14, 16. [q] Ps 14, 4; Jer 10, 25.
[o] Pss 44, 14; 80, 7; 123, 3-4; Jb 12, 4;

Ps 79: A communal lament complaining that the nations have defiled the temple and murdered the holy people, leaving their corpses unburied (1-4). The occasion is probably the destruction of Jerusalem by the Babylonian army in 587 B.C. The people ask how long the withdrawal of divine favor will last (5), pray for action now (6-7), and admit that their own sins have brought about the catastrophe (8-9). They seek to persuade God to act for reasons of honor: the nations who do not call upon the Name are running amok (6); the divine honor is compromised (1. 10. 12); God's own servants suffer (2-4. 11).

8 Do not hold past iniquities against us;
    may your compassion come quickly,
        for we have been brought very low.[r]

III
9 Help us, God our savior,
    for the glory of your name.
Deliver us, pardon our sins
    for your name's sake.[s]
10 Why should the nations say,
    "Where is their God?"[t]
Before our eyes make clear to the nations
    that you avenge the blood of your servants.[u]

IV
11 Let the groans of prisoners come before you;
    by your great power free those doomed to death.[v]
12 Lord, inflict on our neighbors sevenfold
    the disgrace they inflicted on you.[w]
13 Then we, your people, the sheep of your pasture,
    will give thanks to you forever;
        through all ages we will declare your praise.

Psalm 80
Prayer to Restore God's Vineyard

1 *For the leader; according to "Lilies." Eduth. A psalm of Asaph.*

I
2 Shepherd of Israel, listen,
    guide of the flock of Joseph!

---

[r] Ps 142, 7.
[s] Ez 20, 44; 36, 22.
[t] Pss 42, 4; 115, 2; Jl 2, 17.
[u] Jl 4, 21.
[v] Ps 102, 21.
[w] Ps 89, 51-52.

Ps 80: A community lament in time of military defeat. Using the familiar image of Israel as a vineyard, the people complain that God has broken down the wall protecting the once splendid vine brought from Egypt (9-14). They pray that God will again turn to them and use the Davidic king to lead them to victory (15-20).

80, 1: *Lilies . . . Eduth:* the first term is probably the title of the melody to which the psalm was to be sung; the second is unexplained.

From your throne upon the cherubim reveal yourself[x]

3   to Ephraim, Benjamin, and Manasseh.

Stir up your power, come to save us.

4   O LORD of hosts, restore us;

Let your face shine upon us,

        that we may be saved.[y]

II

5 LORD of hosts,

        how long will you burn with anger

        while your people pray?[z]

6 You have fed them the bread of tears,

        made them drink tears in abundance.[a]

7 You have left us to be fought over by our neighbors;

        our enemies deride us.[b]

8 O LORD of hosts, restore us;

        let your face shine upon us,

        that we may be saved.

III

9 You brought a vine out of Egypt;

        you drove away the nations and planted it.

10 You cleared the ground;

        it took root and filled the land.

11 The mountains were covered by its shadow,

        the cedars of God by its branches.

12 It sent out boughs as far as the sea,

        shoots as far as the river.

13 Why have you broken down the walls,

        so that all who pass by pluck its fruit?[c]

---

[x] Pss 23, 1-3; 95, 7; 100, 3; Gn 48, 15; Ex 25, 22; 1 Sm 4, 4; 2 Sm 6, 2; Mi 7, 14.
[y] 4. 8. 20: Pss 4, 7; 31, 17; 67, 2; 85, 5; Nm 6, 25; Dn 9, 17.
[z] Pss 13, 2; 44, 24; 74, 1; 79, 5; 89, 47; Dt 4, 24.
[a] Pss 42, 4; 102, 10.
[b] Pss 44, 14; 79, 4; 123, 3-4; Jb 12, 4; Dn 9, 16; Zep 2, 8.
[c] Ps 89, 41.

80, 9: *A vine:* a frequent metaphor for Israel. Cf Is 5, 1-7; 27, 2-5; Jer 2, 21; Hos 10, 1; Mt 21, 33.

80, 12: *The sea:* the Mediterranean. *The river:* the Euphrates. Cf Gn 15, 18; 1 Kgs 5, 1. The terms may also have a mythic nuance the seas that surround the earth; sea and river are sometimes paralleled in poetry.

14 The boar from the forest strips the vine;
        the beast of the field feeds upon it.[d]
15 Turn again, Lord of hosts;
        look down from heaven and see;
    Attend to this vine,
16   the shoot your right hand has planted.
17 Those who would burn or cut it down—
        may they perish at your rebuke.
18 May your help be with the man at your right hand,
        with the one whom you once made strong.
19 Then we will not withdraw from you;
        revive us, and we will call on your name.
20 Lord of hosts, restore us;
        let your face shine upon us,
        that we may be saved.

Psalm 81
An Admonition to Fidelity

1   *For the leader; "upon the* gittith." *Of Asaph.*

    I
2   Sing joyfully to God our strength;[e]
        shout in triumph to the God of Jacob!
3   Take up a melody, sound the timbrel,
        the sweet-sounding harp and lyre.

---

[d] Hos 2, 14.   16, 1.
[e] Pss 43, 4; 68, 26; 149, 3; 150, 3-4; Jdt

80, 18: *The man at your right hand . . . the one:* the Davidic king who will lead the army in battle.

Ps 81: At a pilgrimage feast, probably harvest in the fall, the people assemble in the temple in accord with the Sinai ordinances (2-6a). They hear a divine word (mediated by a temple speaker) telling how God rescued them from slavery in Egypt (7-9), gave them the fundamental commandment of fidelity (9-11), which would bring punishment if they refused to obey (12-13). But if Israel repents, God will be with them once again, bestowing protection and fertility (14-17).

81, 1: *Upon the gittith:* probably the title of the melody to which the psalm was to be sung or a musical instrument.

4 Blow the trumpet at the new moon,
      at the full moon, on our solemn feast.[f]
5 For this is a law in Israel,
      an edict of the God of Jacob,[g]
6 Who made it a decree for Joseph
      when he came out of the land of Egypt.

   II
   I hear a new oracle:
7   "I relieved their shoulders of the burden;
         their hands put down the basket.[h]
8 In distress you called and I rescued you;
      unseen, I spoke to you in thunder;
   At the waters of Meribah I tested you and said:[i]   *Selah*
9   'Listen, my people, I give you warning!
         If only you will obey me, Israel![j]
10 There must be no foreign god among you;[k]
      you must not worship an alien god.
11 I, the LORD, am your God,
      who brought you up from the land of Egypt.
      Open wide your mouth that I may fill it.'
12 But my people did not listen to my words;
      Israel did not obey me.

---

f Lv 23, 24; Nm 29, 1.
g Ex 23, 14ff.
h Ex 1, 14; 6, 6.
i Ps 95, 8; Ex 2, 23ff; 17, 7; 19, 16; Nm

20, 13; 27, 14.
j Ex 15, 26; Is 55, 2-3.
k 10-11: Ex 20, 2-6; Dt 5, 6-10.

81, 4: *New moon . . . full moon:* the pilgrimage feast of harvest began with a great assembly (Lv 23, 24; Nm 29, 1), used the new moon as a sign (Nm 29, 6), and included trumpets (Lv 23, 24).

81, 6: *I hear a new oracle:* literally, "a tongue I do not know I hear." A temple official speaks the word of God (6b-17), which is authoritative and unlike merely human words (cf Nm 24, 4. 16).

81, 7: *I relieved their shoulders of the burden:* literally, "his [Israel's] shoulder," hence the plural translation. A reference to the liberation of Israel from slavery in Egypt. *The basket:* for carrying clay to make bricks. Cf Ex 1, 14.

81, 8: *Meribah:* place of rebellion in the wilderness; cf Ex 17, 7; Nm 20, 13.

81, 10: *There must be no foreign god among you:* as in Pss 50 and 95, Israel is challenged to obey the first commandment of fidelity to God after the proclamation of the exodus.

150

13 So I gave them over to hardness of heart;
    they followed their own designs.[l]
14 But even now if my people would listen,
    if Israel would walk in my paths,[m]
15 In a moment I would subdue their foes,
    against their enemies unleash my hand.[n]
16 Those who hate the LORD would tremble,
    their doom sealed forever.
17 But Israel I would feed with the finest wheat,
    satisfy them with honey from the rock."[o]

Psalm 82
The Downfall of Unjust Gods

1 *A psalm of Asaph.*

I
God rises in the divine council,
    gives judgment in the midst of the gods.[p]
2 "How long will you judge unjustly
    and favor the cause of the wicked?[q]   *Selah*
3 Defend the lowly and fatherless;
    render justice to the afflicted and needy.
4 Rescue the lowly and poor;
    deliver them from the hand of the wicked."[r]

II
5 The gods neither know nor understand,
    wandering about in darkness,

---

[l] Jer 3, 17; 7, 24.   [p] Is 3, 13-14.
[m] Is 48, 18.   [q] Ps 58, 2.
[n] Lv 26, 7-8.   [r] Dt 1, 17.
[o] Ps 147, 14; Dt 32, 13-14.

Ps 82: As in Ps 58, the pagan gods are seen as subordinate divine beings to whom Israel's God had delegated oversight of the foreign countries in the beginning (Dt 32, 8-9 LXX). Now God arises in the heavenly assembly (1) to rebuke the unjust "gods" (2-4), who are stripped of divine status and reduced in rank to mortals (5-7). They are accused of misruling the earth by not upholding the poor. A short prayer for universal justice concludes the psalm (8).
82, 5: The gods are blind and unable to declare what is right. Their

and all the world's foundations shake.

6 I declare: "Gods though you be,
    offspring of the Most High all of you,

7 Yet like any mortal you shall die;
    like any prince you shall fall."

8 Arise, O God, judge the earth,
    for yours are all the nations.

Psalm 83
Prayer against a Hostile Alliance

1 *A song; a psalm of Asaph.*

I

2 God, do not be silent;
    God, be not still and unmoved![s]

3 See how your enemies rage;
    your foes proudly raise their heads.

4 They conspire against your people,
    plot against those you protect.[t]

5 They say, "Come, let us wipe out their nation;
    let Israel's name be mentioned no more!"

6 They scheme with one mind,
    in league against you:[u]

---

[s] Pss 10, 1; 44, 24; 109, 1.   [u] Ps 2, 2.
[t] Jer 11, 9.

---

misrule shakes earth's foundations (cf Pss 11, 3; 75, 4), which God made firm in creation (Ps 96, 10).

82, 6: *I declare: "Gods though you be":* in Jn 10, 34 Jesus uses the verse to prove that those to whom the word of God is addressed can fittingly be called "gods."

82, 8: *Judge the earth:* according to Dt 32, 8-9 LXX, Israel's God had originally assigned jurisdiction over the foreign nations to the subordinate deities, keeping Israel as a personal possession. Now God will directly take over the rulership of the whole world.

Ps 83: The community lament complains to God of the nations' attempts to wipe out the name of Israel (2-9). The psalmist sees all Israel's enemies throughout its history united in a conspiracy (3-9). May God destroy the current crop of enemies as the enemies of old were destroyed (10-13), and may they be pursued until they acknowledge the name of Israel's God (14-19).

7 The tents of Ishmael and Edom,
    the people of Moab and Hagar,[v]
8 Gebal, Ammon, and Amalek,[w]
    Philistia and the inhabitants of Tyre.[x]
9 Assyria, too, in league with them
    gives aid to the descendants of Lot.   *Selah*

    II
10 Deal with them as with Midian;
    as with Sisera and Jabin at the torrent Kishon,[y]
11 Those destroyed at Endor,
    who became dung for the ground.[z]
12 Make their nobles like Oreb and Zeeb,
    all their princes like Zebah and Zalmunna,
13 Who made a plan together,
    "Let us seize the pastures of God."
14 My God, turn them into withered grass,
    into chaff flying before the wind.[a]
15 As a fire raging through a forest,
    a flame setting mountains ablaze,[b]
16 Pursue them with your tempest;
    terrify them with your storm.[c]
17 Cover their faces with shame,
    till they pay you homage, LORD.
18 Let them be dismayed and shamed forever;
    let them perish in disgrace.
19 Show them you alone are the LORD,
    the Most High over all the earth.[d]

---

[v] Nm 20, 23; 1 Chr 5, 10. 19.
[w] Ex 17, 8.
[x] Jos 13, 2.
[y] Ex 2, 15; Is 9, 3; 10, 26.
[z] Jer 8, 2.

[a] Pss 1, 4; 35, 5; 58, 10; Is 5, 24; 10, 17; 17, 13; 29, 5; Ez 21, 3.
[b] Ps 50, 3.
[c] Jb 25, 32; 27, 21.
[d] Ps 97, 9; Dt 4, 39; Dn 3, 45.

83, 7-9: Apart from the Assyrians, all the nations listed here were neighbors of Israel. *The people of . . . Hagar:* a tribe of the desert regions east of *Ammon* and *Moab* (1 Chr 5, 10. 19-22). *Gebal* is the Phoenician city of Byblos or perhaps a mountain region south of the Dead Sea. *The descendants of Lot* are Moab and Edom (Gn 19, 36-38 and Dt 2, 9). These nations were never united against Israel in the same period; the psalm has lumped them all together.

83, 10-13: For the historical events, see Jgs 4-8.

Psalm 84
Prayer of a Pilgrim to Jerusalem

1   *For the leader; "upon the* gittith." *A psalm of the Korahites.*

I
2   How lovely your dwelling,
        O LORD of hosts!e
3   My soul yearns and pines
        for the courts of the LORD.f
    My heart and flesh cry out
        for the living God.
4   As the sparrow finds a home
        and the swallow a nest to settle her young,
    My home is by your altars,
        LORD of hosts, my king and my God!g
5   Happy are those who dwell in your house!
        They never cease to praise you.   *Selah*

II
6   Happy are those who find refuge in you,
        whose hearts are set on pilgrim roads.
7   As they pass through the Baca valley,
        they find spring water to drink.
    Also from pools the Lord provides water
        for those who lose their way.
8   They pass through outer and inner wall
        and see the God of gods on Zion.

III
9   LORD of hosts, hear my prayer;
        listen, God of Jacob.   *Selah*

---

e Pss 43, 3-4; 122, 1.   g Ps 5, 3.
f Pss 42, 2-3; 63, 2-3; 143, 6; Is 26, 9.

Ps 84: Israelites celebrated three pilgrimage feasts in Jerusalem annually. The psalm expresses the sentiments of the pilgrims eager to enjoy the divine presence.

84, 4: The desire of a restless bird for a secure home is an image of the desire of a pilgrim for the secure house of God. Cf Ps 42, 2-3, where the image for the desire of the pilgrim is the thirst of the deer for water.

84, 7: *Baca valley:* Hebrew obscure; probably a valley on the way to Jerusalem.

10 O God, look kindly on our shield;
      look upon the face of your anointed.[h]

    IV

11 Better one day in your courts
      than a thousand elsewhere.
    Better the threshold of the house of my God
      than a home in the tents of the wicked.
12 For a sun and shield is the LORD God,
      bestowing all grace and glory.
    The LORD withholds no good thing
      from those who walk without reproach.
13 O LORD of hosts,
      happy are those who trust in you!

Psalm 85
Prayer for Divine Favor

1 *For the leader. A psalm of the Korahites.*

    I

2 You once favored, LORD, your land,
      restored the good fortune of Jacob.[i]
3 You forgave the guilt of your people,
      pardoned all their sins.   *Selah*
4 You withdrew all your wrath,
      turned back your burning anger.[j]

    II

5 Restore us once more, God our savior;
      abandon your wrath against us.[k]

---

[h] Ps 89, 19.
[i] Pss 14, 7; 126, 4.
[j] Ps 78, 38; Ex 32, 14; Is 48, 9.
[k] Ps 80, 4.

84, 10: *Our shield . . . your anointed:* the king had a role in the liturgical celebration. For the king as shield, cf Ps 89, 19.

Ps 85: A national lament reminding God of past favors and forgiveness (2-4) and begging for forgiveness and grace now (5-8). A speaker represents the people who wait humbly with open hearts (9-10): God will be active on their behalf (11-14). The situation suggests the conditions of Judea during the early postexilic period, the fifth century B.C.; the thoughts are similar to those of postexilic prophets (Hg 1, 5-11; 2, 6-9).

6 Will you be angry with us forever,
  drag out your anger for all generations?[i]
7 Please give us life again,
  that your people may rejoice in you.
8 Show us, LORD, your love;
  grant us your salvation.

III

9 I will listen for the word of God;
  surely the LORD will proclaim peace
To his people, to the faithful,
  to those who trust in him.
10 Near indeed is salvation for the loyal;
  prosperity will fill our land.
11 Love and truth will meet;
  justice and peace will kiss.[m]
12 Truth will spring from the earth;
  justice will look down from heaven.[n]
13 The LORD will surely grant abundance;
  our land will yield its increase.[o]
14 Prosperity will march before the Lord,
  and good fortune will follow behind.

Psalm 86
Prayer in Time of Distress

1 *A prayer of David.*

I

Hear me, LORD, and answer me,
  for I am poor and oppressed.

---

[i] Pss 79, 5; 89, 47.
[m] Pss 89, 15; 97, 2.
[n] Is 45, 8.

[o] Ps 67, 7; Lv 26, 4; Ez 34, 27; Hos 2, 23-24; Zec 8, 12.

85, 9: The prophet listens to God's revelation. Cf Hb 2, 1.

85, 11-14: Divine activity is personified as pairs of virtues.

Ps 86: An individual lament. The psalmist, "poor and oppressed" (1), "devoted" (2), "your servant" (2. 4. 16), "rescued from the depths of Sheol" (13), attacked by the ruthless (14), desires only God's protection (1-7. 11-17).

2   Preserve my life, for I am loyal;
     save your servant who trusts in you.

3   You are my God; pity me, Lord;
     to you I call all the day.

4   Gladden the soul of your servant;
     to you, Lord, I lift up my soul.[p]

5   Lord, you are kind and forgiving,
     most loving to all who call on you.[q]

6   LORD, hear my prayer;
     listen to my cry for help.[r]

7   In this time of trouble I call,
     for you will answer me.

II

8   None among the gods can equal you, O Lord;
     nor can their deeds compare to yours.[s]

9   All the nations you have made shall come
     to bow before you, Lord,
     and give honor to your name.[t]

10 For you are great and do wondrous deeds;
     and you alone are God.

III

11 Teach me, LORD, your way
     that I may walk in your truth,[u]
     single-hearted and revering your name.

12 I will praise you with all my heart,
     glorify your name forever, Lord my God.

13 Your love for me is great;
     you have rescued me from the depths of Sheol.[v]

14 O God, the arrogant have risen against me;
     a ruthless band has sought my life;
     to you they pay no heed.

15 But you, Lord, are a merciful and gracious God,
     slow to anger, most loving and true.[w]

p Pss 25, 1; 143, 8.
q Jl 2, 13.
r Pss 5, 2; 130, 1-2.
s Pss 35, 10; 89, 9; Ex 15, 11; Dt 3, 24; Jer 10, 6.
t Ps 22, 28; Zec 14, 16; Rv 15, 4.
u Pss 25, 4; 26, 3; 27, 11; 119, 12. 35; 143, 8. 10.
v Pss 30, 4; 40, 3; Jon 2, 7.
w Pss 103, 8; 130, 7; 145, 8; Ex 34, 6.

16 Turn to me, have pity on me;
>> give your strength to your servant;
>> save this child of your handmaid.[x]
17 Give me a sign of your favor:
>> make my enemies see, to their confusion,
>> that you, Lord, help and comfort me.

Psalm 87
Zion the True Birthplace of Diaspora Pilgrims

1 *A psalm of the Korahites. A song.*

I
The Lord loves the city[y]
>> founded on holy mountains,
2 Loves the gates of Zion
>> more than any dwelling in Jacob.
3 Glorious things are said of you,
>> O city of God!   *Selah*

II
4 From Babylon and Egypt I count
>> those who acknowledge the Lord.
>> Philistia, Ethiopia, Tyre,
>>> of them it can be said:
>>> "This one was born there."
5 But of Zion it must be said:
>> "They all were born here."[z]
>> The Most High confirms this;[a]

---

x Pss 25, 16; 116, 16; Wis 9, 5.   z Gal 4, 26.
y 1-2: Pss 76, 2-3; 78, 68-69.   a Ps 48, 9.

Ps 87: A song of Zion, like Psalms 46, 48, 76, and 132. After the Exile of the sixth century B.C., diaspora Jews from all over the world (4) made the long pilgrimage to Jerusalem, the city of God (1-3). Such Jews may have hailed from distant lands, but the psalm sees them as children of Zion (5-7). The original occasion may have been Pentecost, which always attracted a large number of diaspora Jews.

87, 2: *The gates:* the city itself, a common Hebrew idiom.

87, 5-6: The bond between the exile and the holy city was so strong as to override the exile's citizenship of lesser cities.

6   the Lord notes in the register of the peoples:
         "This one was born here."[b]   *Selah*
7   So all sing in their festive dance:
         "Within you is my true home."[c]

Psalm 88
A Despairing Lament

1   *A song; a psalm of the Korahites. For the leader; according to* Mahalath.
    For singing; a maskil *of Heman the Ezrahite.*

    I
2   LORD, my God, I call out by day;
         at night I cry aloud in your presence.[d]
3   Let my prayer come before you;
         incline your ear to my cry.[e]
4   For my soul is filled with troubles;[f]
         my life draws near to Sheol.
5   I am reckoned with those who go down to the pit;
         I am weak, without strength.
6   My couch is among the dead,
         with the slain who lie in the grave.
    You remember them no more;
         they are cut off from your care.
7   You plunged me into the bottom of the pit,
         into the darkness of the abyss.
8   Your wrath lies heavy upon me;
         all your waves crash over me.[g]   *Selah*
9   Because of you my friends shun me;
         you make me loathsome to them;[h]

---

[b] Is 4, 3.
[c] Pss 68, 26; 149, 3.
[d] Ps 77, 3.
[e] Ps 119, 170.
[f] 4-7: Pss 28, 1; 30, 4; 40, 3; 86, 13;

143, 7; Nm 16, 33; Jb 17, 1; Jon 2, 7.
[g] Pss 18, 5; 32, 6; 42, 8; 69, 2; Jon 2, 4.
[h] Pss 38, 12; 79, 4; 80, 7; 123, 3-4; 142,
8; Jb 12, 4; 19, 13; Lam 3, 7; Dn 9, 16.

Ps 88: A lament in which the psalmist prays for rescue from the
alienation of approaching death. Each of the three stanzas begins with
a call to God (2. 10b. 14) and complains of the death that separates one
from God. The tone is persistently grim.

88, 4-8: In imagination the psalmist already experiences the alienation of Sheol.

Caged in, I cannot escape;
10   my eyes grow dim from trouble.

II

All day I call on you, LORD;
    I stretch out my hands to you.
11 Do you work wonders for the dead?
    Do the shades arise and praise you?[i]   *Selah*
12 Is your love proclaimed in the grave,
    your fidelity in the tomb?
13 Are your marvels declared in the darkness,
    your righteous deeds in the land of oblivion?

III

14 But I cry out to you, LORD;
    in the morning my prayer comes before you.
15 Why do you reject me, LORD?
    Why hide your face from me?
16 I am mortally afflicted since youth;
    lifeless, I suffer your terrible blows.
17 Your wrath has swept over me;
    your terrors have reduced me to silence.[j]
18 All the day they surge round like a flood;
    from every side they close in on me.
19 Because of you companions shun me;[k]
    my only friend is darkness.

Psalm 89
A Lament over God's Promise to David

1 *A* maskil *of Ethan the Ezrahite.*

I

2 The promises of the LORD I will sing forever,[l]
    proclaim your loyalty through all ages.

---

[i] Pss 6, 6; 30, 10; 38, 18; 115, 17.   [k] Jb 19, 13.
[j] Jb 6, 4; 20, 25.   [l] Is 63, 7.

88, 11-13: The psalmist seeks to persuade God to act out of concern for divine honor: the shades give you no worship, so keep me alive to offer you praise.

Ps 89: The community laments the defeat of the Davidic king, to whom

3 For you said, "My love is established forever;
my loyalty will stand as long as the heavens.
4 I have made a covenant with my chosen one;
I have sworn to David my servant:
5 I will make your dynasty stand forever
and establish your throne through all ages."[m] *Selah*

II

6 The heavens praise your marvels, LORD,
your loyalty in the assembly of the holy ones.[n]
7 Who in the skies ranks with the LORD?
Who is like the LORD among the gods?[o]
8 A God dreaded in the council of the holy ones,
greater and more awesome than all who sit there!
9 LORD, God of hosts, who is like you?
Mighty LORD, your loyalty is always present.
10 You rule the raging sea;[p]
you still its swelling waves.
11 You crushed Rahab with a mortal blow;
your strong arm scattered your foes.
12 Yours are the heavens, yours the earth;
you founded the world and everything in it.[q]
13 Zaphon and Amanus you created;
Tabor and Hermon rejoice in your name.

---

[m] Pss 61, 7-8; 132, 11; 2 Sm 7, 8-16.
[n] Pss 29, 1; 82, 1; Jb 1, 6; 5, 1.
[o] 7-9: Pss 35, 10; 86, 8; 113, 5; Ex 15, 11; Jer 10, 6.
[p] 10-11: Pss 65, 8; 74, 13-15; 107, 29; Jb 7, 12; Is 51, 9-10.
[q] Pss 24, 1-2; 50, 12; Dt 10, 14; 1 Cor 10, 26.

God promised kingship as enduring as the heavens (2-5). The psalm narrates how God became king of the divine beings (6-9) and how the Davidic king became king of earthly kings (20-38). Since the defeat of the king calls into question God's promise, the community ardently prays God to be faithful to the original promise to David (39-52).

89, 3-5: avid's dynasty is to be as long-lasting as the heavens, a statement reinforced by using the same verbs (establish, stand) both of the divine love and loyalty and of the Davidic dynasty and throne. Cf 29-30.

89, 7: *The gods:* literally, "the sons of gods," "the holy ones" and "courtiers" of 6 and 8. These heavenly spirits are members of God's court.

89, 11: *Rahab:* a mythological sea monster whose name is used in the Bible mainly as a personification of primeval chaos. Cf Jb 9, 13; 26, 12; Ps 74, 13-14; Is 51, 9.

89, 13: *Zaphon and Amanus:* two sacred mountains in northern Syria.

14 Mighty your arm, strong your hand,
        your right hand is ever exalted.
15 Justice and judgment are the foundation of your throne;
        love and loyalty march before you.[r]
16 Happy the people who know you, LORD,
        who walk in the radiance of your face.
17 In your name they sing joyfully all the day;
        at your victory they raise the festal shout.[s]
18 You are their majestic strength;
        by your favor our horn is exalted.[t]
19 Truly the LORD is our shield,
        the Holy One of Israel, our king![u]

    III
20 Once you spoke in vision;[v]
        to your faithful ones you said:
    "I have set a leader over the warriors;
        I have raised up a hero from the army.
21 I have chosen David, my servant;
        with my holy oil I have anointed him.
22 My hand will be with him;[w]
        my arm will make him strong.
23 No enemy shall outwit him,
        nor shall the wicked defeat him.
24 I will crush his foes before him,
        strike down those who hate him.
25 My loyalty and love will be with him;
        through my name his horn will be exalted.
26 I will set his hand upon the sea,
        his right hand upon the rivers.

---

[r] Pss 85, 11-12; 97, 2.
[s] Ps 47, 2; Zep 3, 14.
[t] Pss 112, 9; 148, 14.
[u] Pss 47, 9; 96, 10; 97, 1; 99, 1; Is 6, 3.

[v] 20-21: Pss 78, 70; 132, 11-12; 2 Sm 7, 4. 8-16; 1 Chr 17, 3. 7-14; Is 42, 1; Acts 13, 22.
[w] 22-25: 1 Sm 2, 9-10.

Tabor: a high hill in the valley of Jezreel in northern Israel. *Hermon:* a mountain in Lebanon, forming the southern spur of the Anti-Lebanon range.

89, 18. 25: *Horn:* a concrete noun for an abstract quality; horn is a symbol of strength.

89, 26: *The sea . . . the rivers:* geographically the limits of the Davidic

27 He shall cry to me, 'You are my father,[x]
    my God, the Rock that brings me victory!'
28 I myself make him firstborn,
    Most High over the kings of the earth.
29 Forever I will maintain my love for him;[y]
    my covenant with him stands firm.
30 I will establish his dynasty forever,
    his throne as the days of the heavens.
31 If his descendants forsake my law,[z]
    do not follow my decrees,
32 If they fail to observe my statutes,
    do not keep my commandments,
33 I will punish their crime with a rod
    and their guilt with lashes.
34 But I will not take my love from him,
    nor will I betray my bond of loyalty.[a]
35 I will not violate my covenant;
    the promise of my lips I will not alter.[b]
36 By my holiness I swore once for all:[c]
    I will never be false to David.
37 His dynasty will continue forever,[d]
    his throne, like the sun before me.
38 Like the moon it will stand eternal,
    forever firm like the sky!''   *Selah*

    IV
39 But now you have rejected and spurned,[e]
    been enraged at your anointed.

---

[x] 27-28: Pss 2, 7; 110, 2-3; 2 Sm 7, 9.
14; Col 1, 15. 18; Rv 1, 5.
[y] 29-30: Pss 18, 51; 61, 8; 144, 10; 2
Sm 7, 11; Is 55, 3.
[z] 31-33: Lv 26, 14-33.

[a] Ps 40, 12; Sir 47, 22.
[b] Jer 33, 20-21.
[c] Am 4, 2.
[d] 37-38: Pss 61, 8; 72, 5; Sir 43, 6.
[e] 39-47: Ps 44, 10-25.

Empire (the Mediterranean and the Euphrates); mythologically, the traditional forces of chaos. See note on v 11.

89, 28: *Most High:* a divine title, which is here extended to David as God's own king. Cf Ps 2, 7-9; Is 9, 5. As God rules over the members of the heavenly council (6-9), so David, God's surrogate, rules over earthly kings.

89, 37-38: *Like the sun before me . . . like the sky:* as enduring as the heavenly lights. Cf 2-5 and Ps 72, 5. 17.

40   You renounced the covenant with your servant,
      defiled his crown in the dust.
41   You broke down all his defenses,[f]
      left his strongholds in ruins.
42   All who pass through seize plunder;
      his neighbors deride him.
43   You have exalted the right hand of his foes,
      have gladdened all his enemies.[g]
44   You turned back his sharp sword,
      did not support him in battle.
45   You brought to an end his splendor,
      hurled his throne to the ground.
46   You cut short the days of his youth,
      covered him with shame.   *Selah*
47   How long, LORD?
      Will you stay hidden forever?
      Must your wrath smolder like fire?[h]
48   Remember how brief is my life,
      how frail the race you created![i]
49   What mortal can live and not see death?
      Who can escape the power of Sheol?[j]   *Selah*
50   Where are your promises of old, Lord,
      the loyalty sworn to David?
51   Remember, Lord, the insults to your servants,
      how I bear all the slanders of the nations.[k]
52   Your enemies, LORD, insult your anointed;
      they insult my every endeavor.

* * *

53   Blessed be the LORD forever! Amen and amen![l]

---

[f] 41-42: Ps 80, 13-14.
[g] Lam 1, 5.
[h] Pss 13, 2; 44, 25; 74, 10; 79, 5; Dt 4, 24.
[i] Pss 39, 5-6; 62, 10; 90, 9-10; 144, 4; Jb 7, 6. 16; 14, 1. 5; Eccl 6, 12; Wis 2, 5.
[j] Ps 90, 3.
[k] Ps 79, 12.
[l] Pss 41, 14; 72, 18; 106, 48.

89, 53: The doxology at the end of the third book of the Psalms; it is not part of Ps 89.

FOURTH BOOK—PSALMS 90–106

Psalm 90
God's Eternity and Human Frailty

1   *A prayer of Moses, the man of God.*

I
Lord, you have been our refuge
    through all generations.
2   Before the mountains were born,
      the earth and the world brought forth,
      from eternity to eternity you are God.[m]
4   A thousand years in your eyes
    are merely a yesterday,[n]
3   But humans you return to dust,
    saying, "Return, you mortals!"[o]
4c Before a watch passes in the night,
5   you have brought them to their end;[p]
They disappear like sleep at dawn;
    they are like grass that dies.

---

[m] Pss 48, 15; 55, 20; 93, 2; 102, 13; Hb 1, 12.
[n] 2 Pt 3, 8.
[o] Pss 103, 14; 104, 29; 146, 4; Gn 3, 19; 1 Mc 2, 63; Jb 34, 14-15; Eccl 3, 20; 12, 7; Sir 40, 11.
[p] Ps 89, 48.
[q] Pss 37, 2; 102, 11; 103, 15-16; Jb 14, 1-2; Is 40, 6-8.

Ps 90: A communal lament that describes only in general terms the cause of the community's distress. After confidently invoking God (1), the psalm turns to a complaint contrasting God's eternity with the brevity of human life (2-6) and sees in human suffering the punishment for sin (7-12). The psalm concludes with a plea for God's intervention (13-17).

90, 3: *Return:* one word of God is enough to return mortals to the dust from which they were created. Humans were created from earth in Gn 2, 7; 3, 19.

90, 4: The translation reverses the order of the difficult Hebrew verses 3 and 4 to get the probable original order. *A watch in the night:* the night was divided into three sentry periods or watches. Cf Jgs 7, 19.

90, 5: *You have brought them to their end:* an interpretation of the unclear Hebrew.

6   It sprouts green in the morning;
        by evening it is dry and withered.[q]

    II

7   Truly we are consumed by your anger,
        filled with terror by your wrath.
8   You have kept our faults before you,
        our hidden sins exposed to your sight.[r]
9   Our life ebbs away under your wrath;[s]
        our years end like a sigh.
10 Seventy is the sum of our years,
        or eighty, if we are strong;
    Most of them are sorrow and toil;
        they pass quickly, we are all but gone.
11 Who comprehends your terrible anger?
        Your wrath matches the fear it inspires.
12 Teach us to count our days aright,
        that we may gain wisdom of heart.
13 Relent, O Lᴏʀᴅ! How long?
        Have pity on your servants!
14 Fill us at daybreak with your love,[t]
        that all our days we may sing for joy.
15 Make us glad as many days as you humbled us,
        for as many years as we have seen trouble.[u]
16 Show your deeds to your servants,
        your glory to their children.
17 May the favor of the Lord our God be ours.[v]
        Prosper the work of our hands!
        Prosper the work of our hands!

---

[r] Ps 109, 14-15; Hos 7, 2.
[s] 9-10: Pss 39, 5-7; 62, 10; 102, 24-25; 144, 4; Gn 6, 3; Jb 7, 6. 16; 14, 5; Prv 10, 27; Eccl 6, 12; Wis 2, 5; Sir 18, 8; Is 65, 20.
[t] Ps 17, 15.
[u] Nm 14, 34; Jer 31, 13.
[v] Ps 33, 22.

90, 6: *It is dry and withered:* the transitory nature of the grass under the scorching sun was proverbial. Cf Ps 129, 6; Is 40, 6-8.

Psalm 91
Security under God's Protection

I

1 You who dwell in the shelter of the Most High,
  who abide in the shadow of the Almighty,

2 Say to the LORD, "My refuge and fortress,
  my God in whom I trust."[w]

3 God will rescue you from the fowler's snare,
  from the destroying plague,

4 Will shelter you with pinions,
  spread wings that you may take refuge;[x]
  God's faithfulness is a protecting shield.

5 You shall not fear the terror of the night
  nor the arrow that flies by day,[y]

6 Nor the pestilence that roams in darkness,
  nor the plague that ravages at noon.[z]

7 Though a thousand fall at your side,
  ten thousand at your right hand,
  near you it shall not come.

8 You need simply watch;
  the punishment of the wicked you will see.[a]

9 You have the LORD for your refuge;
  you have made the Most High your stronghold.

10 No evil shall befall you,
  no affliction come near your tent.[b]

---

[w] Pss 18, 3; 31, 3-4; 42, 10; 142, 6; 2
 Sm 22, 3.
[x] Pss 17, 8; 36, 8; 57, 2; 63, 8; Dt 32,
 11; Ru 2, 12; Mt 23, 37.
[y] Prv 3, 25; Song 3, 8.
[z] Dt 32, 24.
[a] Ps 92, 12.
[b] Prv 12, 21; Dt 7, 15.

Ps 91: A prayer of someone who has taken refuge in the security of the temple (1-2). The psalmist is confident that God's presence will protect the people in every dangerous situation (3-13). The final verses are an oracle of salvation promising salvation to those who trust in God (14-16).

91, 1: *The shelter of the Most High:* basically "hiding place" but in the psalms a designation for the protected temple precincts. Cf Pss 27, 5; 31, 21; 61, 5. *The shadow of the Almighty:* literally, "the shadow of the wings of the Almighty." Cf Pss 17, 8; 36, 8; 57, 2; 63, 8. V 4 makes clear that the shadow is an image of the safety afforded by the outstretched wings of the cherubim in the holy of holies.

11 For God commands the angels[c]
   to guard you in all your ways.[d]
12 With their hands they shall support you,
   lest you strike your foot against a stone.[e]
13 You shall tread upon the asp and the viper,
   trample the lion and the dragon.[f]

   II
14 Whoever clings to me I will deliver;
   whoever knows my name I will set on high.[g]
15 All who call upon me I will answer;[h]
   I will be with them in distress;[i]
   I will deliver them and give them honor.
16 With length of days I will satisfy them
   and show them my saving power.[j]

Psalm 92
A Hymn of Thanksgiving for God's Fidelity

1 *A psalm. A sabbath song.*

   I
2 It is good to give thanks to the LORD,
   to sing praise to your name, Most High,[k]
3 To proclaim your love in the morning,
   your faithfulness in the night,
4 With the ten-stringed harp,
   with melody upon the lyre.[l]
5 For you make me jubilant, LORD, by your deeds;
   at the works of your hands I shout for joy.

---

[c] 11-12: Mt 4, 6; Lk 4, 10f.
[d] Heb 1, 14.
[e] Ps 121, 3; Prv 3, 23.
[f] Is 11, 8; Lk 10, 19.
[g] Pss 9, 11; 119, 132.
[h] Jer 33, 3; Zec 13, 9.
[i] Is 43, 2.
[j] Prv 3, 2.
[k] Pss 33, 1; 147, 1.
[l] Pss 33, 2; 144, 9.

91, 11-12: The words are cited in Lk 4, 10-11; Mt 4, 6, as Jesus' reply to Satan in the desert.

Ps 92: A hymn of praise and thanks for God's faithful deeds (2-5). The wicked, deluded by their prosperity (6-9), are punished (10), whereas the psalmist has already experienced God's protection (11-16).

II
6 How great are your works, Lord!^m
      How profound your purpose!
7 A senseless person cannot know this;
      a fool cannot comprehend.
8 Though the wicked flourish like grass
      and all sinners thrive,ⁿ
   They are destined for eternal destruction;
9   for you, Lord, are forever on high.
10 Indeed your enemies, Lord,
      indeed your enemies shall perish;
      all sinners shall be scattered.^o

III
11 You have given me the strength of a wild bull;^p
      you have poured rich oil upon me.^q
12 My eyes look with glee on my wicked enemies;
      my ears delight in the fall of my foes.^r
13 The just shall flourish like the palm tree,
      shall grow like a cedar of Lebanon.^s
14 Planted in the house of the Lord,
      they shall flourish in the courts of our God.
15 They shall bear fruit even in old age,
      always vigorous and sturdy,
16 As they proclaim: "The Lord is just;
      our rock, in whom there is no wrong."^t

---

^m 6-7: Pss 131, 1; 139, 6. 17; Wis 13, 1; 17, 1.
ⁿ Ps 37, 35.
^o Pss 68, 1-2; 125, 5.
^p Ps 75, 10; Dt 33, 17.
^q Ps 23, 5.
^r Ps 91, 8.
^s Pss 1, 3; 52, 10; Jer 17, 8.
^t Dt 32, 4.

92, 14: *Planted:* the just are likened to trees growing in the sacred precincts of the temple, which is often seen as the source of life and fertility because of God's presence. Cf Ps 36, 9. 10; Ez 47, 1-12.

Psalm 93
God Is a Mighty King

1 The LORD is king, robed with majesty;
      the LORD is robed, girded with might.[u]
   The world will surely stand in place,
      never to be moved.[v]

2 Your throne stands firm from of old;
      you are from everlasting, LORD.[w]

3 The flood has raised up, LORD;
      the flood has raised up its roar;
      the flood has raised its pounding waves.

4 More powerful than the roar of many waters,
      more powerful than the breakers of the sea,
      powerful in the heavens is the LORD.

5 Your decrees are firmly established;
      holiness belongs to your house, LORD,
      for all the length of days.

---

[u] Pss 47, 8; 96, 10; 97, 1; 99, 1.   [w] Pss 55, 20; 90, 2; 102, 13; Hb 1, 12.
[v] Pss 75, 2-3; 104, 5.

Ps 93: A hymn celebrating the kingship of God, who created the world (1-2) by defeating the sea (3-4). In the ancient myth that is alluded to here, Sea completely covered the land, making it impossible for the human community to live. Sea, or Flood, roars in anger against God, who is personified in the storm. God's utterances or decrees are given authority by the victory over Sea (5).

93, 1: *The LORD is king:* literally, "the LORD reigns." This psalm, and Pss 47 and 96–99, are sometimes called enthronement psalms. They may have been used in a special liturgy during which God's ascent to the throne was ritually reenacted. They have also been interpreted eschatologically, pointing to the coming of God as king at the end-time.

93, 3: *The flood:* the primordial sea was tamed by God in the act of creation. It is a figure of chaos and rebellion. Cf Ps 46, 4.

Psalm 94
A Prayer for Deliverance from the Wicked

I

1 LORD, avenging God,
    avenging God, shine forth!ˣ
2 Rise up, judge of the earth;
    give the proud what they deserve.ʸ

II

3 How long, LORD, shall the wicked,
    how long shall the wicked glory?ᶻ
4 How long will they mouth haughty speeches,
    go on boasting, all these evildoers?ᵃ
5 They crush your people, LORD,
    torment your very own.
6 They kill the widow and alien;
    the fatherless they murder.ᵇ
7 They say, "The LORD does not see;
    the God of Jacob takes no notice."ᶜ

III

8 Understand, you stupid people!
    You fools, when will you be wise?ᵈ
9 Does the one who shaped the ear not hear?
    The one who formed the eye not see?ᵉ
10 Does the one who guides nations not rebuke?
    The one who teaches humans not have knowledge?

ˣ Na 1, 2.
ʸ Jer 51, 56; Lam 3, 64.
ᶻ Pss 13, 2; 75, 5; Jer 12, 1.
ᵃ Ps 73; Mal 2, 17; 3, 14.
ᵇ Ex 22, 21-22; Dt 24, 17-22.

ᶜ Pss 10, 11; 64, 6; 73, 11; Jb 22, 13-14;
   Ez 9, 9.
ᵈ Prv 1, 22; 8, 5.
ᵉ Ex 4, 11; Prv 20, 12.

Ps 94: A lament of an individual who is threatened by wicked people. The danger affects the whole community. Calling upon God as judge (1-2), the psalm complains about oppression of the holy community by people within (3-7). Bold declarations of faith follow: denunciation of evildoers (8-11) and assurance to the just (12-15). The psalm continues with further lament (16-19) and ends with strong confidence in God's response (20-23).

11 The LORD does know human plans;
        they are only puffs of air.[f]

    IV

12 Happy those whom you guide, LORD,[g]
        whom you teach by your instruction.
13 You give them rest from evil days,
        while a pit is being dug for the wicked.
14 You, LORD, will not forsake your people,
        nor abandon your very own.[h]
15 Judgment shall again be just,
        and all the upright of heart will follow it.

    V

16 Who will rise up for me against the wicked?
        Who will stand up for me against evildoers?
17 If the LORD were not my help,
        I would long have been silent in the grave.[i]
18 When I say, "My foot is slipping,"
        your love, LORD, holds me up.[j]
19 When cares increase within me,
        your comfort gives me joy.

    VI

20 Can unjust judges be your allies,
        those who create burdens in the name of law,
21 Those who conspire against the just
        and condemn the innocent to death?
22 No, the LORD is my secure height,
        my God, the rock where I find refuge,
23 Who will turn back their evil upon them[k]
        and destroy them for their wickedness.
        Surely the LORD our God will destroy them![l]

---

[f] Ps 33, 15; 1 Cor 3, 20.
[g] Ps 119, 71; Jb 5, 17.
[h] 1 Sm 12, 22; Sir 47, 22.
[i] Ps 115, 17.
[j] Ps 145, 14.
[k] Pss 7, 16; 9, 16; 35, 8; 57, 7; Prv 26, 27; Eccl 10, 8; Sir 27, 26.
[l] Ps 107, 42.

Psalm 95
A Call to Praise and Obedience

I

1 Come, let us sing joyfully to the LORD;
　　cry out to the rock of our salvation.[m]
2 Let us greet him with a song of praise,
　　joyfully sing out our psalms.
3 For the LORD is the great God,
　　the great king over all gods,[n]
4 Whose hand holds the depths of the earth;
　　who owns the tops of the mountains.
5 The sea and dry land belong to God,
　　who made them, formed them by hand.[o]

II

6 Enter, let us bow down in worship;
　　let us kneel before the LORD who made us.
7 For this is our God,
　　whose people we are,
　　God's well-tended flock.[p]

III

Oh, that today you would hear his voice:[q]
8 　　Do not harden your hearts as at Meribah,
　　as on the day of Massah in the desert.
9 There your ancestors tested me;
　　they tried me though they had seen my works.[r]

---

[m] Dt 32, 15.
[n] Pss 47, 2; 135, 5.
[o] Ps 24, 1-2.
[p] Pss 23, 1-3; 100, 3; Mi 7, 14.

[q] 7c-11: Pss 81, 8; 106, 32; Heb 3, 7-11.
15; 4, 3. 5. 7.
[r] Nm 14, 22; 20, 2-13; Dt 6, 16; 33, 8.

Ps 95: Twice the psalm calls the people to praise and worship God (1-2. 6), the king of all creatures (3-5) and shepherd of the flock (7ab). The last strophe warns the people to be more faithful than were their ancestors in the journey to the promised land (7c-11). This invitation to praise God regularly opens the Church's official prayer, the Liturgy of the Hours.

95, 8: *Meribah:* literally, "contention"; the place where the Israelites quarreled with God. *Massah:* "testing," the place where they put God to the trial. Cf Ex 17, 7; Nm 20, 13.

10 Forty years I loathed that generation;
     I said: "This people's heart goes astray;
     they do not know my ways."[s]
11 Therefore I swore in my anger:
     "They shall never enter my rest."

Psalm 96
God of the Universe

I

1 Sing to the LORD a new song;[t]
     sing to the LORD, all the earth.
2 Sing to the LORD, bless his name;
     announce his salvation day after day.
3 Tell God's glory among the nations;
     among all peoples, God's marvelous deeds.[u]

II

4 For great is the LORD and highly to be praised,
     to be feared above all gods.[v]
5 For the gods of the nations all do nothing,
     but the LORD made the heavens.[w]
6 Splendor and power go before him;
     power and grandeur are in his holy place.

III

7 Give to the LORD, you families of nations,
     give to the LORD glory and might;
8   give to the LORD the glory due his name![x]

---

[s] Ps 78, 8; Nm 14, 34; Dt 32, 5.
[t] Ps 98, 1; Is 42, 10.
[u] Pss 98, 4; 105, 1.

[v] Pss 48, 2; 95, 3; 145, 3.
[w] Ps 97, 7; Is 40, 17; 1 Cor 8, 4.
[x] Ps 29, 2.

95, 11: *My rest:* the promised land as in Dt 12, 9. Heb 4 applies the verse to the eternal rest of heaven.

Ps 96: A hymn inviting all humanity to praise the glories of Israel's God (1-3), who is the sole God (4-6). To the just ruler of all belongs worship (7-10); even inanimate creation is to offer praise (11-13). This psalm has numerous verbal and thematic contacts with Is 40-55, as does Ps 98. Another version of the psalm is 1 Chr 16, 23-33.

96, 4: For references to other gods, see comments on Pss 58 and 82.

Bring gifts and enter his courts;
9   bow down to the LORD, splendid in holiness.
Tremble before God, all the earth;
10   say among the nations: The LORD is king.[y]
The world will surely stand fast, never to be moved.
     God rules the peoples with fairness.

IV

11 Let the heavens be glad and the earth rejoice;
     let the sea and what fills it resound;[z]
12   let the plains be joyful and all that is in them.
Then let all the trees of the forest rejoice
13   before the LORD who comes,
     who comes to govern the earth,[a]
To govern the world with justice
     and the peoples with faithfulness.

Psalm 97
The Divine Ruler of All

I

1   The LORD is king; let the earth rejoice;
     let the many islands be glad.[b]
2   Cloud and darkness surround the Lord;
     justice and right are the foundation of his throne.[c]
3   Fire goes before him;
     everywhere it consumes the foes.
4   Lightning illumines the world;
     the earth sees and trembles.[d]

---

[y] Pss 75, 4; 93, 1.
[z] Ps 98, 7.
[a] Ps 98, 9.
[b] Pss 75, 4; 93, 1; 96, 10.

[c] Pss 85, 11; 89, 15; Ex 19, 6; Dt 4, 11; 5, 22; 1 Kgs 8, 12.
[d] Pss 18, 8; 50, 3; 77, 18; 99, 1; Jgs 5, 4-5.

Ps 97: The hymn begins with God appearing in a storm, a traditional picture of some ancient Near Eastern gods (1-6); cf Ps 18, 8-16; Mi 1, 3-4; Hb 3, 3-15. Israel rejoices in the overthrowing of idol worshipers and their gods (7-9) and the rewarding of the faithful righteous (10-12).

5 The mountains melt like wax before the LORD,
  before the Lord of all the earth.[e]
6 The heavens proclaim God's justice;
  all peoples see his glory.[f]

 II
7 All who serve idols are put to shame,
  who glory in worthless things;
  all gods bow down before you.[g]
8 Zion hears and is glad,
  and the cities of Judah rejoice
  because of your judgments, O LORD.[h]
9 You, LORD, are the Most High over all the earth,[i]
  exalted far above all gods.
10 The LORD loves those who hate evil,
  protects the lives of the faithful,[j]
  rescues them from the hand of the wicked.
11 Light dawns for the just;
  gladness, for the honest of heart.[k]
12 Rejoice in the LORD, you just,
  and praise his holy name.[l]

Psalm 98
The Coming of God

1 *A psalm.*

 I
Sing a new song to the LORD,
  who has done marvelous deeds,[m]

---

[e] Jdt 16, 15; Mi 1, 4.
[f] Ps 50, 6.
[g] Ps 96, 5.
[h] Ps 48, 12.
[i] Ps 83, 19.
[j] Ps 121, 7.
[k] Ps 112, 4.
[l] Ps 30, 5.
[m] Ps 96, 1; Is 42, 10.

97, 7: *All gods:* divine beings thoroughly subordinate to Israel's God. The Greek translates "angels," an interpretation adopted by Heb 1, 6.

Ps 98: A hymn, similar to Ps 96, extolling God for Israel's victory (1-3). All nations (4-6) and even inanimate nature (7-8) are summoned to welcome God's coming to rule over the world (9).

98, 1: *Marvelous deeds . . . victory:* the conquest of all threats to the

    Whose right hand and holy arm
        have won the victory.[n]
2 The LORD has made his victory known;
        has revealed his triumph for the nations to see,
3 Has remembered faithful love
        toward the house of Israel.
    All the ends of the earth have seen
        the victory of our God.

    II

4 Shout with joy to the LORD, all the earth;
        break into song; sing praise.
5 Sing praise to the LORD with the harp,
        with the harp and melodious song.
6 With trumpets and the sound of the horn
        shout with joy to the King, the LORD.[o]

    III

7 Let the sea and what fills it resound,[p]
        the world and those who dwell there.
8 Let the rivers clap their hands,
        the mountains shout with them for joy,[q]
9 Before the LORD who comes,
        who comes to govern the earth,[r]
    To govern the world with justice
        and the peoples with fairness.[s]

---

[n] Is 59, 16; 63, 5.   [q] Is 44, 23; 55, 12.
[o] Ps 47, 6-7.   [r] Ps 96, 13.
[p] Ps 96, 11.   [s] Ps 67, 5.

---

peaceful existence of Israel, depicted in the psalms variously as a cosmic force such as Sea, or nations bent on Israel's destruction, or evildoers seemingly triumphant. *Whose right hand and holy arm:* God is pictured as a powerful warrior.

Psalm 99
The Holy King

I

1 The LORD is king, the peoples tremble;
    God is enthroned on the cherubim, the earth quakes.[t]
2 The LORD is great on Zion,
    exalted above all the peoples.
3 Let them praise your great and awesome name:
    Holy is God![u]

II

4 O mighty king, lover of justice,
    you alone have established fairness;
    you have created just rule in Jacob.[v]
5 Exalt the LORD, our God;
    bow down before his footstool;[w]
    holy is God!

III

6 Moses and Aaron were among his priests,
    Samuel among those who called on God's name;
    they called on the LORD, who answered them.[x]
7 From the pillar of cloud God spoke to them;
    they kept the decrees, the law they received.[y]

---

[t] Pss 18, 8-11; 80, 2; 93, 1; Ex 25, 22;
    1 Sm 4, 4; 2 Sm 6, 2.
[u] Is 6, 3.
[v] Pss 72, 1; 99, 4; Jer 23, 5.
[w] Ps 132, 7.
[x] Jer 15, 1.
[y] Ex 33, 9; Nm 12, 5.

Ps 99: A hymn to God as the king whose grandeur is most clearly seen on Mount Zion (2) and in the laws given to Israel (4). Israel is special because of God's word of justice, which was mediated by the revered speakers, Moses, Aaron, and Samuel (6-8). The poem is structured by the threefold statement that God is holy (3. 5. 9) and by the twice-repeated command to praise (5. 9).

99, 1: *Enthroned on the cherubim:* cherubim were composite beings with animal and human features, common in ancient Near Eastern art. Two cherubim were placed on the ark (or box) of the covenant in the holy of holies. Upon them God was believed to dwell invisibly. Cf Ex 25, 20-22; 1 Sm 4, 4; 2 Sm 6, 2; Ps 80, 2.

99, 5: *Footstool:* a reference to the ark. Cf 1 Chr 28, 2; Ps 132, 7.

8 O LORD, our God, you answered them;
  you were a forgiving God,
  though you punished their offenses.[z]
9 Exalt the LORD, our God;
  bow down before his holy mountain;
  holy is the LORD, our God.

Psalm 100
Processional Hymn

1 *A psalm of thanksgiving.*

  Shout joyfully to the LORD, all you lands;
2   worship the LORD with cries of gladness;
    come before him with joyful song.
3 Know that the LORD is God,
    our maker to whom we belong,
    whose people we are, God's well-tended flock.[a]
4 Enter the temple gates with praise,
    its courts with thanksgiving.
  Give thanks to God, bless his name;[b]
5   good indeed is the LORD,
  Whose love endures forever,
    whose faithfulness lasts through every age.

Psalm 101
Norm of Life for Rulers

1 *A psalm of David.*

  I
  I sing of love and justice;
    to you, LORD, I sing praise.

---

[z] Ex 32, 11; Nm 20, 12.
[a] Pss 23, 1; 95, 7; Mi 7, 14; Is 64, 7.
[b] 4-5: Pss 106, 1; 107, 1; 118, 1; 136, 1; 138, 8; Jer 33, 11.

Ps 100: A hymn inviting the people to enter the temple courts with thank offerings for the God who created them.
100, 3: Although the people call on all the nations of the world to join in their hymn, they are conscious of being the chosen people of God.
Ps 101: The king, grateful at being God's chosen (1), promises to be

2   I follow the way of integrity;^c
        when will you come to me?
    I act with integrity of heart
        within my royal court.^d
3   I do not allow into my presence
        anyone who speaks perversely.
    Whoever acts shamefully I hate;
        no such person can be my friend.^e
4   I shun the devious of heart;
        the wicked I do not tolerate.
5   Whoever slanders another in secret
        I reduce to silence.^f
    Haughty eyes and arrogant hearts^g
        I cannot endure.

    II
6   I look to the faithful of the land;
        they alone can be my companions.
    Those who follow the way of integrity,^h
        they alone can enter my service.
7   No one who practices deceit
        can hold a post in my court.
    No one who speaks falsely
        can be among my advisors.ⁱ
8   Each morning I clear the wicked from the land,
        and rid the LORD's city of all evildoers.

---

^c Ps 26, 11.
^d 1 Kgs 9, 4; Is 33, 15.
^e Prv 11, 20.
^f Prv 17, 20; 30, 10.
^g Prv 21, 4.
^h Ps 26, 11; Prv 20, 7.
ⁱ Ps 5, 5; Prv 25, 5.

a ruler after God's own heart (2-3), allowing into the royal service only the God-fearing (3-8).

101, 2: *Within my royal court:* the king promises to make his own household a model for Israel, banning all officials who abuse their power.

101, 6: *I look to the faithful of the land:* the king seeks companions only among those faithful to God.

101, 8: *Each morning:* the normal time for the administration of justice (2 Sm 15, 2; Jer 21, 12) and for the arrival of divine aid (Pss 59, 17; 143, 8; Is 33, 2). *I clear the wicked from the land:* the king, as God's servant, is responsible for seeing that divine justice is carried out.

Psalm 102
Prayer in Time of Distress

1 *The prayer of one afflicted and wasting away whose anguish is poured out before the* LORD.

I

2 LORD, hear my prayer;
  let my cry come to you.
3 Do not hide your face from me
  now that I am in distress.[j]
 Turn your ear to me;
  when I call, answer me quickly.
4 For my days vanish like smoke;[k]
  my bones burn away as in a furnace.
5 I am withered, dried up like grass,
  too wasted to eat my food.
6 From my loud groaning
  I become just skin and bones.
7 I am like a desert owl,
  like an owl among the ruins.
8 I lie awake and moan,
  like a lone sparrow on the roof.
9 All day long my enemies taunt me;
  in their rage, they make my name a curse.
10 I eat ashes like bread,
  mingle my drink with tears.[l]
11 Because of your furious wrath,
  you lifted me up just to cast me down.

---

[j] Pss 69, 18; 143, 7.   [l] Pss 42, 4; 80, 6.
[k] 4-6: Ps 38, 7-9.

Ps 102: A lament, one of the Penitential Psalms. The psalmist, experiencing psychic and bodily disintegration (4-12), cries out to God (1-3). In the temple precincts where God has promised to be present, the psalmist recalls God's venerable promises to save the poor (13-23). The final part (24-29) restates the original complaint and prayer, and emphasizes God's eternity.

102, 9: *They make my name a curse:* enemies use the psalmist's name in phrases such as, "May you be as wretched as this person!"

12 My days are like a lengthening shadow;[m]
    I wither like the grass.[n]

II

13 But you, LORD, are enthroned forever;
    your renown is for all generations.[o]
14 You will again show mercy to Zion;
    now is the time for pity;
    the appointed time has come.
15 Its stones are dear to your servants;
    its dust moves them to pity.
16 The nations shall revere your name, LORD,
    all the kings of the earth, your glory,[p]
17 Once the LORD has rebuilt Zion
    and appeared in glory,
18 Heeding the plea of the lowly,
    not scorning their prayer.
19 Let this be written for the next generation,
    for a people not yet born,
    that they may praise the LORD:[q]
20 "The LORD looked down from the holy heights,
    viewed the earth from heaven,[r]
21 To attend to the groaning of the prisoners,
    to release those doomed to die."[s]
22 Then the LORD's name will be declared on Zion,
    the praise of God in Jerusalem,
23 When all peoples and kingdoms gather
    to worship the LORD.[t]

III

24 God has shattered my strength in mid-course,
    has cut short my days.

---

[m] Pss 109, 23; 144, 4; Jb 8, 9; 14, 2; Eccl 6, 12; Wis 2, 5.
[n] Ps 90, 5-6.
[o] Pss 55, 20; 90, 2; 93, 2; 102, 13; 135, 13; 145, 13; Lam 5, 19; Hb 1, 12.
[p] Is 59, 19; 66, 18.
[q] Ps 22, 31-32.
[r] Pss 11, 4; 14, 2.
[s] Ps 79, 11.
[t] Is 60, 3-4; Zec 2, 15; 8, 22.

102, 20-23: Both 20-21 and 22-23 depend on 19.

25 I plead, O my God,
>   do not take me in the midst of my days.ᵘ
>   Your years last through all generations.
26 Of old you laid the earth's foundations;ᵛ
>   the heavens are the work of your hands.
27 They perish, but you remain;
>   they all wear out like a garment;
>   Like clothing you change them and they are changed,
28 but you are the same, your years have no end.
29 May the children of your servants live on;
>   may their descendants live in your presence.ʷ

Psalm 103
Praise of Divine Goodness

1 *Of David.*

I

Bless the LORD, my soul;
>   all my being, bless his holy name!
2 Bless the LORD, my soul;
>   do not forget all the gifts of God,
3 Who pardons all your sins,
>   heals all your ills,
4 Delivers your life from the pit,ˣ
>   surrounds you with love and compassion,
5 Fills your days with good things;
>   your youth is renewed like the eagle's.

ᵘ Pss 39, 5; 90, 10; Jb 14, 5.
ᵛ 26-28: Heb 1, 10-12.
ʷ Ps 69, 36-37.

ˣ Pss 28, 1; 30, 4; 40, 3; 69, 16; 88, 5; 143, 7; Prv 1, 12; Jon 2, 7.

102, 25: *In the midst of my days:* when the normal span of life is but half completed. Cf Is 38, 10; Jer 17, 11.

Ps 103: The speaker in this hymn begins by praising God for personal benefits (1-5), then moves on to God's mercy toward all the people (6-18). Even sin cannot destroy that mercy (11-13), for the eternal God is well aware of the people's human fragility (14-18). The psalmist invites the heavenly beings to join in praise (19-22).

103, 5: *Your youth is renewed like the eagle's:* because of the eagle's long life it was a symbol of perennial youth and vigor. Cf Is 40, 31.

II

6 The LORD does righteous deeds,
    brings justice to all the oppressed.[y]

7 His ways were revealed to Moses,
    mighty deeds to the people of Israel.

8 Merciful and gracious is the LORD,
    slow to anger, abounding in kindness.[z]

9 God does not always rebuke,
    nurses no lasting anger,

10 Has not dealt with us as our sins merit,
    nor requited us as our deeds deserve.

III

11 As the heavens tower over the earth,
    so God's love towers over the faithful.[a]

12 As far as the east is from the west,
    so far have our sins been removed from us.

13 As a father has compassion on his children,
    so the LORD has compassion on the faithful.

14 For he knows how we are formed,
    remembers that we are dust.[b]

15 Our days are like the grass;
    like flowers of the field we blossom.[c]

16 The wind sweeps over us and we are gone;
    our place knows us no more.

17 But the LORD's kindness is forever,
    toward the faithful from age to age.
    He favors the children's children

18   of those who keep his covenant,
    who take care to fulfill its precepts.

IV

19 The LORD's throne is established in heaven;
    God's royal power rules over all.

20 Bless the LORD, all you angels,[d]
    mighty in strength and attentive,
    obedient to every command.

---

y Ps 146, 6-7.
z Pss 86, 15; 145, 8; Ex 34, 6-7; Nm 14,
   18; Jer 3, 12; Jl 2, 13; Jon 4, 2.
a Is 55, 9.

b Ps 90, 3.
c Pss 37, 2; 90, 5-6; Is 40, 7.
d Ps 148, 2; Dn 3, 58.

21 Bless the LORD, all you hosts,
        ministers who do God's will.
22 Bless the LORD, all creatures,
        everywhere in God's domain.
     Bless the LORD, my soul!

Psalm 104
Praise of God the Creator

I
1 Bless the LORD, my soul!
        LORD, my God, you are great indeed!
     You are clothed with majesty and glory,
2   robed in light as with a cloak.
     You spread out the heavens like a tent;[e]
3   you raised your palace upon the waters.
     You make the clouds your chariot;
        you travel on the wings of the wind.
4 You make the winds your messengers;
        flaming fire, your ministers.[f]

II
5 You fixed the earth on its foundation,
        never to be moved.
6 The ocean covered it like a garment;
        above the mountains stood the waters.

---

[e] Prv 8, 27-28; Jb 9, 8; Is 40, 22; Gn 1,   [f] Heb 1, 7.
  6-7; Am 9, 6.

Ps 104: A hymn praising God who easily and skillfully made rampaging waters and primordial night into a world vibrant with life. The psalmist describes God's splendor in the heavens (1-4), how the chaotic waters were tamed to fertilize and feed the world (5-18), and how primordial night was made into a gentle time of refreshment (19-23). The picture is like Gn 1, 1-2: a dark and watery chaos is made dry and lighted so that creatures might live. The psalmist reacts to the beauty of creation with awe (24-34). May sin not deface God's work (35)!

104, 3: *Your palace upon the waters:* God's heavenly dwelling above the upper waters of the sky. Cf Gn 1, 6-7; Ps 29, 10.

104, 5-9: God places the gigantic disk of the earth securely on its foundation and then, as a warrior, chases away the enveloping waters and confines them under, above, and around the earth.

7 At your roar they took flight;
    at the sound of your thunder they fled.[g]
8 They rushed up the mountains, down the valleys
    to the place you had fixed for them.
9 You set a limit they cannot pass;
    never again will they cover the earth.[h]

III

10 You made springs flow into channels
    that wind among the mountains.
11 They give drink to every beast of the field;[i]
    here wild asses quench their thirst.
12 Beside them the birds of heaven nest;
    among the branches they sing.
13 You water the mountains from your palace;
    by your labor the earth abounds.
14 You raise grass for the cattle
    and plants for our beasts of burden.
    You bring bread from the earth,
15   and wine to gladden our hearts,
    Oil to make our faces gleam,
    food to build our strength.
16 The trees of the LORD drink their fill,
    the cedars of Lebanon, which you planted.
17 There the birds build their nests;
    junipers are the home of the stork.[j]
18 The high mountains are for wild goats;
    the rocky cliffs, a refuge for badgers.

IV

19 You made the moon to mark the seasons,[k]
    the sun that knows the hour of its setting.
20 You bring darkness and night falls,
    then all the beasts of the forest roam abroad.

---

g Ps 29, 3.
h Jer 5, 22; Gn 9, 11-15.
i 11-14: Ps 147, 8-9.

j Ez 31, 6.
k Sir 43, 6.

104, 16-18: Even the exotic flora and fauna of the high mountains of the Lebanon range receive adequate water.

21 Young lions roar for prey;
        they seek their food from God.[l]
22 When the sun rises, they steal away
        and rest in their dens.
23 People go forth to their work,
        to their labor till evening falls.

V

24 How varied are your works, LORD!
        In wisdom you have wrought them all;
        the earth is full of your creatures.[m]
25 Look at the sea, great and wide!
        It teems with countless beings,
        living things both large and small.[n]
26 Here ships ply their course;
        here Leviathan, your creature, plays.[o]

VI

27 All of these look to you
        to give them food in due time.[p]
28 When you give to them, they gather;
        when you open your hand, they are well filled.
29 When you hide your face, they are lost.
        When you take away their breath, they perish
        and return to the dust from which they came.[q]
30 When you send forth your breath, they are created,
        and you renew the face of the earth.

VII

31 May the glory of the LORD endure forever;
        may the LORD be glad in these works!

---

[l] Jb 38, 39.
[m] Ps 92, 6; Sir 39, 16.
[n] Sir 43, 26.
[o] Jb 3, 8; 40, 25.
[p] Pss 136, 25; 145, 15-16.
[q] Jb 34, 14-15; Eccl 3, 20; Ps 90, 3.

104, 26: *Leviathan:* a sea monster symbolizing primeval chaos. Cf Ps 74, 14; Is 27, 1; Jb 40, 25. God does not destroy chaos but makes it part of the created order.

104, 29-30: On one level, the spirit (or wind) of God is the fall and winter rains that provide food for all creatures. On another, it is the breath (or spirit) of God that makes beings live.

32 If God glares at the earth, it trembles;
　　if God touches the mountains, they smoke![r]
33 I will sing to the LORD all my life;
　　I will sing praise to my God while I live.[s]
34 May my theme be pleasing to God;
　　I will rejoice in the LORD.
35 May sinners vanish from the earth,
　　and the wicked be no more.
　Bless the LORD, my soul! Hallelujah!

Psalm 105
God's Fidelity to the Promise

I

1 Give thanks to the LORD, invoke his name;[t]
　　make known among the peoples his deeds![u]
2 Sing praise, play music;
　　proclaim all his wondrous deeds!
3 Glory in his holy name;
　　rejoice, O hearts that seek the LORD!
4 Rely on the mighty LORD;
　　constantly seek his face.[v]
5 Recall the wondrous deeds he has done,
　　his signs and his words of judgment,
6 You descendants of Abraham his servant,
　　offspring of Jacob the chosen one!

---

[r] Ps 144, 5.
[s] Ps 146, 2.
[t] 1-15: 1 Chr 16, 8-22.

[u] Pss 18, 50; 96, 3; 145, 5; Is 12, 4-5.
[v] Pss 24, 6; 27, 8.

104, 35: *Hallelujah:* a frequent word in the last third of the Psalter. The word combines the plural imperative of praise *(hallelu)* with an abbreviated form of the divine name Yah(weh).

Ps 105: A hymn to God who promised the land of Canaan to the holy people. Cf Pss 78; 106; 136. Israel is invited to praise and seek the presence of God (1-6), who is faithful to the promise of land to the ancestors (7-11). In every phase of the national story—the ancestors in the land of Canaan (12-15), Joseph in Egypt (16-22), Israel in Egypt (23-38), Israel in the desert on the way to Canaan (39-45)—God remained faithful, reiterating the promise of the land to successive servants.

II

7 The LORD is our God
   who rules the whole earth.
8 He remembers forever his covenant,
   the pact imposed for a thousand generations,
9 Which was made with Abraham,
   confirmed by oath to Isaac,ʷ
10 And ratified as binding for Jacob,
    an everlasting covenant for Israel:
11 "To you I give the land of Canaan,
    your own allotted heritage."ˣ

III

12 When they were few in number,ʸ
    a handful, and strangers there,
13 Wandering from nation to nation,
    from one kingdom to another,
14 He let no one oppress them;
    for their sake he rebuked kings:
15 "Do not touch my anointed,
    to my prophets do no harm."

IV

16 Then he called down a famine on the land,
    destroyed the grain that sustained them.ᶻ
17 He had sent a man ahead of them,
    Joseph, sold as a slave.ᵃ
18 They shackled his feet with chains;
    collared his neck in iron,ᵇ
19 Till his prediction came to pass,
    and the word of the LORD proved him true.ᶜ

ʷ Gn 15, 1ff; 26, 3.   ᵃ Gn 37, 28. 36; 45, 5.
ˣ Gn 12, 7; 15, 18.   ᵇ Gn 39, 20.
ʸ 12-13: Dt 4, 27; 26, 5.   ᶜ Gn 40-41.
ᶻ Gn 41, 54. 57.

105, 14: *Kings:* Pharaoh and Abimelech of Gerar. Cf Gn 12, 17; 20, 6-7.
105, 15: *My anointed . . . my prophets:* the patriarchs Abraham, Isaac, and Jacob, who were "anointed" in the sense of being consecrated and recipients of God's revelation.

20 The king sent and released him;
  the ruler of peoples set him free.[d]

21 He made him lord over his palace,
  ruler over all his possessions,[e]

22 To instruct his princes by his word,
  to teach his elders wisdom.

  V

23 Then Israel entered Egypt;[f]
  Jacob lived in the land of Ham.

24 God greatly increased his people,
  made them too many for their foes.[g]

25 He turned their hearts to hate his people,
  to treat his servants unfairly.[h]

26 He sent his servant Moses,
  Aaron whom he had chosen.[i]

27 They worked his signs in Egypt[j]
  and wonders in the land of Ham.

28 He sent darkness and it grew dark,
  but they rebelled against his word.

29 He turned their waters into blood
  and killed all their fish.

30 Their land swarmed with frogs,
  even the chambers of their kings.

31 He spoke and there came swarms of flies,
  gnats through all their country.

32 For rain he gave them hail,
  flashes of lightning throughout their land.

33 He struck down their vines and fig trees,
  shattered the trees of their country.

34 He spoke and the locusts came,
  grasshoppers without number.[k]

---

[d] Gn 41, 14.
[e] Gn 41, 41-44.
[f] Gn 46, 1-47, 12; Acts 7, 15.
[g] Ex 1, 7; Acts 7, 17.

[h] Ex 1, 8-14.
[i] Ex 3, 10; 4, 27.
[j] 27-36: Ps 78, 43-51; Ex 7-12.
[k] Jl 1, 4.

105, 23. 27: *The land of Ham:* a synonym for Egypt. Cf Gn 10, 6.

105, 27-38: This psalm and Ps 78, 43-51 have an account of the plagues differing in number or in order from Ex 7, 14-12, 30. Several versions of the exodus story were current.

35 They devoured every plant in the land;
       they ravaged the crops of their fields.
36 He struck down every firstborn in the land,
       the first fruits of all their vigor.
37 He brought his people out,
       laden with silver and gold;[l]
       no stragglers among the tribes.
38 Egypt rejoiced when they left,
       for panic had seized them.

VI

39 He spread a cloud as a cover,
       and made a fire to light up the night.[m]
40 They asked and he brought them quail;
       with bread from heaven he filled them.[n]
41 He split the rock and water gushed forth;
       it flowed through the desert like a river.[o]
42 For he remembered his sacred word
       to Abraham his servant.
43 He brought his people out with joy,
       his chosen ones with shouts of triumph.
44 He gave them the lands of the nations,
       the wealth of the peoples to own,[p]
45 That they might keep his laws
       and observe his teachings.[q]
   Hallelujah!

Psalm 106
Israel's Confession of Sin

1 *Hallelujah!*

A

Give thanks to the LORD, who is good,
   whose love endures forever.[r]

---

[l] Ex 12, 33-36.
[m] Ps 78, 14; Ex 13, 21-22; Wis 18, 3.
[n] Ps 78, 24-28; Ex 16, 13-15; Nm 11, 31ff; Wis 16, 20.
[o] Ps 78, 15-16; Ex 17, 1-7; Nm 20, 11.

[p] Dt 4, 37-40.
[q] Dt 6, 20-25; 7, 8-11.
[r] Pss 100, 5; 107, 1; 1 Chr 16, 34; Jer 33, 11; Dn 3, 89.

Ps 106: Israel is invited to praise the God whose mercy has always tempered judgment of Israel (1-3). The speaker, on behalf of all, seeks

2 Who can tell the mighty deeds of the LORD,
  proclaim in full God's praise?
3 Happy those who do what is right,
  whose deeds are always just.[s]
4 Remember me, LORD, as you favor your people;
  come to me with your saving help,[t]
5 That I may see the prosperity of your chosen,
  rejoice in the joy of your people,
  and glory with your heritage.

B

6 We have sinned like our ancestors;[u]
  we have done wrong and are guilty.

I

7 Our ancestors in Egypt
  did not attend to your wonders.
They did not remember your great love;
  they defied the Most High at the Red Sea.
8 Yet he saved them for his name's sake
  to make his power known.[v]
9 He roared at the Red Sea and it dried up.
  He led them through the deep as through a desert.[w]

---

s Is 56, 1-2.
t Ps 25, 7; Neh 5, 19.
u 6-7: Ps 78, 11-17; Ex 14, 11; Lv 26, 40; 1 Kgs 8, 47; Bar 2, 12; Dn 9, 5.

v Ez 36, 20-22.
w Ex 14, 21-31; Is 50, 2; 63, 11-14; Na 1, 4.

solidarity with the people, who can always count on God's fidelity despite their sin (4-5). Confident of God's mercy, the speaker invites national repentance (6) by reciting from Israel's history eight instances of sin, judgment, and forgiveness. The sins are the rebellion at the Red Sea (6-12; see Ex 14-15), the craving for meat in the desert (13-15; see Nm 11), the challenge to Moses' authority (16-18; see Nm 16), the golden calf episode (19-23; see Ex 32-34), the refusal to take Canaan by the southern route (24-27; see Nm 13-14 and Dt 1-2), the rebellion at Baal-Peor (28-31; see Nm 25, 1-10), the anger of Moses (32-33; see Nm 20, 1-13), and mingling with the nations (34-47). The last, as suggested by its length and generalized language, may be the sin that invites the repentance of the present generation. The text gives the site of each sin: Egypt (7), the desert (14), the camp (16), Horeb (19), in their tents (25), Baal-Peor (28), the waters of Meribah (32), Canaan (38).

10 He rescued them from hostile hands,
        freed them from the power of the enemy.
11 The waters covered their oppressors;
        not one of them survived.
12 Then they believed his words
        and sang songs of praise.[x]

    II
13 But they soon forgot all he had done;
        they had no patience for his plan.
14 In the desert they gave way to their cravings,
        tempted God in the wasteland.[y]
15 So he gave them what they asked
        and sent among them a wasting disease.[z]

    III
16 In the camp they challenged Moses[a]
        and Aaron, the holy one of the LORD.
17 The earth opened and swallowed Dathan,
        it closed on the followers of Abiram.
18 Against that company the fire blazed;
        flames consumed the wicked.

    IV
19 At Horeb they fashioned a calf,[b]
        worshiped a metal statue.
20 They exchanged their glorious God
        for the image of a grass-eating bull.
21 They forgot the God who saved them,
        who did great deeds in Egypt,[c]
22 Amazing deeds in the land of Ham,
        fearsome deeds at the Red Sea.
23 He would have decreed their destruction,
        had not Moses, the chosen leader,

---

[x] Ex 15, 1-21.
[y] Ps 78, 18; Ex 15, 24; 16, 3; Nm 11, 1-6.
[z] Ps 78, 26-31; Nm 11, 33.
[a] 16-18: Nm 16; Dt 11, 6; Is 26, 11.

[b] 19-20: Ex 32; Dt 9, 8-21; Jer 2, 11; Acts 7, 41; Rom 1, 23.
[c] Ps 78, 42-58; Dt 32, 18; Jer 2, 32.

106, 23: *Withstood him in the breach:* the image is that of Moses standing in a narrow break made in the wall to keep anyone from entering.

Withstood him in the breach
        to turn back his destroying anger.[d]

V

24 Next they despised the beautiful land,[e]
        they did not believe the promise.
25 In their tents they complained;
        they did not obey the LORD.
26 So with raised hand he swore
        to destroy them in the desert,
27 To scatter their descendants among the nations,
        disperse them in foreign lands.

VI

28 They joined in the rites of Baal of Peor,[f]
        ate food sacrificed to dead gods.
29 They provoked him by their actions,
        and a plague broke out among them.
30 Then Phinehas rose to intervene,
        and the plague was brought to a halt.
31 This was counted for him as a righteous deed
        for all generations to come.

VII

32 At the waters of Meribah they angered God,[g]
        and Moses suffered because of them.
33 They so embittered his spirit
        that rash words crossed his lips.

VIII

34 They did not destroy the peoples
        as the LORD had commanded them,[h]
35 But mingled with the nations
        and imitated their ways.[i]

---

[d] Ex 32, 11; Dt 9, 25; Ez 22, 30.
[e] 24-27: Lv 26, 33; Nm 14; Dt 1, 25-36; Ez 20, 15. 23.
[f] 28-31: Nm 25; Dt 26, 14; Sir 45, 23-24.
[g] 32-33: Ps 95, 8-9; Ex 17, 1-7; Nm 20, 2-13; Dt 6, 16; 33, 8.
[h] Dt 7, 1; Jgs 2, 1-5.
[i] Lv 18, 3; Jgs 1, 27-35; 3, 5.

106, 32: *Moses suffered because of them:* Moses was not allowed to enter the promised land because of his rash words (Nm 20, 12). According to Dt 1, 37, Moses was not allowed to cross because of the people's sin, not his own.

36 They worshiped their idols
     and were ensnared by them.[j]
37 They sacrificed to the gods
     their own sons and daughters,
38 Shedding innocent blood,
     the blood of their own sons and daughters,
   Whom they sacrificed to the idols of Canaan,
     desecrating the land with bloodshed.
39 They defiled themselves by their actions,
     became adulterers by their conduct.
40 So the LORD grew angry with his people,
     abhorred his own heritage.
41 He handed them over to the nations,
     and their adversaries ruled them.[k]
42 Their enemies oppressed them,
     kept them under subjection.
43 Many times did he rescue them,
     but they kept rebelling and scheming
     and were brought low by their own guilt.[l]
44 Still God had regard for their affliction
     when he heard their wailing.
45 For their sake he remembered his covenant
     and relented in his abundant love,[m]
46 Winning for them compassion
     from all who held them captive.

C

47 Save us, LORD, our God;
     gather us from among the nations
   That we may give thanks to your holy name
     and glory in praising you.[n]

* * *

---

[j] 36-38: Lv 18, 21; Nm 35, 33; Dt 32,
   17; Jgs 2, 11-13. 17. 19; 2 Kgs 16, 3;
   Bar 4, 7; 1 Cor 10, 20.
[k] Jgs 2, 14-23.
[l] Is 63, 7-9.
[m] Lv 26, 42.
[n] 1 Chr 16, 35.

106, 37: *The gods:* Hebrew *shedim,* customarily translated "demons,"
occurs in parallelism with "gods" in an important inscription from Trans-
jordan and hence is translated "gods."

48 Blessed be the LORD, the God of Israel,
from everlasting to everlasting!
Let all the people say, Amen![o]
Hallelujah!

FIFTH BOOK—PSALMS 107-150

Psalm 107
God the Savior of Those in Distress

1 "Give thanks to the LORD who is good,
whose love endures forever!"[p]
2 Let that be the prayer of the LORD's redeemed,
those redeemed from the hand of the foe,[q]
3 Those gathered from foreign lands,
from east and west, from north and south.[r]

I

4 Some had lost their way in a barren desert;
found no path toward a city to live in.
5 They were hungry and thirsty;
their life was ebbing away.[s]
6 In their distress they cried to the LORD,
who rescued them in their peril,
7 Guided them by a direct path[t]
so they reached a city to live in.[u]

[o] Pss 41, 14; 72, 18; 89, 53; 1 Chr 16, 36; Neh 9, 5.
[p] Pss 100, 4-5; 106, 1; Jer 33, 11.
[q] Is 63, 12.
[r] Is 43, 5-6; 49, 12; Zec 8, 7.
[s] Dt 8, 15; 32, 10; Is 49, 10.
[t] Is 35, 8; 40, 3; 43, 19.
[u] Dt 6, 10.

106, 48: A doxology ending Book IV of the Psalter. It is not part of the psalm.

Ps 107: A hymn inviting those who have been rescued by God to give praise (1-3). Four archetypal divine rescues are described, each ending in thanksgiving: from the sterile desert (4-9), from imprisonment in gloom (10-16), from mortal illness (17-22), and from the angry sea (23-32). The number four connotes totality, all the possible varieties of rescue. The same saving activity of God is shown in Israel's history (33-41); whenever the people were endangered God rescued them. The last verses invite people to ponder the persistent saving acts of God (42-43).

8 Let them thank the LORD for such kindness,
        such wondrous deeds for mere mortals.
9 For he satisfied the thirsty,
        filled the hungry with good things.[v]

II

10 Some lived in darkness and gloom,
        in prison, bound with chains,
11 Because they rebelled against God's word,
        scorned the counsel of the Most High,[w]
12 Who humbled their hearts through hardship;
        they stumbled with no one to help.[x]
13 In their distress they cried to the LORD,
        who saved them in their peril,
14 Led them forth from darkness and gloom
        and broke their chains asunder.[y]
15 Let them thank the LORD for such kindness,
        such wondrous deeds for mere mortals.
16 For he broke down the gates of bronze
        and snapped the bars of iron.

III

17 Some fell sick from their wicked ways,
        afflicted because of their sins.
18 They loathed all manner of food;[z]
        they were at the gates of death.
19 In their distress they cried to the LORD,
        who saved them in their peril,
20 Sent forth the word to heal them,[a]
        snatched them from the grave.
21 Let them thank the LORD for such kindness,
        such wondrous deeds for mere mortals.
22 Let them offer a sacrifice in thanks,
        declare his works with shouts of joy.

---

[v] Lk 1, 53.
[w] Is 42, 7. 22; Jb 36, 8-9; Prv 1, 25.
[x] Ps 106, 43.
[y] Is 42, 7; 49, 9; 51, 14.
[z] Jb 6, 6-7; 33, 20.
[a] Ps 147, 15; Wis 16, 12; Is 55, 11; Mt 8, 8.

IV

23 Some went off to sea in ships,
    plied their trade on the deep waters.[b]

24 They saw the works of the LORD,
    the wonders of God in the deep.

25 He spoke and roused a storm wind;
    it tossed the waves on high.[c]

26 They rose up to the heavens, sank to the depths;
    their hearts trembled at the danger.

27 They reeled, staggered like drunkards;
    their skill was of no avail.[d]

28 In their distress they cried to the LORD,
    who brought them out of their peril,

29 Hushed the storm to a murmur;
    the waves of the sea were stilled.[e]

30 They rejoiced that the sea grew calm,
    that God brought them to the harbor they longed for.

31 Let them thank the LORD for such kindness,
    such wondrous deeds for mere mortals.

32 Let them praise him in the assembly of the people,
    give thanks in the council of the elders.

V

33 God changed rivers into desert,
    springs of water into thirsty ground,[f]

34 Fruitful land into a salty waste,
    because of the wickedness of its people.[g]

35 He changed the desert into pools of water,
    arid land into springs of water,[h]

36 And settled the hungry there;
    they built a city to live in.[i]

---

b Sir 43, 25.
c Jon 1, 4.
d Is 29, 9.
e Pss 65, 8; 89, 10; Mt 8, 26 par.
f Is 35, 7; 42, 15; 50, 2.
g Gn 19, 23-28; Dt 29, 22; Sir 39, 23.
h Ps 114, 8; Is 41, 8.
i Ez 36, 35.

107, 33-41: God destroyed Sodom and Gomorrah in Gn 18-19, which the psalm sees as the destruction of the wicked inhabitants of Canaan to prepare the way for Israel (33-34). God then led Israel through the desert to give them a fertile land (35-38) and protected them from every danger (39-41).

37 They sowed fields and planted vineyards,
       brought in an abundant harvest.[j]
38 God blessed them, they became very many,
       and their livestock did not decrease.[k]
40 But he poured out contempt on princes,
       made them wander the trackless wastes,[l]
39 Where they were diminished and brought low
       through misery and cruel oppression,
41 While the poor were released from their affliction;
       their families increased like their flocks.[m]
42 The upright saw this and rejoiced;[n]
       all wickedness shut its mouth.
43 Whoever is wise will take note of these things,[o]
       will ponder the merciful deeds of the LORD.

Psalm 108
Prayer for Victory

1 *A song; a psalm of David.*

   I
2 My heart is steadfast, God;[p]
       my heart is steadfast.
    I will sing and chant praise.
3 Awake, my soul; awake, lyre and harp!
       I will wake the dawn.[q]
4 I will praise you among the peoples, LORD;
       I will chant your praise among the nations.[r]
5 For your love towers to the heavens;
       your faithfulness, to the skies.[s]

---

[j] Is 65, 21; Jer 31, 5.
[k] Dt 7, 13-14.
[l] Jb 12, 23-25.
[m] Ps 113, 7.
[n] Pss 58, 11; 63, 12.
[o] Hos 14, 10.
[p] 2-6: Ps 57, 8-12.
[q] Jb 38, 12.
[r] Pss 9, 12; 18, 50; 148, 13.
[s] Pss 36, 6; 71, 19.

Ps 108: A prayer compiled from two other psalms: 2-6 are virtually the same as Ps 57, 8-12; 7-14 are the same as Ps 60, 7-14. An old promise of salvation (8-10) is combined with a confident assurance (1-6. 14) and petition (7. 12-13).

6 Appear on high over the heavens, God;
    may your glory appear above all the earth.
7 Help with your right hand and answer us
    that your loved ones may escape.

II

8 God promised in the sanctuary:[t]
    "I will exult, I will apportion Shechem;
    the valley of Succoth I will measure out.
9 Gilead is mine, mine is Manasseh;
    Ephraim is the helmet for my head,
    Judah, my own scepter.
10 Moab is my washbowl;
    upon Edom I cast my sandal;[u]
    I will triumph over Philistia."

III

11 Who will bring me to the fortified city?
    Who will lead me into Edom?
12 Was it not you who rejected us, God?
    Do you no longer march with our armies?[v]
13 Give us aid against the foe;
    worthless is human help.
14 We will triumph with the help of God,
    who will trample down our foes.

Psalm 109
Prayer of a Person Falsely Accused

1 *For the leader. A psalm of David.*

I

O God, whom I praise, do not be silent,[w]
2   for wicked and treacherous mouths attack me.

---

[t] 8-14: Ps 60, 8-14.
[u] Ru 4, 7-8.

[v] Ps 44, 10.
[w] Pss 35, 22; 83, 1.

Ps 109: A lament notable for the length and vehemence of its prayer against evildoers (6-20); the cry to God (1) and the complaint (22-25) are brief in comparison. The psalmist is apparently the victim of a slander

They speak against me with lying tongues;
3   with hateful words they surround me,
         attacking me without cause.
4 In return for my love they slander me,
         even though I prayed for them.
5 They repay me evil for good,
         hatred for my love.[x]

II
My enemies say of me:
6 "Find a lying witness,
         an accuser to stand by his right hand,
7 That he may be judged and found guilty,
         that his plea may be in vain.
8 May his days be few;
         may another take his office.[y]
9 May his children be fatherless,
         his wife, a widow.[z]
10 May his children be vagrant beggars,
         driven from their hovels.
11 May the usurer snare all he owns,
         strangers plunder all he earns.
12 May no one treat him kindly
         or pity his fatherless children.
13 May his posterity be destroyed,[a]
         his name cease in the next generation.

---

[x] Pss 35, 12; 38, 21; Prv 17, 13; Jer 18, 20.
[y] Acts 1, 20.
[z] Ex 22, 23; Jer 18, 21.
[a] Ps 21, 11; Prv 10, 7.

campaign, potentially devastating in a society where reputation and honor are paramount. In the emotional perspective of the psalm, there are only two types of people: the wicked and their poor victims. The psalmist is a poor victim (22. 31) and by that fact a friend of God and enemy of the wicked. The psalmist seeks vindication not on the basis of personal virtue but because of God's promise to protect the poor.

109, 6: *An accuser:* Hebrew *satan,* a word occurring in Jb 1-2 and Zec 3, 1-2. In the latter passage *Satan* stands at the right hand of the high priest to bring false accusations against him before God. Here the accuser is human.

14 May the Lord remember his fathers' guilt;
   his mother's sin not be canceled.[b]
15 May their guilt be always before the Lord,[c]
   till their memory is banished from the earth,[d]
1̀6 For he did not remember to show kindness,
   but hounded the wretched poor
   and brought death to the brokenhearted.
17 He loved cursing; may it come upon him;
   he hated blessing; may none come to him.
18 May cursing clothe him like a robe;
   may it enter his belly like water,
   seep into his bones like oil.
19 May it be near as the clothes he wears,
   as the belt always around him.''

   III
20 May the Lord bring all this upon my accusers,
   upon those who speak evil against me.
21 But you, Lord, my God,
   deal kindly with me for your name's sake;
   in your great mercy rescue me.
22 For I am sorely in need;
   my heart is pierced within me.
23 Like a lengthening shadow I near my end,
   all but swept away like the locust.
24 My knees totter from fasting;[e]
   my flesh has wasted away.
25 I have become a mockery to them;
   when they see me, they shake their heads.
26 Help me, Lord, my God;
   save me in your kindness.
27 Make them know this is your hand,
   that you, Lord, have acted.

---

[b] Ex 20, 5.   [d] Ps 34, 16.
[c] Ps 90, 8.   [e] 24-25: Ps 69, 11-13.

109, 20: *May the Lord bring all this:* the psalmist prays that God ratify the curses of 6-19 and bring them upon the wicked.

28 Though they curse, may you bless;
     shame my foes, that your servant may rejoice.
29 Clothe my accusers with disgrace;
     make them wear shame like a mantle.
30 I will give fervent thanks to the LORD;
     before all I will praise my God.[f]
31 For God stands at the right hand of the poor
     to defend them against unjust accusers.

Psalm 110
God Appoints the King both King and Priest

1 *A psalm of David.*

    The LORD says to you, my lord:
      "Take your throne at my right hand,
      while I make your enemies your footstool."[g]
2 The scepter of your sovereign might
     the LORD will extend from Zion.
    The LORD says: "Rule over your enemies!
3   Yours is princely power from the day of your birth.
    In holy splendor before the daystar,
      like the dew I begot you."[h]

---

[f] Ps 111, 1.
[g] Mt 22, 44; Acts 2, 34-35; 1 Cor 15, 25;

Heb 1, 13; 8, 1; 10, 12-13; 1 Pt 3, 22.
[h] Pss 2, 7; 89, 27; Is 49, 1.

Ps 110: A royal psalm in which a court singer recites three oracles in which God assures the king that his enemies are conquered (1-2), makes the king "son" in traditional adoption language (3), gives priestly status to the king and promises to be with him in future military ventures (4-7).

110, 1: *The LORD says to you, my lord:* literally, "The LORD says to my lord," a polite form of address of an inferior to a superior. Cf 1 Sm 25, 25; 2 Sm 1, 10. The court singer refers to the king. Jesus in the synoptic gospels (Mt 22, 41-46 and parallels) takes the psalmist to be David and hence "my lord" refers to the messiah, who must be someone greater than David. *Your footstool:* in ancient times victorious kings put their feet on the prostrate bodies of their enemies.

110, 3: *Like the dew I begot you:* an adoption formula as in Pss 2, 7; 89, 27-28. *Before the daystar:* possibly an expression for before the world began (Prv 8, 22).

4 The LORD has sworn and will not waver:
   "Like Melchizedek you are a priest forever."[i]
5 At your right hand is the Lord,
   who crushes kings on the day of wrath,[j]
6 Who, robed in splendor, judges nations,
   crushes heads across the wide earth,
7 Who drinks from the brook by the wayside
   and thus holds high the head.[k]

Psalm 111
Praise of God for Goodness to Israel

1 *Hallelujah.*

   I will praise the LORD with all my heart[l]
   in the assembled congregation of the upright.
2 Great are the works of the LORD,
   to be treasured for all their delights.
3 Majestic and glorious is your work,
   your wise design endures forever.

---

[i] Pss 89, 35; 132, 11; Gn 14, 18; Heb 5, 6; 7, 21.
[j] Ps 2, 9; Rv 2, 27; 12, 5; 19, 15.
[k] Ps 3, 4.
[l] Ps 138, 1.

110, 4: *Like Melchizedek:* Melchizedek was the ancient king of Salem (Jerusalem) who blessed Abraham (Gn 14, 18-20); like other kings of the time he performed priestly functions. Heb 7 sees in Melchizedek a type of Christ.

110, 7: *Who drinks from the brook by the wayside:* the meaning is uncertain. Some see an allusion to a rite of royal consecration at the Gihon spring (cf 1 Kgs 1, 33. 38). Others find here an image of the divine warrior (or king) pursuing enemies so relentlessly that he does not stop long enough to eat and drink.

Ps 111: A temple singer (1) tells how God is revealed in Israel's history (2-10). The deeds reveal God's very self, powerful, merciful, faithful. The poem is an acrostic, each verse beginning with a successive letter of the Hebrew alphabet.

111, 1: *In the assembled congregation of the upright:* in the temple. Cf Ps 149, 1.

111, 3: *Your:* the psalm refers to God in the third person throughout; the shift to the second person is for the sake of inclusive language.

4 You won renown for your wondrous deeds;
    gracious and merciful is the LORD.[m]
5 You gave food to those who fear you,
    mindful of your covenant forever.
6 You showed powerful deeds to your people,
    giving them the lands of the nations.
7 The works of your hands are right and true,
    reliable all your decrees,
8 Established forever and ever,
    to be observed with loyalty and care.
9 You sent deliverance to your people,
    ratified your covenant forever;
    holy and awesome is your name.
10 The fear of the LORD is the beginning of wisdom;[n]
    prudent are all who live by it.
    Your praise endures forever.

Psalm 112
The Blessings of the Just

1 *Hallelujah!*

Happy are those who fear the LORD,
    who greatly delight in God's commands.[o]

---

m Ps 103, 8; 112, 4.   o Pss 1, 1-2; 119, 1-2; 128, 1.
n Prv 1, 7; 9, 10; Sir 1, 16.

111, 5: *Food to those who fear you:* probably a reference to the manna in the desert, which elsewhere is seen as a type of the Eucharist. Cf Jn 6, 31-33. 49-51.

111, 6: *Lands:* literally, "inheritance, heritage."

111, 10: *The fear of the LORD:* reverence for God, the Hebrew term for religion.

Ps 112: An acrostic poem detailing the blessings received by those who remain close to God by obedience to the commandments. Among their blessings are children (2), wealth that enables them to be magnanimous (3. 5. 9), and virtue by which they encourage others (4). The just person is an affront to the wicked, whose hopes remain unfulfilled (10). The logic resembles Pss 1 and 111.

112, 1: *Happy are those:* literally, "Happy the person." "Person" is used typically, hence the plural translation.

2   Their descendants shall be mighty in the land,
    a generation upright and blessed.

3   Wealth and riches shall be in their homes;
    their prosperity shall endure forever.

4   They shine through the darkness, a light for the upright;[p]
    they are gracious, merciful, and just.

5   All goes well for those gracious in lending,
    who conduct their affairs with justice.

6   They shall never be shaken;
    the just shall be remembered forever.[q]

7   They shall not fear an ill report;
    their hearts are steadfast, trusting the LORD.

8   Their hearts are tranquil, without fear,
    till at last they look down on their foes.

9   Lavishly they give to the poor;
    their prosperity shall endure forever;[r]
    their horn shall be exalted in honor.

10   The wicked shall be angry to see this;
    they will gnash their teeth and waste away;
    the desires of the wicked come to nothing.

Psalm 113
Praise of God's Care of the Poor

1   *Hallelujah!*

I

Praise, you servants of the LORD,
    praise the name of the LORD.[s]

---

p Pss 37, 6; 97, 11; Prv 13, 9; Is 58, 10.   r Prv 22, 9; 2 Cor 9, 9.
q Prv 10, 7; Wis 8, 13.   s Ps 135, 1.

112, 3: *Prosperity:* literally, "justice." In the Second Temple Period the word acquired the nuance of liberality and almsgiving. Cf Sir 3, 30; 7, 10; Mt 6, 1-4.

112, 9: *Their horn:* the symbol for vitality and honor.

Ps 113: A hymn exhorting the congregation to praise God's name, i.e., the way in which God is present in the world; the name is mentioned three times in 1-3. The divine name is especially honored in the temple (1) but its recognition is not limited by time (2) and space (3), for God is everywhere active (4-5) especially in rescuing the lowly faithful (7-9).

2 Blessed be the name of the LORD
    both now and forever.
3 From the rising of the sun to its setting
    let the name of the LORD be praised.

II

4 High above all nations is the LORD;
    above the heavens God's glory.ᵗ
5 Who is like the LORD,
    our God enthroned on high,
6   looking down on heaven and earth?ᵘ
7 The LORD raises the needy from the dust,
    lifts the poor from the ash heap,ᵛ
8 Seats them with princes,
    the princes of the people,
9 Gives the childless wife a home,
    the joyful mother of children.ʷ
    Hallelujah!

Psalm 114
The Lord's Wonders at the Exodus

1 When Israel came forth from Egypt,
    the house of Jacob from an alien people,
2 Judah became God's holy place,
    Israel, God's domain.ˣ
3 The sea beheld and fled;
    the Jordan turned back.ʸ

ᵗ Ps 148, 13.
ᵘ Ps 89, 7-9.
ᵛ Ps 107, 41; 1 Sm 2, 7-8.
ʷ 1 Sm 2, 5; Is 54, 1.

ˣ Ex 19, 6.
ʸ Ex 14, 21f; Jos 3, 14ff; Pss 66, 6; 74, 15.

Ps 114: A hymn celebrating Israel's escape from Egypt, journey through the wilderness, and entry into the promised land, and the miracles of nature that bore witness to God's presence in their midst. In the perspective of the psalm, the people proceed directly from Egypt into the promised land (1-2). Sea and Jordan, which stood like soldiers barring the people from their land, flee before the mighty God as the earth recoils from the battle (3-4). The poet taunts the natural elements as one taunts defeated enemies (5-6).

114, 3-4: Pairs of cosmic elements such as sea and rivers, mountains and hills, are sometimes mentioned in creation accounts. Personified here

4 The mountains skipped like rams;
    the hills, like lambs of the flock.[z]
5 Why was it, sea, that you fled?
    Jordan, that you turned back?
6 You mountains, that you skipped like rams?
    You hills, like lambs of the flock?
7 Tremble, earth, before the Lord,[a]
    before the God of Jacob,
8 Who turned rock into pools of water,
    stone into flowing springs.[b]

Psalm 115
The Greatness of the True God

I
1 Not to us, LORD, not to us
    but to your name give glory
    because of your faithfulness and love.[c]
2 Why should the nations say,
    "Where is their God?"[d]
3 Our God is in heaven;
    whatever God wills is done.[e]

---

[z] Ps 29, 6; Wis 19, 9.
[a] Ps 68, 9.
[b] Ex 17, 6; Nm 20, 11.
[c] Ez 36, 22-23.
[d] Ps 79, 10.
[e] Ps 135, 6.

---

as warriors, the pairs tremble in fear before the Divine Warrior. The quaking also recalls the divine appearance in the storm at Sinai (Ex 19, 16-19) and elsewhere (Jgs 5, 4-5; Ps 18, 8-16).

114, 8: The miracles of giving drink to the people in the arid desert. Cf Ex 17, 1-7; Is 41, 17-18.

Ps 115: A response to the enemy taunt, "Where is your God?" This hymn to the glory of Israel's God (1-3) ridicules the lifeless idols of the nations (4-8), expresses in a litany the trust of the various classes of the people in God (9-11), invokes God's blessing on them as they invoke the divine name (12-15), and concludes as it began with praise of God. Ps 135, 15-18 similarly mocks the Gentile gods and has a similar litany and hymn (Ps 135, 19-21).

115, 2: *Where is their God?:* implies that God cannot help them.

II

4   Their idols are silver and gold,[f]
        the work of human hands.[g]
5   They have mouths but do not speak,
        eyes but do not see.
6   They have ears but do not hear,
        noses but do not smell.
7   They have hands but do not feel,
        feet but do not walk,
        and no sound rises from their throats.
8   Their makers shall be like them,
        all who trust in them.

III

9   The house of Israel trusts in the LORD,[h]
        who is their help and shield.[i]
10 The house of Aaron trusts in the LORD,
        who is their help and shield.
11 Those who fear the LORD trust in the LORD,
        who is their help and shield.
12 The LORD remembers us and will bless us,
        will bless the house of Israel,
        will bless the house of Aaron,
13 Will bless those who fear the LORD,
        small and great alike.
14 May the LORD increase your number,
        you and your descendants.
15 May you be blessed by the LORD,
        who made heaven and earth.

---

[f] 4-10: Ps 135, 15-19; Wis 15, 15-16; Is   [h] Ps 118, 2-4.
    44, 9f; Jer 10, 1-5.   [i] Ps 33, 20.
[g] Is 40, 19.

115, 9-11: *The house of Israel . . . the house of Aaron . . . those fear the LORD:* the laity of Israelite birth, the priests, and the converts to Judaism. Cf Pss 118, 2-4; 135, 19-21. In the New Testament likewise "those who fear the Lord" means converts to Judaism (cf Act 10, 2. 22. 35; 13, 16. 26).

16 The heavens belong to the LORD,
> but the earth is given to us.[j]
17 The dead do not praise the LORD,
> all those gone down into silence.[k]
18 It is we who bless the LORD,
> both now and forever.
Hallelujah!

Psalm 116
Thanksgiving to God Who Saves from Death

I

1 I love the LORD, who listened
> to my voice in supplication,
2 Who turned an ear to me
> on the day I called.
3 I was caught by the cords of death;[l]
> the snares of Sheol had seized me;
> I felt agony and dread.
4 Then I called on the name of the LORD,
> "O LORD, save my life!"

II

5 Gracious is the LORD and just;
> yes, our God is merciful.[m]
6 The LORD protects the simple;
> I was helpless, but God saved me.

---

j Gn 1, 28.   l Ps 18, 5; Jon 2, 3.
k Pss 6, 6; 88, 11ff; Sir 17, 22f; Is 38, 18.   m Ex 34, 6.

115, 16: *The heavens:* literally "the heaven of heavens" or "the highest heavens," i.e., above the firmament. See note on Ps 148, 4.

115, 17: See note on Ps 6, 6.

Ps 116: A thanksgiving in which the psalmist responds to divine rescue from mortal danger (3-4) and from near despair (10-11) with vows and temple sacrifices (13-14. 17-19). The Greek and Latin versions divide the psalm into two parts: 1-9 and 10-19, corresponding to its two major divisions.

116, 3: *The cords of death:* death is personified here; it attempts to capture the psalmist with snares and nets. Cf Ps 18, 6.

7   Return, my soul, to your rest;
        the LORD has been good to you.[n]
8   For my soul has been freed from death,
        my eyes from tears, my feet from stumbling.[o]
9   I shall walk before the LORD
        in the land of the living.[p]

    III
10 I kept faith, even when I said,
        "I am greatly afflicted!"[q]
11 I said in my alarm,
        "No one can be trusted!"[r]
12 How can I repay the LORD
        for all the good done for me?
13 I will raise the cup of salvation
        and call on the name of the LORD.
14 I will pay my vows to the LORD
        in the presence of all his people.
15 Too costly in the eyes of the LORD
        is the death of his faithful.[s]
16 LORD, I am your servant,
        your servant, the child of your maidservant;[t]
        you have loosed my bonds.
17 I will offer a sacrifice of thanksgiving
        and call on the name of the LORD.[u]

---

n Ps 13, 6.
o Ps 56, 14; Is 25, 8; Rv 21, 4.
p Pss 27, 13; 56, 14; Is 38, 11.
q 2 Cor 4, 13.

r Ps 12, 2.
s Ps 72, 14; Is 43, 4.
t Pss 86, 16; 143, 12; Wis 9, 5.
u Lv 7, 12ff.

116, 9: *The land of the living:* the phrase elsewhere is an epithet of the Jerusalem Temple (cf Pss 27, 13; 52, 7; Is 38, 11). Hence the psalmist probably refers to being present to God in the temple.

116, 10: *I kept faith, even when I said:* even in the days of despair, the psalmist did not lose all hope.

116, 13: *The cup of salvation:* probably the libation of wine poured out in gratitude for rescue. Cf Ex 25, 29; Nm 15, 5. 7. 10.

116, 15: *Too costly in the eyes of the LORD:* the meaning is that the death of God's faithful is grievous to God, not that God is pleased with the death. Cf Ps 72, 14. In Wis 3, 5-6 God accepts the death of the righteous as a sacrificial burnt offering.

18 I will pay my vows to the LORD^v
        in the presence of all his people,
19 In the courts of the house of the LORD,
        in your midst, O Jerusalem.
    Hallelujah!

Psalm 117
The Nations Called to Praise

1 Praise the LORD, all you nations!
        Give glory, all you peoples!^w
2 The LORD's love for us is strong;
        the LORD is faithful forever.
    Hallelujah!

Psalm 118
Hymn of Thanksgiving

I
1 Give thanks to the LORD, who is good,^x
        whose love endures forever.
2 Let the house of Israel say:
        God's love endures forever.
3 Let the house of Aaron say,
        God's love endures forever.

---

v Jon 2, 10.   x Pss 100, 5; 136, 1f.
w Rom 15, 11.

Ps 117: This shortest of hymns calls on the nations to acknowledge God's supremacy. The supremacy of Israel's God has been demonstrated to them by the people's secure existence, which is owed entirely to God's gracious fidelity.

Ps 118: A thanksgiving liturgy accompanying a victory procession of the king and the people into the temple precincts. After an invocation in the form of a litany (1-4), the psalmist (very likely speaking in the name of the community) describes how the people confidently implored God's help (5-9) when hostile peoples threatened its life (10-14); vividly God's rescue is recounted (15-18). Then follows a dialogue at the temple gates between the priests and the psalmist as the latter enters to offer the thanksgiving sacrifice (19-25). Finally, the priests impart their blessing (26-27), and the psalmist sings in gratitude (28-29).

4 Let those who fear the LORD say,[y]
     God's love endures forever.

II

5 In danger I called on the LORD;
     the LORD answered me and set me free.
6 The LORD is with me; I am not afraid;
     what can mortals do against me?[z]
7 The LORD is with me as my helper;
     I shall look in triumph on my foes.
8 Better to take refuge in the LORD[a]
     than to put one's trust in mortals.
9 Better to take refuge in the LORD
     than to put one's trust in princes.

III

10 All the nations surrounded me;
     in the LORD's name I crushed them.
11 They surrounded me on every side;
     in the LORD's name I crushed them.
12 They surrounded me like bees;[b]
     they blazed like fire among thorns;
     in the LORD's name I crushed them.
13 I was hard pressed and falling,
     but the LORD came to my help.[c]
14 The LORD, my strength and might,
     came to me as savior.[d]

IV

15 The joyful shout of deliverance
     is heard in the tents of the victors:
    "The LORD's right hand strikes with power;
16   the LORD's right hand is raised;
     the LORD's right hand strikes with power."
17 I shall not die but live
     and declare the deeds of the LORD.

---

[y] Ps 115, 9-11.
[z] Ps 27, 1; Heb 13, 6.
[a] 8f: Ps 146, 3.

[b] Dt 1, 44.
[c] Ps 129, 1-2.
[d] Ex 15, 2; Is 12, 2.

18 The LORD chastised me harshly,
       but did not hand me over to death.

    V
19 Open the gates of victory;
       I will enter and thank the LORD.[e]
20 This is the LORD's own gate,
       where the victors enter.
21 I thank you for you answered me;
       you have been my savior.
22 The stone the builders rejected
       has become the cornerstone.[f]
23 By the LORD has this been done;
       it is wonderful in our eyes.
24 This is the day the LORD has made;
       let us rejoice in it and be glad.
25 LORD, grant salvation!
       LORD, grant good fortune!

    VI
26 Blessed is he
       who comes in the name of the LORD.[g]
    We bless you from the LORD's house.
27   The LORD is God and has given us light.
    Join in procession with leafy branches
       up to the horns of the altar.

---

[e] Is 26, 2.
[f] Mt 21, 42; Lk 20, 17; Acts 4, 11; Rom   9, 33; 1 Pt 2, 7.
[g] Mt 21, 9; 23, 39.

118, 20: *Where the victors enter:* their victory has demonstrated that God favors them; they are "just" in the biblical sense.

118, 22: *The stone the builders rejected:* a proverb: what is insignificant to human beings has become great through divine election. The "stone" may originally have meant the foundation stone or capstone of the temple. The New Testament interpreted the verse as referring to the death and resurrection of Christ (Mt 21, 42; Acts 4, 11; cf Is 28, 16 and Rom 9, 33; 1 Pt 2, 7).

118, 25: *Grant salvation:* the Hebrew for this cry has come into English as "Hosanna." This cry and the words in 26 were used in the gospels to welcome Jesus entering the temple on Palm Sunday (Mk 11, 9-10).

VII

28 You are my God, I give you thanks;
    my God, I offer you praise.
29 Give thanks to the LORD, who is good,
    whose love endures forever.

Psalm 119
A Prayer to God, the Lawgiver

Aleph

1 Happy those whose way is blameless,
    who walk by the teaching of the LORD.[h]
2 Happy those who observe God's decrees,
    who seek the LORD with all their heart.[i]
3 They do no wrong;
    they walk in God's ways.
4 You have given them the command
    to keep your precepts with care.
5 May my ways be firm
    in the observance of your laws!

---

[h] Pss 1, 1-2; 15, 2; 112, 1.   [i] Dt 4, 29.

Ps 119: This psalm, the longest by far in the psalter, praises God for giving such splendid laws and instruction for people to live by. The author glorifies and thanks God for the Torah, prays for protection from sinners enraged by others' fidelity to the law, laments the cost of obedience, delights in the law's consolations, begs for wisdom to understand the precepts, and asks for the rewards of keeping them. Several expected elements do not appear in the psalm: Mount Sinai with its story of God's revelation and gift to Israel of instruction and commandments, the temple and other institutions related to revelation and laws (frequent in other psalms). The psalm is fascinated with God's word directing and guiding human life.

The poem is an acrostic; its twenty-two stanzas (of eight verses each) are in the order of the Hebrew alphabet. Each of the eight verses within a stanza begins with the same letter. Each verse contains one word for "instruction." The translation here given attempts to translate each Hebrew word for "instruction" with the same English word. There are, however, nine words for "instruction," not eight, so the principle of a different word for "instruction" in each verse cannot be maintained with perfect consistency. The nine words for "instruction" in the translation are: law, edict, command, precept, word, utterance, way, decree, and teaching.

6 Then I will not be ashamed
    to ponder all your commands.
7 I will praise you with sincere heart
    as I study your just edicts.
8 I will keep your laws;
    do not leave me all alone.

Beth

9 How can the young walk without fault?
    Only by keeping your words.
10 With all my heart I seek you;
    do not let me stray from your commands.
11 In my heart I treasure your promise,
    that I may not sin against you.
12 Blessed are you, O Lord;
    teach me your laws.[j]
13 With my lips I recite
    all the edicts you have spoken.
14 I find joy in the way of your decrees
    more than in all riches.
15 I will ponder your precepts
    and consider your paths.
16 In your laws I take delight;
    I will never forget your word.

Gimel

17 Be kind to your servant that I may live,
    that I may keep your word.
18 Open my eyes to see clearly
    the wonders of your teachings.
19 I am a sojourner in the land;[k]
    do not hide your commands from me.
20 At all times my soul is stirred
    with longing for your edicts.
21 With a curse you rebuke the proud
    who stray from your commands.

---

[j] Pss 25, 4; 27, 11; 86, 11; 143, 8. 10.   [k] Ps 39, 13.

119, 19: *A sojourner in the land:* like someone without the legal protection of a native inhabitant, the psalmist has a special need for the guidance of God's teaching.

22 Free me from disgrace and contempt,
    for I observe your decrees.
23 Though princes meet and talk against me,
    your servant studies your laws.
24 Your decrees are my delight;
    they are my counselors.

Daleth

25 I lie prostrate in the dust;[l]
    give me life in accord with your word.
26 I disclosed my ways and you answered me;
    teach me your laws.
27 Make me understand the way of your precepts;
    I will ponder your wondrous deeds.
28 I weep in bitter pain;
    in accord with your word to strengthen me.
29 Lead me from the way of deceit;
    favor me with your teaching.
30 The way of loyalty I have chosen;
    I have set your edicts before me.
31 I cling to your decrees, LORD;
    do not let me come to shame.
32 I will run the way of your commands,
    for you open my docile heart.

He

33 LORD, teach me the way of your laws;
    I shall observe them with care.[m]
34 Give me insight to observe your teaching,
    to keep it with all my heart.
35 Lead me in the path of your commands,[n]
    for that is my delight.
36 Direct my heart toward your decrees
    and away from unjust gain.
37 Avert my eyes from what is worthless;
    by your way give me life.

---

l Ps 44, 26.   n Pss 25, 4; 27, 11; 86, 11; 143, 8. 10.
m Ps 19, 12.

119, 32: *For you open my docile heart:* literally, "you make broad my heart."

38 For your servant fulfill your promise
   made to those who fear you.
39 Turn away from me the taunts I dread,
   for your edicts bring good.
40 See how I long for your precepts;
   in your justice give me life.

Waw

41 Let your love come to me, LORD,
   salvation in accord with your promise.
42 Let me answer my taunters with a word,
   for I trust in your word.
43 Do not take the word of truth from my mouth,
   for in your edicts is my hope.
44 I will keep your teachings always,
   for all time and forever.
45 I will walk freely in an open space
   because I cherish your precepts.
46 I will speak openly of your decrees
   without fear even before kings.
47 I delight in your commands,
   which I dearly love.
48 I lift up my hands to your commands;
   I study your laws, which I love.

Zayin

49 Remember your word to your servant
   by which you give me hope.
50 This is my comfort in affliction,
   your promise that gives me life.
51 Though the arrogant utterly scorn me,
   I do not turn from your teaching.
52 When I recite your edicts of old
   I am comforted, LORD.
53 Rage seizes me because of the wicked;
   they forsake your teaching.
54 Your laws become my songs
   wherever I make my home.

119, 48: *I lift up my hands to your commands:* to lift up the hands was an ancient gesture of reverence to God. Here the picture is applied to God's law.

55 Even at night I remember your name
        in observance of your teaching, LORD.
56 This is my good fortune,
        for I have observed your precepts.

Heth

57 My portion is the LORD;
        I promise to keep your words.
58 I entreat you with all my heart:
        have mercy on me in accord with your promise.
59 I have examined my ways
        and turned my steps to your decrees.
60 I am prompt, I do not hesitate
        in keeping your commands.
61 Though the snares of the wicked surround me,
        your teaching I do not forget.
62 At midnight I rise to praise you
        because your edicts are just.
63 I am the friend of all who fear you,
        of all who keep your precepts.
64 The earth, LORD, is filled with your love;°
        teach me your laws.

Teth

65 You have treated your servant well,
        according to your word, O LORD.
66 Teach me wisdom and knowledge,
        for in your commands I trust.
67 Before I was afflicted I went astray,
        but now I hold to your promise.
68 You are good and do what is good;
        teach me your laws.
69 The arrogant smear me with lies,
        but I observe your precepts with all my heart.
70 Their hearts are gross and fat;ᵖ
        as for me, your teaching is my delight.
71 It was good for me to be afflicted,
        in order to learn your laws.

° Ps 33, 5.   ᵖ Pss 17, 10; 73, 7; Jb 15, 27.

72 Teaching from your lips is more precious to me
than heaps of silver and gold.

Yodh

73 Your hands made me and fashioned me;
give me insight to learn your commands.
74 Those who fear you rejoice to see me,
because I hope in your word.
75 I know, LORD, that your edicts are just;
though you afflict me, you are faithful.
76 May your love comfort me
in accord with your promise to your servant.
77 Show me compassion that I may live,
for your teaching is my delight.
78 Shame the proud for oppressing me unjustly,
that I may study your precepts.
79 Let those who fear you turn to me,
those who acknowledge your decrees.
80 May I be wholehearted toward your laws,
that I may not be put to shame.

Kaph

81 My soul longs for your salvation;
I put my hope in your word.[q]
82 My eyes long to see your promise.[r]
When will you comfort me?
83 I am like a wineskin shriveled by smoke,[s]
but I have not forgotten your laws.
84 How long can your servant survive?
When will your edict doom my foes?
85 The arrogant have dug pits for me;
defying your teaching.
86 All your commands are steadfast.
Help me! I am pursued without cause.
87 They have almost ended my life on earth,
but I do not forsake your precepts.
88 In your kindness give me life,
to keep the decrees you have spoken.

[q] Ps 130, 6.
[r] Pss 25, 15; 123, 1-2; 141, 8.
[s] Jb 30, 30.

Lamedh

89 Your word, Lord, stands forever;[t]
       it is firm as the heavens.
90 Through all generations your truth endures;
       fixed to stand firm like the earth.
91 By your edicts they stand firm to this day,
       for all things are your servants.
92 Had your teaching not been my delight,
       I would have perished in my affliction.
93 I will never forget your precepts;
       through them you give me life.
94 I am yours; save me,
       for I cherish your precepts.
95 The wicked hope to destroy me,
       but I pay heed to your decrees.
96 I have seen the limits of all perfection,
       but your command is without bounds.

Mem

97 How I love your teaching, Lord!
       I study it all day long.
98 Your command makes me wiser than my foes,
       for it is always with me.
99 I have more understanding than all my teachers,
       because I ponder your decrees.
100 I have more insight than my elders,
       because I observe your precepts.[u]
101 I keep my steps from every evil path,
       that I may obey your word.
102 From your edicts I do not turn,
       for you have taught them to me.
103 How sweet to my tongue is your promise,
       sweeter than honey to my mouth![v]
104 Through your precepts I gain insight;
       therefore I hate all false ways.

---

t Is 40, 8.   v Ps 19, 11.
u Jb 32, 6; Wis 4, 8-9.

119, 89-91: God's word creates the world, which manifests that word by its permanence and reliability.

Nun

105 Your word is a lamp for my feet,
     a light for my path.^w

106 I make a solemn vow
     to keep your just edicts.

107 I am very much afflicted, LORD;
     give me life in accord with your word.

108 Accept my freely offered praise;^x
     LORD, teach me your decrees.

109 My life is always at risk,
     but I do not forget your teaching.

110 The wicked have set snares for me,
     but from your precepts I do not stray.

111 Your decrees are my heritage forever;
     they are the joy of my heart.

112 My heart is set on fulfilling your laws;
     they are my reward forever.

Samekh

113 I hate every hypocrite;
     your teaching I love.

114 You are my refuge and shield;
     in your word I hope.

115 Depart from me, you wicked,^y
     that I may observe the commands of my God.

116 Sustain me by your promise that I may live;
     do not disappoint me in my hope.

117 Strengthen me that I may be safe,
     ever to contemplate your laws.

118 You reject all who stray from your laws,
     for vain is their deceit.

119 Like dross you regard all the wicked on earth;
     therefore I love your decrees.

120 My flesh shudders with dread of you;
     I hold your edicts in awe.

Ayin

121 I have fulfilled your just edict;
     do not abandon me to my oppressors.

---

^w Ps 18, 29; Prv 6, 23.   ^y Pss 6, 9; 139, 19; Jb 21, 14.
^x Ps 50, 14. 23; Heb 13, 15.

122 Guarantee your servant's welfare;
    do not let the arrogant oppress me.
123 My eyes long to see your salvation
    and the justice of your promise.
124 Act with kindness toward your servant;
    teach me your laws.
125 I am your servant; give me discernment
    that I may know your decrees.
126 It is time for the LORD to act;
    they have disobeyed your teaching.
127 Truly I love your commands
    more than the finest gold.
128 Thus I follow all your precepts;
    every wrong way I hate.

Pe

129 Wonderful are your decrees;
    therefore I observe them.
130 The revelation of your words sheds light,
    gives understanding to the simple.
131 I sigh with open mouth,
    yearning for your commands.
132 Turn to me and be gracious,[z]
    your edict for lovers of your name.
133 Steady my feet in accord with your promise;
    do not let iniquity lead me.
134 Free me from human oppression,
    that I may keep your precepts.
135 Let your face shine upon your servant;
    teach me your laws.
136 My eyes shed streams of tears
    because your teaching is not followed.

Sadhe

137 You are righteous, LORD,
    and just are your edicts.[a]
138 You have issued your decrees in justice
    and in surpassing faithfulness.

---

[z] Pss 25, 16; 86, 16.   [a] Tb 3, 2.

139 I am consumed with rage,
>   because my foes forget your words.
140 Your servant loves your promise;
>   it has been proved by fire.
141 Though belittled and despised,
>   I do not forget your precepts.
142 Your justice is forever right,
>   your teaching forever true.
143 Though distress and anguish come upon me,
>   your commands are my delight.
144 Your decrees are forever just;
>   give me discernment that I may live.

Qoph

145 I call with all my heart, O LORD;
>   answer me that I may observe your laws.
146 I call to you to save me
>   that I may keep your decrees.
147 I rise before dawn and cry out;
>   I put my hope in your words.
148 My eyes greet the night watches
>   as I meditate on your promise.[b]
149 Hear my voice in your love, O LORD;
>   by your edict give me life.
150 Malicious persecutors draw near me;
>   they are far from your teaching.
151 You are near, O LORD;
>   reliable are all your commands.
152 Long have I known from your decrees
>   that you have established them forever.

Resh

153 Look at my affliction and rescue me,
>   for I have not forgotten your teaching.
154 Take up my cause and redeem me;[c]
>   for the sake of your promise give me life.
155 Salvation is far from sinners
>   because they do not cherish your laws.

---

b Pss 63, 7; 77, 7.   c Ps 43, 1.

156 Your compassion is great, O LORD;
    in accord with your edicts give me life.
157 Though my persecutors and foes are many
    I do not turn from your decrees.
158 I view the faithless with loathing,[d]
    because they do not heed your promise.
159 See how I love your precepts, LORD;
    in your kindness give me life.
160 Your every word is enduring;
    all your just edicts are forever.

Shin

161 Princes persecute me without reason,
    but my heart reveres only your word.
162 I rejoice at your promise,
    as one who has found rich spoil.
163 Falsehood I hate and abhor;
    your teaching I love.
164 Seven times a day I praise you
    because your edicts are just.
165 Lovers of your teaching have much peace;[e]
    for them there is no stumbling block.
166 I look for your salvation, LORD,
    and I fulfill your commands.
167 I observe your decrees;
    I love them very much.
168 I observe your precepts and decrees;
    all my ways are before you.

Taw

169 Let my cry come before you, LORD;[f]
    in keeping with your word give me discernment.
170 Let my prayer come before you;
    rescue me according to your promise.
171 May my lips pour forth your praise,
    because you teach me your laws.
172 May my tongue sing of your promise,
    for all your commands are just.

---

[d] Ps 139, 22.
[e] Ps 72, 7.   [f] Ps 88, 3.

173 Keep your hand ready to help me,
      for I have chosen your precepts.
174 I long for your salvation, LORD;
      your teaching is my delight.
175 Let me live to praise you;
      may your edicts give me help.
176 I have wandered like a lost sheep;
      seek out your servant,
      for I do not forget your commands.[g]

Psalm 120
Prayer of a Returned Exile

1   *A song of ascents.*

    I
    The LORD answered me
      when I called in my distress:[h]
2   LORD, deliver me from lying lips,
      from treacherous tongues.[i]

    II
3   What will the Lord inflict on you,
      O treacherous tongue,

---

g Is 53, 6; Jer 50, 6; Lk 15, 1-7.   i Ps 12, 3-5; Sir 51, 3.
h Jon 2, 3.

Ps 120: A thanksgiving, reporting divine rescue (1) yet with fervent prayer for further protection against lying attackers (2-4). The psalmist is acutely conscious of living away from God's own land where divine peace prevails (5-7).

120, 1: *Song of ascents:* Pss 120–134 all begin with this superscription. Most probably these fifteen psalms once formed a collection of psalms sung when pilgrims went to Jerusalem, since one "ascended" to Jerusalem (1 Kgs 12, 28; Pss 24, 3; 122, 4; Lk 2, 42) or to the house of God or to an altar (1 Kgs 12, 33; 2 Kgs 23, 2; Ps 24, 3). Less probable is the explanation that these psalms were sung by the exiles when they "ascended" to Jerusalem from Babylonia (cf Ezr 7, 9). The idea, found in the Mishnah, that the fifteen steps on which the Levites sang corresponded to these fifteen psalms (*Middot* 2, 5) must underlie the Vulgate translation *canticum graduum,* "song of the steps" or "gradual song."

120, 3: *More besides:* a common curse formula in Hebrew was "May the Lord do such and such evils to you [the evils being specified], and

and what more besides?
4   A warrior's sharpened arrows
       and fiery coals of brushwood!ʲ

III

5   Alas, I was an alien in Meshech,
       I lived near the tents of Kedar!
6   Too long did I live
       among those who hated peace.
7   When I spoke of peace,
       they were for war.ᵏ

Psalm 121
The Lord My Guardian

1   *A song of ascents.*

I

I raise my eyes toward the mountains.
   From where will my help come?ˡ
2   My help comes from the LORD,
       the maker of heaven and earth.ᵐ

ʲ Pss 11, 6; 140, 11; Prv 16, 27.   ˡ Jer 3, 23.
ᵏ Pss 35, 20; 140, 3-4.   ᵐ Pss 124, 8; 146, 6.

---

add *still more* to them." Cf 1 Sm 3, 17; 14, 44; 25, 22. Here the psalmist
is at a loss for a suitable malediction.

120, 4: *Coals of brushwood:* coals made from the stalk of the broom
plant burn with intense heat. The psalmist thinks of lighted coals cast
at his enemies.

120, 5: *Meshech* was in the far north (Gn 10, 2) and *Kedar* was a tribe
of the north Arabian desert (Gn 25, 13). The psalmist may be thinking
generally of all aliens living among inhospitable peoples.

Ps 121: A blessing given to someone embarking on a dangerous journey, whether a soldier going on a campaign or a pilgrim returning home
from the temple. People look anxiously at the wooded hills. Will God protect them on their journey (1)? The speaker declares that God is not confined to a place or a time (2), that every step is guarded (3-4); night and
day (5-6) God watches over their every movement (7-8).

121, 1: *The mountains:* possibly Mount Zion, the site of the temple and
hence of safety, but more probably mountains as a place of dangers,
causing anxiety to the psalmist.

II

3 God will not allow your foot to slip;[n]
  your guardian does not sleep.
4 Truly, the guardian of Israel
  never slumbers nor sleeps.
5 The LORD is your guardian;
  the LORD is your shade
  at your right hand.[o]
6 By day the sun cannot harm you,
  nor the moon by night.[p]
7 The LORD will guard you from all evil,
  will always guard your life.[q]
8 The LORD will guard your coming and going
  both now and forever.[r]

Psalm 122
A Pilgrim's Prayer for Jerusalem

1 *A song of ascents. Of David.*

I

I rejoiced when they said to me,
  "Let us go to the house of the LORD."[s]
2 And now our feet are standing
  within your gates, Jerusalem.
3 Jerusalem, built as a city,
  walled round about.[t]

---

[n] Pss 66, 9; 91, 12; 1 Sm 2, 9; Prv 3, 23.
[o] Pss 16, 8; 73, 23.
[p] Wis 18, 3; Is 25, 4; 49, 10.
[q] Ps 97, 10.
[r] Dt 28, 6.
[s] Pss 43, 3-4; 84, 2-5.
[t] Ps 48, 13-14.

121, 5-6: The image of shade, a symbol of protection, is apt: God as shade protects from the harmful effects that ancients believed were caused by the sun and moon.

Ps 122: A song of Zion, sung by pilgrims obeying the law to visit Jerusalem three times on a journey. The singer anticipates joining the procession into the city (1-3). Jerusalem is a place of encounter, where the people praise God (4) and hear the divine justice mediated by the king (5). The very buildings bespeak God's power (cf Ps 48, 13-15). May the grace of this place transform the people's lives (6-9)!

122, 3: *Walled round about:* literally, "which is joined to it," probably referring both to the density of the buildings and to the dense population.

4 Here the tribes have come,
>   the tribes of the LORD,
>   As it was decreed for Israel,
>   to give thanks to the name of the LORD.[u]
5 Here are the thrones of justice,
>   the thrones of the house of David.

II

6 For the peace of Jerusalem pray:
>   "May those who love you prosper!
7 May peace be within your ramparts,
>   prosperity within your towers."[v]
8 For family and friends I say,
>   "May peace be yours."
9 For the house of the LORD, our God, I pray,
>   "May blessings be yours."

Psalm 123
Reliance on the Lord

1   *A song of ascents.*

To you I raise my eyes,
>   to you enthroned in heaven.[w]
2 Yes, like the eyes of a servant
>   on the hand of his master,
>   Like the eyes of a maid
>   on the hand of her mistress,
>   So our eyes are on the LORD our God,
>   till we are shown favor.
3 Show us favor, LORD, show us favor,
>   for we have our fill of contempt.[x]
4 We have our fill of insult from the insolent,
>   of disdain from the arrogant.

---

[u] Dt 16, 16.   [w] Pss 25, 15; 119, 82; 141, 8.
[v] Ps 128, 5.   [x] Ps 44, 13-14; Jb 12, 4.

Ps 123: A lament that begins as a prayer of an individual (1), who expresses by a touching comparison exemplary confidence in God (2). The psalm ends in prayer that God relieve the people's humiliation at the hands of the arrogant (3-4).

Psalm 124
God, the Rescuer of the People

1   *A song of ascents. Of David.*

I

Had not the LORD been with us,
   let Israel say,[y]

2   Had not the LORD been with us,
   when people rose against us,

3   They would have swallowed us alive,[z]
   for their fury blazed against us.

4   The waters would have engulfed us,
   the torrent overwhelmed us;[a]

5   seething waters would have drowned us.

II

6   Blessed be the LORD, who did not leave us
   to be torn by their fangs.

7   We escaped with our lives
   like a bird from the fowler's snare;
   the snare was broken and we escaped.

8   Our help is the name of the LORD,
   the maker of heaven and earth.[b]

Psalm 125
Israel's Protector

1   *A song of ascents.*

I

Like Mount Zion are they
   who trust in the LORD,

---

y Ps 129, 1.   a Pss 18, 5; 69, 2.
z Prv 1, 12.   b Pss 121, 2; 146, 6.

Ps 124: A thanksgiving which teaches that Israel's very existence is owed to God who rescues them. In the first part Israel's enemies are compared to the mythic sea dragon (2b-3a; cf Jer 51, 34) and Flood (3b-5; cf Is 51, 9-10). The psalm heightens the malice of human enemies by linking them to the primordial enemies of God's creation. Israel is a bird freed from the trapper's snare (6-8)—freed originally from Pharaoh and now from the current danger.

124, 8: *Our help is the name:* for the idiom, see Ex 18, 4.

Ps 125: In response to exilic anxieties about the ancient promises of

unshakable, forever enduring.[c]
2 As mountains surround Jerusalem,
 the LORD surrounds his people
 both now and forever.[d]

II
3 The scepter of the wicked will not prevail
 in the land given to the just,
Lest the just themselves
 turn their hands to evil.

III
4 Do good, LORD, to the good,
 to those who are upright of heart.[e]
5 But those who turn aside to crooked ways
 may the LORD send down with the wicked.[f]
Peace upon Israel![g]

Psalm 126
The Reversal of Zion's Fortunes

1 *A song of ascents.*

I
When the LORD restored the fortunes of Zion,[h]
 then we thought we were dreaming.

---

[c] Prv 10, 25.	[f] Prv 3, 32.
[d] Dt 32, 11.	[g] Ps 128, 6.
[e] Ps 18, 25ff.	[h] Ps 14, 7.

---

restoration, the psalm expresses confidence that God will surround the people as the mountains surround Zion (1-2). The just will not be contaminated by the wicked (3). May God judge between the two groups (4-5).

125, 3: *The land given to the just:* literally, "the lot of the just." The promised land was divided among the tribes of Israel by lot (Nm 26, 55; Jos 18). *The just* are the members of the people who are obedient to God. If the domination of the wicked were to continue in the land, even the just would be infected by their evil attitudes.

Ps 126: A lament probably sung shortly after Israel's return from exile. The people rejoice that they are in Zion (1-3) but mere presence in the holy city is not enough; they must pray for the prosperity and the fertility of the land (4). The last verses are probably an oracle of promise: the painful work of sowing will be crowned with life (5-6).

2 Our mouths were filled with laughter;
>   our tongues sang for joy.[i]
> Then it was said among the nations,
>   "The LORD had done great things for them."
3 The LORD has done great things for us;
>   Oh, how happy we were!
4 Restore again our fortunes, LORD,
>   like the dry stream beds of the Negeb.

II

5 Those who sow in tears
>   will reap with cries of joy.[j]
6 Those who go forth weeping,
>   carrying sacks of seed,
> Will return with cries of joy,
>   carrying their bundled sheaves.

Psalm 127
The Need of God's Blessing

1 *A song of ascents. Of Solomon.*

I

Unless the LORD build the house,
>   they labor in vain who build.
Unless the LORD guard the city,
>   in vain does the guard keep watch.
2 It is vain for you to rise early
>   and put off your rest at night,
> To eat bread earned by hard toil—
>   all this God gives to his beloved in sleep.[k]

---

i Jb 8, 21.   k Eccl 2, 24.
j Bar 4, 23; Is 65, 19.

126, 4: *Like the dry stream beds of the Negeb:* the psalmist prays for rain in such abundance that the dry riverbeds will run.

Ps 127: The psalm puts together two proverbs (1-2 and 3-5) on God establishing "houses" or families. The prosperity of human groups is not the work of humans but the gift of God.

II
3 Children too are a gift from the LORD,
        the fruit of the womb, a reward.[l]
4 Like arrows in the hand of a warrior
        are the children born in one's youth.
5   Blessed are they whose quivers are full.
   They will never be shamed
        contending with foes at the gate.

Psalm 128
The Happy Home of the Just

1 *A song of ascents.*

I
Happy are all who fear the LORD,
        who walk in the ways of God.[m]
2 What your hands provide you will enjoy;
        you will be happy and prosper:[n]
3 Like a fruitful vine
        your wife within your home,
   Like olive plants
        your children around your table.[o]
4 Just so will they be blessed
        who fear the LORD.

---

[l] Pss 115, 14; 128, 3; Dt 28, 11; Prv 17,   [n] Ps 112, 3.
   6.   [o] Jb 29, 5; Ps 144, 12.
[m] Ps 112, 1.

127, 5: *At the gate:* the reference is not to enemies besieging the walls of a city but to adversaries in litigation. Lawcourts functioned in the open area near the main city gate. The more adult sons a man had, the more forceful he would appear in disputes. Cf Prv 31, 23.

Ps 128: A statement that the ever-reliable God will bless the reverent (1). God's blessing is concrete: satisfaction and prosperity, a fertile spouse and abundant children (2-4). The perspective is that of the adult male, ordinarily the ruler and representative of the household to the community. The last verses extend the blessing to all the people for generations to come (5-6).

128, 1: *All who fear the LORD:* literally, singular: "the one fearing," is used in a typical sense and so is translated by the plural.

II

5 May the LORD bless you from Zion,
    all the days of your life[p]
  That you may share Jerusalem's joy
6   and live to see your children's children.[q]
  Peace upon Israel![r]

Psalm 129
Against Israel's Enemies

1 *A song of ascents.*

I

Much have they oppressed me from my youth,
    now let Israel say.[s]
2 Much have they oppressed me from my youth,[t]
    yet they have not prevailed.
3 Upon my back the plowers plowed,
    as they traced their long furrows.[u]
4 But the just LORD set me free
    from the ropes of the yoke of the wicked.

II

5 May they be scattered in disgrace,
    all who hate Zion.
6 May they be like grass on the rooftops
    withered in early growth,[v]

---

p Pss 20, 3; 134, 3.
q Jb 42, 16; Prv 17, 6.
r Ps 125, 5.
s Ps 124, 1.

t Ps 118, 13.
u Is 51, 23.
v Is 37, 27.

Ps 129: A psalm giving thanks for God's many rescues of Israel over the long course of their history (1-4); the people pray that their oppressors never know the joy of harvest (5-8).

129, 4: *The ropes of the yoke of the wicked:* usually understood as the rope for yoking animals to the plow. If it is severed, the plowing (cf 3) comes to a halt.

129, 6: *Like grass on the rooftops:* after the spring rains, grass would sprout from the coat of mud with which the flat roofs of simple houses were covered, but when the dry summer began there was no moisture in the thin roof-covering to sustain the grass.

7 Never to fill the reaper's hands,
      nor the arms of the binders of sheaves,
8 With none passing by to call out:
      "The blessing of the LORD be upon you!
      We bless you in the name of the LORD!"[w]

Psalm 130
Prayer for Pardon and Mercy

1 *A song of ascents.*

I

Out of the depths I call to you, LORD;
2   Lord, hear my cry!
May your ears be attentive
      to my cry for mercy.[x]
3 If you, LORD, mark our sins,
      Lord, who can stand?[y]
4 But with you is forgiveness
      and so you are revered.

II

5 I wait with longing for the LORD,
      my soul waits for his word.[z]
6 My soul looks for the Lord
      more than sentinels for daybreak.[a]
More than sentinels for daybreak,

---

[w] Ps 118, 26.
[x] Pss 5, 2-3; 55, 2-3; 86, 6; Lam 3, 55-56; Jon 2, 3.
[y] Na 1, 6.
[z] Ps 119, 81.
[a] Is 21, 11; 26, 9.

129, 8: *The blessing of the LORD be upon you:* harvesters greeted one another with such blessings. Cf Ru 2, 4.

Ps 130: This lament, a Penitential Psalm, is the *De profundis* used in liturgical prayers for the faithful departed. In deep sorrow the psalmist cries to God (1-2), asking for mercy (3-4). The psalmist's trust (5-6) becomes a model for the people (7-8).

130, 1: *The depths:* Sheol here is a metaphor of total misery. Deep anguish makes the psalmist feel "like those descending to the pit" (Ps 143, 7).

130, 4: *And so you are revered:* the experience of God's mercy leads one to a greater sense of God.

7   let Israel look for the LORD,
For with the LORD is kindness,
        with him is full redemption,[b]
8 And God will redeem Israel
        from all their sins.[c]

Psalm 131
Humble Trust in God

1   *A song of ascents. Of David.*

LORD, my heart is not proud;
        nor are my eyes haughty.
I do not busy myself with great matters,
        with things too sublime for me.[d]
2   Rather, I have stilled my soul,
        hushed it like a weaned child.
Like a weaned child on its mother's lap,
        so is my soul within me.[e]
3   Israel, hope in the LORD,
        now and forever.

Psalm 132
The Covenant between David and God

1   *A song of ascents.*

I
LORD, remember David
        and all his anxious care;

---

b Pss 86, 15; 100, 5; 103, 8.   d Ps 139, 6.
c Ps 25, 22; Mt 1, 21.   e Is 66, 12-13.

Ps 131: A song of trust, in which the psalmist gives up self-sufficiency (1), like a babe enjoying the comfort of its mother's lap (2), thus providing a model for Israel's faith (3).

Ps 132: A song for a liturgical ceremony in which the ark, the throne of Israel's God, was carried in procession to the temple. The singer asks that David's care for the proper housing of the ark be regarded with favor (1-5), and tells how it was brought to Jerusalem (6-10). There follows God's promise of favor to the Davidic dynasty (11-12) and to Zion (13-17). The transfer of the ark to the tent in Jerusalem is described in 2 Sm 6.

132, 1: *All his anxious care:* to build the temple. Cf 2 Sm 7, 1-17 and 1 Kgs 8, 17.

2 How he swore an oath to the LORD,
　　vowed to the Mighty One of Jacob:
3 "I will not enter the house where I live,[f]
　　nor lie on the couch where I sleep;
4 I will give my eyes no sleep,
　　my eyelids no rest,
5 Till I find a home for the LORD,
　　a dwelling for the Mighty One of Jacob."
6 "We have heard of it in Ephrathah;
　　we have found it in the fields of Jaar.
7 Let us enter God's dwelling;
　　let us worship at God's footstool."[g]
8 "Arise, LORD, come to your resting place,[h]
　　you and your majestic ark.
9 Your priests will be clothed with justice;
　　your faithful will shout for joy."
10 For the sake of David your servant,
　　do not reject your anointed.

II

11 The LORD swore an oath to David,
　　a pledge never to be broken:[i]
　　"Your own offspring[j] I will set upon your throne.
12 If your sons observe my covenant,
　　the laws I shall teach them,
　　Their sons, in turn,
　　shall sit forever on your throne."
13 Yes, the LORD has chosen Zion,
　　desired it for a dwelling:
14 "This is my resting place forever;
　　here I will dwell, for I desire it.

---

f 2 Sm 7; 1 Chr 28, 2.
g Ps 99, 5.
h 8-10: Pss 2, 2; 89, 21; 95, 11; Nm 10, 35; 2 Chr 6, 41-42; Sir 24, 7.
i Ps 110, 4; 2 Sm 7, 12.
j 11-14: Ps 68, 17; 1 Kgs 8, 13; Sir 24, 7.

132, 2. 5: *Mighty One of Jacob:* one of the titles of Israel's God. Cf Gn 49, 24; Is 49, 26; 60, 16.

132, 6: *Ephrathah:* the homeland of David. Cf Ru 4, 11. *The fields of Jaar:* poetic for Kiriath-jearim, a town west of Jerusalem, where the ark remained for several generations. Cf 1 Sm 7, 1-2 ; 2 Sm 6, 2; 1 Chr 13, 5-6.

15 I will bless Zion with meat;
    its poor I will fill with bread.
16 I will clothe its priests with blessing;
    its faithful shall shout for joy.[k]
17 There I will make a horn sprout for David's line;[l]
    I will set a lamp for my anointed.
18 His foes I will clothe with shame,
    but on him my crown shall gleam."

Psalm 133
A Vision of a Blessed Community

1 *A song of ascents. Of David.*

How good it is, how pleasant,
    where the people dwell as one!
2 Like precious ointment on the head,[m]
    running down upon the beard,
Upon the beard of Aaron,
    upon the collar of his robe.
3 Like dew of Hermon coming down
    upon the mountains of Zion.[n]

---

[k] 2 Chr 6, 41; Is 61, 10.
[l] Is 11, 1; Jer 33, 15; Ez 29, 21; Zec 3, 8; Lk 1, 69.
[m] Ex 30, 25. 30.
[n] Hos 14, 6.

132, 17: *A horn sprout for David's line:* the image of the horn, a symbol of strength, is combined with that of a "sprout," a term used for the Davidic descendant (cf Jer 23, 5; 33, 15; Zec 3, 8; 6, 12). Early Christians referred the latter designation to Christ as son of David (Lk 1, 69).

Ps 133: A benediction over a peaceful community, most probably the people Israel, but appropriate too for Israelite families (1). The history of Israel, whether of its ancestors in the book of Genesis or of later periods, was a history of distinct groups struggling to live in unity. Here that unity is declared blessed, like the holy oils upon the priest Aaron or the dew of the rainless summer that waters the crops (2-3).

133, 1: *The people:* literally, "brothers," i.e., male and female members of a kin group or people—most probably, the people Israel.

133, 2: *Ointment:* oil was used at the consecration of the high priest (Ex 30, 22-33).

133, 3: *Dew:* dew was an important source of moisture in the dry cli-

There the LORD has lavished blessings,
life for evermore![o]

Psalm 134
Exhortation to the Night Watch To Bless God

1 *A song of ascents.*

Come, bless the LORD,
all you servants of the LORD
Who stand in the house of the LORD
through the long hours of night.[p]
2 Lift up your hands toward the sanctuary,[q]
and bless the LORD.
3 May the LORD who made heaven and earth[r]
bless you from Zion.

Psalm 135
Praise of God, the Ruler and Benefactor of Israel

1 *Hallelujah!*

I
Praise the name of the LORD!
Praise, you servants of the LORD,[s]

[o] Dt 28, 8; 30, 20.
[p] Ps 135, 1-2; 1 Chr 9, 33.
[q] Pss 28, 2; 141, 2.
[r] Pss 20, 3; 128, 5; Nm 6, 24.
[s] Ps 113, 1.

mate (Gn 27, 28; Hos 14, 6). *Hermon:* the majestic snow-capped mountain visible in the north of Palestine.

Ps 134: A brief liturgy exhorting the temple singers to acknowledge the great deeds of God at a night service (cf Is 30, 29). Mount Zion is the place from which blessings affect the lives of humans, for there Israel's God dwells.

134, 1: *Servants of the LORD:* priests and Levites. Cf Dt 10, 8; Pss 113, 1; 135, 1; Dn 3, 84-85.

Ps 135: The hymn begins and ends with an invitation to praise God (1-3, 19-20) for the great act of choosing Israel (4). The story of Israel's emergence as a people is told in 5-14; God created and redeemed the people, easily conquering all opposition. God's defeat of hostile powers means that the powers themselves and their images are useless (15-18). The last three verses appear also in Ps 115, 4-8.

2 Who stand in the house of the LORD,
  in the courts of the house of our God!ᵗ
3 Praise the LORD; the LORD is good!
  Sing to God's name; it is gracious!
4 For the LORD has chosen Jacob,
  Israel as a treasured possession.ᵘ

  II

5 I know that the LORD is great,
  our Lord is greater than all gods.ᵛ
6 Whatever the LORD wishes
   he does in heaven and on earth,
   in the seas and in all the deeps.ʷ
7 He raises storm clouds from the end of the earth,
   makes lightning and rain,
   brings forth wind from the storehouse.ˣ

  III

8 He struck down Egypt's firstborn,ʸ
  human and beast alike,
9 And sent signs and portents against you, Egypt,
  against Pharaoh and all his servants.
10 The Lord struck down many nations,ᶻ
  slew mighty kings—
11 Sihon, king of the Amorites,
  Og, king of Bashan,
  all the kings of Canaan—
12 And made their land a heritage,
  a heritage for Israel his people.
13 O LORD, your name is forever,
  your renown, from age to age!ᵃ
14 For the LORD defends his people,
  shows mercy to his servants.ᵇ

ᵗ Ps 134, 1.
ᵘ Pss 33, 12; 144, 15; Ex 19, 6; Dt 7, 6.
ᵛ Ps 95, 3; Ex 18, 11.
ʷ Ps 115, 3.
ˣ Ps 148, 8; Jer 10, 13; 51, 16; Jb 37, 9.
ʸ 8-9: Pss 78, 51; 105, 27. 36; 136, 10;
Ex 12, 29.
ᶻ 10-12: Nm 21, 21-35; Dt 2, 24-3, 17;
Ps 136, 17-22.
ᵃ Ps 102, 13; Ex 3, 15.
ᵇ Dt 32, 36.

135, 4: Though all nations are God's, Israel has a special status as God's "treasured" people: Ex 19, 5; Dt 7, 6; 14, 2; 26, 18; Mal 3, 17.

IV

15 The idols of the nations are silver and gold,[c]
the work of human hands.
16 They have mouths but speak not;
they have eyes but see not;
17 They have ears but hear not;
no breath is in their mouths.
18 Their makers shall be like them,
all who trust in them.

V

19 House of Israel, bless the LORD![d]
House of Aaron, bless the LORD!
20 House of Levi, bless the LORD!
You who fear the LORD, bless the LORD!
21 Blessed from Zion be the LORD,
who dwells in Jerusalem!
Hallelujah!

Psalm 136
Hymn of Thanksgiving for God's Everlasting Love

I

1 Praise the LORD, who is so good;[e]
God's love endures forever;
2 Praise the God of gods;
God's love endures forever;
3 Praise the Lord of lords;
God's love endures forever;

---

c 15-18: Ps 115, 4-6. 8.   e Pss 100, 5; 118, 1.
d 19-20: Ps 118, 2-4.

Ps 136: The hymn praises Israel's God ("the God of gods," 2), who has created the world in which Israel lives. The refrain occurring after every line suggests that a speaker and chorus sang the psalm in antiphonal fashion. A single act of God is described in 4-25: God arranges the heavens and the earth as the environment for human community, and then creates the community by freeing them and giving them land. In the final section (23-25) God, who created the people and gave them land, continues to protect and nurture them.

II

4 Who alone has done great wonders,[f]
    God's love endures forever;
5 Who skillfully made the heavens,[g]
    God's love endures forever;
6 Who spread the earth upon the waters,[h]
    God's love endures forever;
7 Who made the great lights,
    God's love endures forever;
8 The sun to rule the day,
    God's love endures forever;
9 The moon and stars to rule the night,[i]
    God's love endures forever;

III

10 Who struck down the firstborn of Egypt,[j]
    God's love endures forever;
11 And led Israel from their midst,
    God's love endures forever;
12 With mighty hand and outstretched arm,[k]
    God's love endures forever;
13 Who split in two the Red Sea,
    God's love endures forever;
14 And led Israel through,
    God's love endures forever;
15 But swept Pharaoh and his army into the Red Sea,[l]
    God's love endures forever;
16 Who led the people through the desert,[m]
    God's love endures forever;

IV

17 Who struck down great kings,[n]
    God's love endures forever;
18 Slew powerful kings,
    God's love endures forever;

---

[f] Ps 72, 18.
[g] Gn 1, 9-19.
[h] Ps 24, 2.
[i] Jer 31, 35.
[j] Ex 12, 29. 51; 14, 22. 27; 15, 22; Pss 78, 51-52; 135, 8.
[k] Dt 4, 34.
[l] Ex 14, 21f.
[m] Dt 8, 2. 15.
[n] 17-22: Ps 135, 10-12.

19 Sihon, king of the Amorites,
        God's love endures forever;
20 Og, king of Bashan,
        God's love endures forever;
21 And made their lands a heritage,
        God's love endures forever;
22 A heritage for Israel, God's servant,
        God's love endures forever.

    V
23 The Lord remembered us in our misery,
        God's love endures forever;
24 Freed us from our foes,
        God's love endures forever;
25 And gives food to all flesh,
        God's love endures forever.

    VI
26 Praise the God of heaven,
        God's love endures forever.

Psalm 137
Sorrow and Hope in Exile

    I
1 By the rivers of Babylon
        we sat mourning and weeping
        when we remembered Zion.°
2 On the poplars of that land
        we hung up our harps.ᴾ

° Ez 3, 15; Lam 3, 48.   ᴾ Is 24, 8; Lam 5, 14.

136, 22: *A heritage for Israel:* the land was given to Israel by God to be handed on to future generations.

Ps 137: A temple singer refuses to sing the people's sacred songs in an alien land despite demands from Babylonian captors (1-4). The singer swears an oath by what is most dear to a musician—hands and tongue—to exalt Jerusalem always (5-6). The psalm ends with a prayer that the old enemies of Jerusalem, Edom and Babylon, be destroyed (7-9).

137, 2: *Poplars:* sometimes incorrectly translated "willow." The Euphrates poplar is a high tree common on riverbanks in the Orient.

3 There our captors asked us
for the words of a song;
Our tormentors, for a joyful song:
"Sing for us a song of Zion!"
4 But how could we sing a song of the LORD
in a foreign land?

II
5 If I forget you, Jerusalem,
may my right hand wither.[q]
6 May my tongue stick to my palate
if I do not remember you,
If I do not exalt Jerusalem
beyond all my delights.

III
7 Remember, LORD, against Edom
that day at Jerusalem.
They said: "Level it, level it
down to its foundations!"[r]
8 Fair Babylon, you destroyer,
happy those who pay you back
the evil you have done us![s]
9 Happy those who seize your children
and smash them against a rock.[t]

[q] Jer 51, 50.
[r] Jer 49, 7; Lam 4, 21-22; Ez 25, 12-14.
[s] Is 47, 1-3; Jer 50-51.
[t] Hos 14, 1.

137, 9: *Happy those who seize your children and smash them against a rock:* the infants represent the future generations, and so must be destroyed if the enemy is truly to be eradicated.

Psalm 138
Hymn of a Grateful Heart

1   *Of David.*

I

I thank you, LORD, with all my heart;[u]
>   before the gods to you I sing.
2   I bow low toward your holy temple;
>   I praise your name for your fidelity and love.
For you have exalted over all
>   your name and your promise.
3   When I cried out, you answered;
>   you strengthened my spirit.

II

4   All the kings of earth will praise you, LORD,
>   when they hear the words of your mouth.
5   They will sing of the ways of the LORD:
>   "How great is the glory of the LORD!"
6   The LORD is on high, but cares for the lowly[v]
>   and knows the proud from afar.
7   Though I walk in the midst of dangers,
>   you guard my life when my enemies rage.
You stretch out your hand;
>   your right hand saves me.
8   The LORD is with me to the end.
>   LORD, your love endures forever.
>   Never forsake the work of your hands!

---

u Ps 9, 1.   v Lk 1, 51-52.

Ps 138: A thanksgiving to God, who came to the rescue of the psalmist. Divine rescue was not the result of the psalmist's virtues but of God's loving fidelity (1-3). The act is not a private transaction but a public act that stirs the surrounding nations to praise God's greatness and care for the people (4-6). The psalmist, having experienced salvation, trusts that God will always be there in moments of danger (7-8).

138, 1: *Before the gods:* i.e., heavenly beings, who were completely subordinate to Israel's God. The earthly temple represents the heavenly palace of God.

Psalm 139
The All-knowing and Ever-present God

1 *For the leader. A psalm of David.*

   I

   LORD, you have probed me, you know me:
2   you know when I sit and stand;[w]
       you understand my thoughts from afar.
3 My travels and my rest you mark;
       with all my ways you are familiar.
4 Even before a word is on my tongue,
       LORD, you know it all.
5 Behind and before you encircle me
       and rest your hand upon me.
6 Such knowledge is beyond me,
       far too lofty for me to reach.[x]

   II
7 Where can I hide from your spirit?
       From your presence, where can I flee?
8 If I ascend to the heavens, you are there;
       if I lie down in Sheol, you are there too.[y]
9 If I fly with the wings of dawn
       and alight beyond the sea,
10 Even there your hand will guide me,
       your right hand hold me fast.
11 If I say, "Surely darkness shall hide me,
       and night shall be my light"—

---

[w] 2 Kgs 19, 27; Jb 12, 13.   [y] Jb 23, 8-9; Jer 23, 23-24.
[x] Ps 131, 1.

Ps 139: A hymnic meditation on God's omnipresence and omniscience. The psalmist is keenly aware of God's all-knowing gaze (1-6), of God's presence in every part of the universe (7-12), and of God's control over the psalmist's very self (13-16). Summing up 1-16, 17-18 express wonder. There is only one place hostile to God's rule—wicked people. The psalmist prays to be removed from their company (19-24).

139, 2: *When I sit and stand:* in all my physical movement.

139, 9: *Fly with the wings of dawn:* go to the extremities of the east. *Beyond the sea:* uttermost bounds of the west; the sea is the Mediterranean.

139, 11: *Night shall be my light:* night to me is what day is to others.

12 Darkness is not dark for you,
        and night shines as the day.
        Darkness and light are but one.[z]

    III
13 You formed my inmost being;
        you knit me in my mother's womb.[a]
14 I praise you, so wonderfully you made me;
        wonderful are your works!
    My very self you knew;
15   my bones were not hidden from you,
    When I was being made in secret,
        fashioned as in the depths of the earth.
16 Your eyes foresaw my actions;
        in your book all are written down;[b]
        my days were shaped, before one came to be.

    IV
17 How precious to me are your designs, O God;
        how vast the sum of them!
18 Were I to count, they would outnumber the sands;
        to finish, I would need eternity.[c]
19 If only you would destroy the wicked, O God,
        and the bloodthirsty would depart from me![d]
20 Deceitfully they invoke your name;
        your foes swear faithless oaths.
21 Do I not hate, LORD, those who hate you?
        Those who rise against you, do I not loathe?[e]
22 With fierce hatred I hate them,
        enemies I count as my own.

    V
23 Probe me, God, know my heart;
        try me, know my concerns.[f]

---

z Jb 12, 22.   d Jb 21, 14.
a Wis 7, 1; Eccl 11, 5; Jb 1, 21.   e Ps 119, 158.
b Mal 3, 16.   f Pss 17, 3; 26, 2.
c Jb 11, 7.

139, 15: *The depths of the earth:* figurative language for the womb,
stressing the hidden and mysterious operations that occur there.

24 See if my way is crooked,
    then lead me in the ancient paths.

Psalm 140
Prayer for Deliverance from the Wicked

1 *For the leader. A psalm of David.*

I

2 Deliver me, LORD, from the wicked;
    preserve me from the violent,[g]
3 From those who plan evil in their hearts,
    who stir up conflicts every day,
4 Who sharpen their tongues like serpents,
    venom of asps upon their lips.[h]   *Selah*

II

5 Keep me, LORD, from the clutches of the wicked;
    preserve me from the violent,
    who plot to trip me up.[i]
6 The arrogant have set a trap for me;
    villains have spread a net,
    laid snares for me by the wayside.   *Selah*
7 I say to the LORD: You are my God;[j]
    listen, LORD, to the words of my prayer.

---

g Ps 71, 4.   i Jer 18, 22; Pss 56, 7; 57, 7.
h Ps 64, 4; Rom 3, 13.   j Ps 31, 15.

139, 24: *My way . . . the ancient paths:* the manner of living of our ancestors, who were faithful to God's will. Cf Jer 6, 16.

Ps 140: A lament seeking rescue from violent and treacherous foes (2-6). The psalmist remains trusting (7-8), vigorously praying that the plans of the wicked recoil upon themselves (9-12). A serene statement of praise ends the psalm (13-14). The psalmist is content to be known as one of "the needy," "the poor," "the just," "the upright" (13-14), a class of people expecting divine protection.

140, 4: Similar metaphors for a wicked tongue are used in Pss 52, 4; 55, 22; 58, 5.

140, 6: *Have set a trap . . . have spread a net:* the same figure, of hunters setting traps, occurs in Pss 9, 16; 31, 5; 35, 7; 64, 6. Cf Mt 22, 15; Lk 11, 54.

8 My revered Lord, my strong helper,
    my helmet on the day of battle.
9 Lord, do not grant the desires of the wicked;
    do not let their plots succeed.   *Selah*
10 Around me they raise their proud heads;
    may the mischief they threaten overwhelm them.
11 May God rain burning coals upon them,[k]
    cast them into the grave never more to rise.

III

12 Slanderers will not survive on earth;
    evil will quickly entrap the violent.
13 For I know the Lord will secure
    justice for the needy, their rights for the poor.
14 Then the just will give thanks to your name;
    the upright will dwell in your presence.[l]

Psalm 141
Prayer for Deliverance from the Wicked

1   *A psalm of David.*

    Lord, I call to you;
    come quickly to help me;
    listen to my plea when I call.
2 Let my prayer be incense before you;
    my uplifted hands an evening sacrifice.[m]
3 Set a guard, Lord, before my mouth,
    a gatekeeper at my lips.[n]
4 Do not let my heart incline to evil,
    or yield to any sin.

---

[k] Pss 11, 6; 120, 4; Gn 19, 24.   [m] Ps 134, 2; Ex 30, 8.
[l] Pss 11, 7; 16, 11; 17, 15.   [n] Sir 22, 27.

Ps 141: A lament of an individual (1-2) who is keenly aware that only the righteous can worship God properly and who therefore prays to be protected from the doomed wicked (3-10).

141, 2: *Incense:* literally, "smoke," i.e., the fragrant fumes arising from the altar at the burning of sacrificial animals or of aromatic spices; also used in Rv 5, 8 as a symbol of prayer. *My uplifted hands:* the gesture of supplication. Cf Pss 28, 2; 63, 5; 88, 10; 119, 48; 134, 2; 143, 6.

I will never feast upon
the fine food of evildoers.
5 Let the just strike me; that is kindness;
let them rebuke me; that is oil for my head.[o]
All this I shall not refuse,
but will pray despite these trials.
6 When their leaders are cast over the cliff,
all will learn that my prayers were heard.
7 As when a farmer plows a field into broken clods,
so their bones will be strewn at the mouth of Sheol.
8 My eyes are upon you, O GOD, my Lord;[p]
in you I take refuge; do not strip me of life.
9 Guard me from the trap they have set for me,
from the snares of evildoers.[q]
10 Into their own nets let all the wicked fall,
while I make good my own escape.

Psalm 142
A Prayer in Time of Trouble

1 *A* maskil *of David, when he was in the cave. A prayer.*

2 With full voice I cry to the LORD;
with full voice I beseech the LORD.
3 Before God I pour out my complaint,
lay bare my distress.
4 My spirit is faint within me,[r]
but you know my path.[s]
Along the way I walk
they have hidden a trap for me.[t]

[o] Prv 9, 8; 25, 12.
[p] Pss 25, 15; 123, 1-2.
[q] Ps 142, 4.
[r] Ps 143, 4.
[s] Ps 139, 24.
[t] Ps 141, 9.

141, 5-7: the Hebrew text is obscure.

Ps 142: In this lament imploring God for help (2-4b), the psalmist tells how enemies have set a trap (4c-5), and prays for rescue (6-8). The speaker feels utterly alone (5), exhausted (7), and may even be imprisoned (8a). Prison is possibly a metaphor for general distress. The last two verses are the vow of praise, made after receiving an assurance of divine help (8cd).

142, 1: *In the cave:* cf 1 Sm 22, 1; 24, 1-3; Ps 57, 1.

5 I look to my right hand,[u]
      but no friend is there.
   There is no escape for me;
      no one cares for me.
6 I cry out to you, LORD,
      I say, You are my refuge,[v]
      my portion in the land of the living.[w]
7 Listen to my cry for help,
      for I am brought very low.[x]
   Rescue me from my pursuers,
      for they are too strong for me.
8 Lead me out of my prison,
      that I may give thanks to your name.
   Then the just shall gather around me
      because you have been good to me.

Psalm 143
A Prayer in Distress

1 *A psalm of David.*

   LORD, hear my prayer;
      in your faithfulness listen to my pleading;
      answer me in your justice.
2 Do not enter into judgment with your servant;
      before you no living being can be just.[y]

---

u Pss 16, 8; 73, 23; 121, 5.   x Ps 79, 8.
v Ps 91, 2. 9.   y Eccl 7, 20; Jb 4, 17; Rom 3, 20.
w Pss 16, 5; 27, 13; 116, 9; Is 38, 11.

142, 8: *Then the just shall gather around me:* in the temple, when the psalmist offers a thanksgiving sacrifice.

Ps 143: One of the Church's seven Penitential Psalms, this lament is a prayer to be freed from death-dealing enemies. The psalmist addresses God, aware that there is no equality between God and humans; salvation is a gift (1-2). Victimized by evil people (3-4), the psalmist recites ("remembers") God's past actions on behalf of the innocent (5-6). The psalm continues with fervent prayer (7-9) and a strong desire for guidance and protection (10-12).

3 The enemy has pursued me;
      they have crushed my life to the ground.[z]
   They have left me in darkness
      like those long dead.[a]
4 My spirit is faint within me;
      my heart is dismayed.[b]
5 I remember the days of old;
      I ponder all your deeds;
      the works of your hands I recall.[c]
6 I stretch out my hands to you;
      I thirst for you like a parched land.[d]   *Selah*
7 Hasten to answer me, LORD;
      for my spirit fails me.
   Do not hide your face from me,
      lest I become like those descending to the pit.[e]
8 At dawn let me hear of your kindness,
      for in you I trust.
   Show me the path I should walk,
      for to you I entrust my life.[f]
9 Rescue me, LORD, from my foes,
      for in you I hope.
10 Teach me to do your will,
      for you are my God.
   May your kind spirit guide me
      on ground that is level.
11 For your name's sake, LORD, give me life;
      in your justice lead me out of distress.
12 In your kindness put an end to my foes;
      destroy all who attack me,
      for I am your servant.[g]

---

[z] Ps 7, 6.
[a] Lam 3, 6.
[b] Ps 142, 4; Jb 17, 1.
[c] Ps 77, 6. 12.

[d] Pss 42, 2; 63, 2.
[e] Pss 28, 1; 30, 4; 88, 5; Prv 1, 12.
[f] Pss 25, 4; 27, 11; 86, 11; 119, 12. 35.
[g] Ps 116, 16.

143, 3: *They have crushed:* literally, "he crushed"; the singular is used typically, hence the plural translation.

Psalm 144
A Prayer for Victory and Prosperity

1   *Of David.*

I
Blessed be the LORD, my rock,
    who trains my hands for battle,
    my fingers for war;
2   My safeguard and my fortress,
    my stronghold, my deliverer,
My shield, in whom I trust,
    who subdues peoples under me.

II
3   LORD, what are mortals that you notice them;
    human beings, that you take thought of them?[h]
4   They are but a breath;
    their days are like a passing shadow.[i]
5   LORD, incline your heavens and come;
    touch the mountains and make them smoke.[j]
6   Flash forth lightning and scatter my foes;
    shoot your arrows and rout them.
7   Reach out your hand from on high;
    deliver me from the many waters;
    rescue me from the hands of foreign foes.

---

[h] Jb 7, 17.
[i] Pss 62, 10; 90, 9-10; Jb 7, 16; Eccl
6, 12; Wis 2, 5.
[j] Is 63, 19.

Ps 144: The psalm may reflect a ceremony in which the king, as leader of the army, asked God's help (1-8). In 9 the poem shifts abruptly from pleading to thanksgiving, and (except for 11) shifts again to prayer for the people. The first section (1-2) is a prayer of thanks for victory; the second (3-7a), a humble acknowledgment of human nothingness and a supplication that God show forth saving power; the third (9-11), a promise of future thanksgiving; the fourth (12-15), a wish for prosperity and peace. A prayer for deliverance from treacherous foes serves as a refrain after the second and third sections (7b-8. 11). Except for its final section, the psalm is made up almost entirely of verses from other psalms.
    144, 1-2: Composed of phrases from Ps 18, 3. 35. 47-48.
    144, 3: Similar to Ps 8, 5.
    144, 4: Composed of phrases from Pss 39, 6; 102, 12.
    144, 5-7: Adapted in large part from Pss 18, 10. 15. 17; 104, 32.

8 Their mouths speak untruth;
    their right hands are raised in lying oaths.
9 O God, a new song I will sing to you;
    on a ten-stringed lyre I will play for you.[k]
10 You give victory to kings;
    you delivered David your servant.[l]
From the menacing sword (11) deliver me;
    rescue me from the hands of foreign foes.
Their mouths speak untruth;
    their right hands are raised in lying oaths.

III

12 May our sons be like plants[m]
    well nurtured from their youth,
Our daughters, like carved columns,
    shapely as those of the temple.
13 May our barns be full
    with every kind of store.
May our sheep increase by thousands,
    by tens of thousands in our fields;
    may our oxen be well fattened.
14 May there be no breach in the walls,
    no exile, no outcry in our streets.[n]
15 Happy the people so blessed;
    happy the people whose God is the LORD.[o]

Psalm 145
The Greatness and Goodness of God

1 *Praise. Of David.*

I will extol you, my God and king;
    I will bless your name forever.

---

[k] Ps 33, 2-3.
[l] Ps 18, 51.
[m] Ps 128, 3.

[n] Is 65, 19.
[o] Ps 33, 12.

144, 8b. 11b: *Their right hands are raised in lying oaths:* the psalmist's enemies give false testimony.

Ps 145: A hymn in acrostic form; every verse begins with a successive letter of the Hebrew alphabet. Acrostic poems usually do not de-

2 Every day I will bless you;
    I will praise your name forever.[p]
3 Great is the Lord and worthy of high praise;[q]
    God's grandeur is beyond understanding.
4 One generation praises your deeds to the next
    and proclaims your mighty works.[r]
5 They speak of the splendor of your majestic glory,
    tell of your wonderful deeds.[s]
6 They speak of your fearsome power
    and attest to your great deeds.[t]
7 They publish the renown of your abounding goodness
    and joyfully sing of your justice.
8 The Lord is gracious and merciful,
    slow to anger and abounding in love.[u]
9 The Lord is good to all,
    compassionate to every creature.[v]
10 All your works give you thanks, O Lord
    and your faithful bless you.[w]
11 They speak of the glory of your reign
    and tell of your great works,
12 Making known to all your power,
    the glorious splendor of your rule.
13 Your reign is a reign for all ages,
    your dominion for all generations.[x]
    The Lord is trustworthy in every word,
    and faithful in every work.
14 The Lord supports all who are falling
    and raises up all who are bowed down.[y]

---

[p] Ps 34, 2.
[q] Pss 48, 2; 95, 3; 96, 4; Jb 36, 26.
[r] Pss 22, 31-32; 48, 14-15; 71, 18; 78, 4; Ex 10, 2; Dt 4, 9.
[s] Pss 96, 3; 105, 2.
[t] Ps 66, 3.
[u] Pss 86, 5. 15; 103, 8; Ex 34, 6; Sir 2, 11.
[v] Ps 103, 13; Wis 11, 24.
[w] Dn 3, 57.
[x] Pss 10, 16; 102, 13; 146, 10; Lam 5, 19; Dn 3, 100; Rv 11, 15.
[y] Pss 94, 18; 146, 8.

---

velop ideas but consist rather of loosely connected statements. The singer invites all to praise God (1-3. 21). The "works of God" make God present and invite human praise (4-7); they climax in a confession (8-9). God's mighty acts show forth divine kingship (10-20), a major theme in the literature of early Judaism and in Christianity.

15 The eyes of all look hopefully to you;
    you give them their food in due season.[z]
16 You open wide your hand
    and satisfy the desire of every living thing.
17 You, LORD, are just in all your ways,
    faithful in all your works.[a]
18 You, LORD, are near to all who call upon you,
    to all who call upon you in truth.[b]
19 You satisfy the desire of those who fear you;
    you hear their cry and save them.[c]
20 You, LORD, watch over all who love you,
    but all the wicked you destroy.[d]
21 My mouth will speak your praises, LORD;
    all flesh will bless your holy name forever.[e]

Psalm 146
Trust in God the Creator and Redeemer

1 *Hallelujah!*

2 Praise the LORD, my soul;
    I shall praise the LORD all my life,
    sing praise to my God while I live.[f]

    I
3 Put no trust in princes,
    in mere mortals powerless to save.[g]
4 When they breathe their last, they return to the earth;
    that day all their planning comes to nothing.[h]

---

[z] Pss 136, 25; 104, 27-28; Mt 6, 25-26.
[a] Dt 32, 4.
[b] Dt 4, 7; Is 55, 6; 58, 9.
[c] Ps 34, 18.
[d] Jgs 5, 31.
[e] Sir 40, 35.
[f] Pss 103, 1; 104, 33.
[g] Ps 118, 8-9.
[h] Pss 90, 3; 104, 29; 1 Mc 2, 63; Jb 34, 14-15; Eccl 3, 20; 12, 7; Sir 40, 11; Is 2, 22.

Ps 146: A hymn of someone who has learned there is no other source of strength except the merciful God. Only God, not mortal humans (3-4), can help vulnerable and oppressed people (5-9). The first of the five hymns that conclude the Psalter.

II

5 Happy those whose help is Jacob's God,
    whose hope is in the LORD, their God,

6 The maker of heaven and earth,
    the seas and all that is in them,[i]
Who keeps faith forever,

7   secures justice for the oppressed,[j]
    gives food to the hungry.
The LORD sets prisoners free;[k]

8   the LORD gives sight to the blind.
The LORD raises up those who are bowed down;[l]
    the LORD loves the righteous.

9 The LORD protects the stranger,
    sustains the orphan and the widow,[m]
    but thwarts the way of the wicked.

10 The LORD shall reign forever,
    your God, Zion, through all generations![n]
Hallelujah!

Psalm 147
God's Word Restores Jerusalem

1 *Hallelujah!*

I

How good to celebrate our God in song;
    how sweet to give fitting praise.[o]

2 The LORD rebuilds Jerusalem,
    gathers the dispersed of Israel,[p]

---

[i] Ex 20, 11; Pss 121, 2; 124, 8; Acts 14, 15; Rv 14, 7.
[j] Ps 103, 6.
[k] Ps 68, 7; Is 49, 9; 61, 1.
[l] Ps 145, 14.
[m] Ps 68, 6; Dt 10, 18.
[n] Ps 145, 13; Lam 5, 19.
[o] Pss 33, 1; 92, 2.
[p] Is 11, 12; 56, 8; Jer 31, 10.

Ps 147: The hymn is divided into three sections by the calls to praise in 1, 7, and 12. The first section praises the powerful creator who restores exiled Judah (1-6); the second section, the creator who provides food to animals and humans; the third and climactic section exhorts the holy city to recognize it has been re-created and made the place of disclosure for God's word, a word as life-giving as water.

3 Heals the brokenhearted,
    binds up their wounds,[q]
4 Numbers all the stars,
    calls each of them by name.[r]
5 Great is our Lord, vast in power,
    with wisdom beyond measure.[s]
6 The LORD sustains the poor,
    but casts the wicked to the ground.[t]

II
7 Sing to the LORD with thanksgiving;
    with the lyre celebrate our God,[u]
8 Who covers the heavens with clouds,
    provides rain for the earth,
    makes grass sprout on the mountains,[v]
9 Who gives animals their food
    and ravens what they cry for.[w]
10 God takes no delight in the strength of horses,
    no pleasure in the runner's stride.[x]
11 Rather the LORD takes pleasure in the devout,
    those who await his faithful care.

III
12 Glorify the LORD, Jerusalem;
    Zion, offer praise to your God,
13 Who has strengthened the bars of your gates,
    blessed your children within you,[y]
14 Brought peace to your borders,
    and filled you with finest wheat.[z]
15 The LORD sends a command to earth;
    his word runs swiftly![a]

---

[q] Jb 5, 18; Is 30, 26; 61, 1; Jer 33, 6.
[r] Is 40, 26.
[s] Jdt 16, 13; Jer 51, 15.
[t] Ps 146, 9; 1 Sm 2, 7-8.
[u] Ps 71, 22.
[v] Ps 104, 13f; Jb 5, 10; Jer 14, 22; Jl 2, 23.
[w] Jb 38, 41; Mt 6, 26.
[x] Pss 20, 8; 33, 16-18.
[y] Ps 48, 14.
[z] Ps 81, 17.
[a] Ps 33, 9.

147, 8-9: God clothes the fields and feeds the birds. Cf Mt 6, 26. 30.
147, 10-11: Acknowledging one's dependence upon God rather than claiming self-sufficiency pleases God. Cf Pss 20, 8; 33, 16-19.
147, 15-19: God speaks through the thunder of nature and the word

16 Thus snow is spread like wool,
        frost is scattered like ash,[b]
17 Hail is dispersed like crumbs;
        before such cold the waters freeze.
18 Again he sends his word and they melt;
        the wind is unleashed and the waters flow.
19 The LORD also proclaims his word to Jacob,
        decrees and laws to Israel.[c]
20 God has not done this for other nations;
        of such laws they know nothing.
    Hallelujah!

Psalm 148
All Creation Summoned to Praise

1 *Hallelujah!*

   I
   Praise the LORD from the heavens;
       give praise in the heights.
2 Praise him, all you angels;
       give praise, all you hosts.[d]
3 Praise him, sun and moon;
       give praise, all shining stars.
4 Praise him, highest heavens,
       you waters above the heavens.
5 Let them all praise the LORD's name;
       for the LORD commanded and they were created,[e]
6 Assigned them duties forever,
       gave them tasks that will never change.

---

b Jb 6, 16; 37, 10; 38, 22.   d Dn 3, 58-63; Ps 103, 20f.
c Ps 78, 5; Bar 3, 37; Dt 4, 7-8.   e Ps 33, 9; Gn 1, 3f; Jdt 16, 14.

of revealed law. Cf Is 55, 10-11. The weather phenomena are well known in Jerusalem: a blizzard of snow and hail followed by a thunderstorm that melts the ice.

Ps 148: A hymn inviting the beings of heaven (1-6) and of earth (7-14) to praise God. The hymn does not distinguish between inanimate and animate (and rational) nature.

148, 4: *Highest heavens:* literally, "the heavens of the heavens," i.e., the space above the firmament, where the "upper waters" are stored. Cf Gn 1, 6-7; Dt 10, 14; 1 Kgs 8, 27; Ps 104, 3. 13.

II

7 Praise the LORD from the earth,
       you sea monsters and all deep waters;[f]
8 You lightning and hail, snow and clouds,
       storm winds that fulfill his command;
9 You mountains and all hills,
       fruit trees and all cedars;[g]
10 You animals wild and tame,
       you creatures that crawl and fly;[h]
11 You kings of the earth and all peoples,
       princes and all who govern on earth;
12 Young men and women too,
       old and young alike.
13 Let them all praise the LORD's name,
       for his name alone is exalted,
       majestic above earth and heaven.[i]
14 The LORD has lifted high the horn of his people;
       to the glory of all the faithful,
       of Israel, the people near to their God.
Hallelujah!

Psalm 149
Praise God with Song and Sword

1 *Hallelujah!*

Sing to the LORD a new song,
    a hymn in the assembly of the faithful.[j]
2 Let Israel be glad in their maker,
    the people of Zion rejoice in their king.

---

f Gn 1, 21; Ps 135, 6.
g Is 44, 23.
h Gn 1, 21. 24f; Ps 30, 5; Dt 4, 7.

i Ps 30, 5; Dt 4, 7.
j Pss 22, 23; 26, 12; 35, 18; 40, 10; Jdt 16, 1.

148, 14: *The LORD has lifted high the horn of his people:* horn = strength, the concrete noun for the abstract. Of all peoples God has chosen Israel to return praise and thanks in a special way.

Ps 149: A hymn inviting the people of Israel to celebrate their God in song and festive dance (1-3. 5) because God has chosen them and given them victory (4). The exodus and conquest are the defining acts of Is-

3 Let them praise his name in festive dance,
    make music with tambourine and lyre.[k]
4 For the LORD takes delight in his people,
    honors the poor with victory.
5 Let the faithful rejoice in their glory,
    cry out for joy at their banquet,
6 With the praise of God in their mouths,
    and a two-edged sword in their hands,[l]
7 To bring retribution on the nations,
    punishment on the peoples,[m]
8 To bind their kings with chains,
    shackle their nobles with irons,
9 To execute the judgments decreed for them—
    such is the glory of all God's faithful.
Hallelujah!

Psalm 150
Final Doxology

1 *Hallelujah!*

Praise God in his holy sanctuary;[n]
    give praise in the mighty dome of heaven.

---

[k] Pss 68, 26; 81, 2-3; 87, 7; 150, 3-4.   [m] Wis 3, 8.
[l] Neh 4, 10-12; 2 Mc 15, 27.   [n] Dn 3, 53.

---

rael; the people must be ready to do again those acts in the future at the divine command (6-9).

149, 3: *Make music with tambourine and lyre:* the verse recalls the great exodus hymn of Ex 15, 20.

149, 5: *At their banquet:* literally, "upon their couches." The people reclined to banquet.

149, 9: *The glory:* what brings honor to the people is their readiness to carry out the divine will, here conceived as punishing injustice done by the nations.

Ps 150: The psalm is a closing doxology both for the fifth book of the Psalms (107–149) and for the Psalter as a whole. Temple musicians and dancers are called to lead all beings on earth and in heaven in praise of God. The psalm proclaims to whom praise shall be given, and where (1); what praise shall be given, and why (2); how praise shall be given (3-5), and by whom (6).

150, 1: *His holy sanctuary:* God's temple on earth. *The mighty dome*

2 Give praise for his mighty deeds,[o]
praise him for his great majesty.
3 Give praise with blasts upon the horn,[p]
praise him with harp and lyre.
4 Give praise with tambourines and dance,
praise him with flutes and strings.[q]
5 Give praise with crashing cymbals,
praise him with sounding cymbals.
6 Let everything that has breath
give praise to the LORD![r]
Hallelujah!

---

[o] Dt 3, 24.
[p] 3ff: Pss 81, 3-4; 149, 3; 2 Sm 6, 5; 1 Chr 13, 8; 16, 5. 42; 2 Chr 5, 12-13; 7, 6.
[q] Ps 68, 26; Ex 15, 20.
[r] Rv 5, 13.

---

of the heavens: literally, "[God's] strong vault"; heaven is here imagined as a giant plate separating the inhabited world from the waters of the heavens.